I0043363

UnREAL-ESTATE CANADA

UnREAL-ESTATE CANADA

by Ronald A. Battiston

BATTISTON PUBLISHING
938 Premier Road
North Bay, Ontario Canada
P1A 2H5

BattistonPublishing.com

First Edition, Version 1.0
Copyright 2017 by Battiston Publishing

ISBN 978-1-894241-08-3

Typeset in Verdana 12 pt by SuperiorWebs.com
Printed in North America by Lulu.com USA
Publisher   Publisher@BattistonPublishing.com
The Author: Ron@BattistonPublishing.
Publisher's website : BattistonPublishing.com

Forward

Real Estate is an extremely complex subject and in Canada it is the largest source of the annual GDP. In Canada there are approximately 14 million residential properties each which on average provide living quarters for about 2.4 people. The numbers change hourly. Everyone is involved in Real Estate in some way from owners to renters from agents to inspectors from government workers to police from children to adults from bankers to construction workers and the list goes on and on.

In a very real way real estate is unreal. What some people believe is true is not, what some people believe is a good investment is not, what some people purchase is not what they really wanted. Our governments believe that they are managing real estate well but in 2017 the average Canadian family is not making enough income to afford a home in many areas of Canada. In once area of Canada the average price of a property zoomed up a staggering 33% in one twelve month period.

People from around the world with substantial amounts of available cash see Canada as an excellent opportunity to purchase real estate as an investment and consequently prices have been pushed up in some areas to levels where locals can no longer afford to purchase them.

UnREAL-ESTATE CANADA

I have approached the subject from a different perspective and my objective is to explain how the unreal estate in Canada really works and in doing so explain to you how you can best make decisions on when and if to purchase and how to deal with all the folks involved in the field. I should warn you that I do have a good sense of humor and I hope that you find the book both very informative and amusing.

Cheers!   Ron Battiston

TABLE OF CONTENTS

UnReal-Estate Canada *By Ron Battiston*

WHAT IS CANADIAN REAL ESTATE..it depends..

Some homes are very expensive...

And some homes are very unique, artistic and fun!

INTRODUCTION

There are over 4 trillion dollars of real estate in Canada.   Millions of Canadians and foreigners are involved in residential, commercial and industrial Canadian real estate from Owners to Renters from Realtors to Bankers to Construction Workers to Government Workers to many more people. Each have different points of view about what real estate is all about. Most of them are correct in their area of expertise but wrong in their overall understanding of what real estate really is. . This book will inform you about the reality of real estate in Canada and how best to deal with it. It will save you lots of money and grief. And because I have a rather twisted sense of humor I hope that you will find it entertaining too!

I am approaching real estate from a different viewpoint. Imagine for a moment when you look at a business deal from both the point of view of the person making the profit and then the view from the person paying the price. And today in Canada too many people are paying the price and too many people can't afford real estate. There is a problem here. In fact there are lots of problems and thankfully some solutions. You will find them here.

In 1996 I started Battiston Publishing a registered Canadian Publisher and my objective was to produce books which would both inform and entertain. I admit that I am not a normal person and I walk that line between what some nice people call genius and other meaner people call crazy. And thankfully I am not alone and I know several friends who have similar points of view. With our book **Your Very First Billion** we explained how one could actually make a billion dollars and how relatively easy it was! We showed how business really worked in Canada a topic which people don't normally talk about. Because most of them don't know how business really works in Canada.

Then we published the **Canadian Winter Drivers Handbook** and explained in detail how one could avoid being injured or killed on our winter or summer roads. And again we approached the subject from a different and yet very real point of view. We tried our best to save the lives of over a million people in the world who die in traffic accidents every year. And now in this book on Real Estate in Canada we will again inform and entertain you and you will learn how to buy and sell real estate here and increase your chances of success and happiness. When you read the book you will encounter facts and points of view that will surprise you and some that will anger you and at that point I suggest that you put the book down and think about it a bit. Just consider it. Do some research to confirm or dispute the points. And then continue on and I hope you enjoy our book!

We need to start someplace and I think that the Earth is the best place. You need to understand what Canadian Real Estate really is. So let's start with the planet (Earth) that we all live on. Here are some interesting facts!

UnREAL-ESTATE CANADA

Here are some facts about the planet that we live on that you probably don't know or care about but would be surprised to hear!

The surface of the Earth is mostly water and only about 30% of the surface of the world is land which would be fine if you were a fish or had a good boat. That would be about 148,300,000 square km and the other 70% is water which would be about 361,800,000 sq.km. There are approximately 7.5 billion people in the world and humans have an average lifespan of about 70.78 years and each year the people on the planet have a Gross Domestic Product (GDP) of approximately 76 trillion US dollars. And just to make it a bit more exciting the earth is spinning around it's axis at a speed of about 1000 miles per hour and hurtling around the sun at about 18.5 miles or 30 km per second. So every time you blink you have traveled about 18.5 miles. And you have most likely traveled over 1500 miles through space since you started reading this book! And you might travel over a million miles before you complete it which is 40 times around the world. Now let's look at Canada to see how it fits in with reality.

The Parliament Buildings, Ottawa, Canada where our elected government officials sit down and pass laws to try and fix mistakes they made and to try and get re-elected. They waste billions of tax dollars every year and everybody picks on them. But they try their best and as a result Canada is one of the best countries in the world to live in! Several of them are quite likeable! But they make so many mistakes!! Just like the rest of us. The potential is there to solve problems too!

Canada has the second largest land and water mass in the world! We have a land mass of 9,093,670 sq. km which includes areas of fresh water totaling 891,163 sq km. I have included a table from Stats Can below to show you how the land is distributed by province and territory. The population of Canada is approximately 36,545,459 and 82.1% live in urban areas with an average age of 40.8 years. Canada's population represents only one half of one percent of the world population and on average we have 4 Canadians per square km of land. But remember that is just an average and in fact almost 90% of the Canadian population actually lives in a 100 mile band clinging to the US border and even in that narrow band the population is concentrated in a few communities. Just to give you a better idea in Toronto the population density is approximately 4,149.5 per square km. and in the GTA the Greater Toronto area the population is approximately 945.4 per sq. km. So even though there is enough land in Canada to have only 4 Canadians per square km in our most populated city the population density is over a 1000 times that!

Here is a table that shows you the Canadian population and private dwellings and average density by provinces: Check it out. Where are you on the list?

AREA	LAND AREA km^2	POPULATION 2011 census	Private Dwellings	POP. DENSITY per km^2
CANADA	**8,965,121**	**33,476,688**	**13,320,614**	**3.7**
Nunavut	1,877,787	31,906	8,661	0
NW Territories	1,143,793	41,462	14,700	0
Yukon	474,712	33,897	14,117	0.1
NFLD and Labrador	370,510	514,536	208,842	1.4
Sask.	588,239	1,033,381	409,645	1.8
Manitoba	552,329	1,208,268	466,138	2.2
British	922,509		1,764,637	4.8

Columbia		4,400,057		
Alberta	640,081	3,645,257	1,390,275	5.7
Quebec	1,356,547	7,903,001	3,395,343	5.8
New Brunswick	71,377	751,171	314,007	10.5
Ontario	908,607	12,851,821	4,887,508	14.1
Nova Scotia	52,939	921,727	390,279	17.4
P.E.I.	5,685	140,204	56,462	24.7

Now we are getting into a subject, which is a bit surprising. But don't blame me. All I am doing here is sharing facts with you about what Canadian real estate really is. I have shown you some numbers so that you better understand the available land in Canada compared to the rest of the world. Now let's take a closer look at actual land ownership in Canada.

Most Canadians feel that when they pay off a mortgage or acquire land from their family that they own that land. Others feel that when they are given the keys to a property they just purchased with a large mortgage from their friendly banker that they own the land. We could be paying a mortgage for 30 years and then surely we own the land. That would be only fair right? I will be sharing facts in this book which will surprise you so let's consider just what land ownership means. And who really owns the land?

We will begin by introducing Queen Elizabeth II the Queen of Canada. In the USA they don't have a Queen they have a First Lady but she does not own as much real estate as our Queen does.

UnREAL-ESTATE CANADA

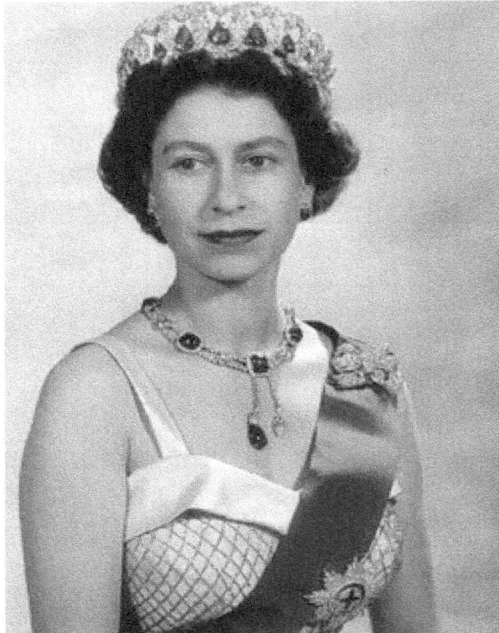

Queen Elizabeth II a truly excellent Queen who actually owns all of Canada. But one could not ask for a better Queen! In WW2 she drove a British Army Truck and served as a mechanic in the Auxiliary Territorial Service. Pretty Impressive!

The Crown of Canada, Queen Elizabeth II owns ALL the land in Canada. All of it. 89% of the land is not dedicated or assigned and is managed by the provincial and federal governments. The remaining 11% is freehold land held (but not owned) by individuals and businesses.

That means you if you have paid off your mortgage and think that you actually own it you are wrong. You are only holding it. If we compare this situation with our friends in the USA here is how it works there. The US Federal government owns approximately 28% of the land in the USA. And if you include state owned and municipal owned land the Governments own approximately 40% of the land while approximately 60% is privately owned. So if you compare private ownership in the USA with free hold private land in Canada Americans own a much higher percentage of their land over 5 times as much as Canadians do. And that is very interesting.

Americans have approximately ten times the population density per square km that Canada has. Canada has slightly more total land and water area than the USA but the USA has slightly more land area. The USA has four times the arable land that Canada has one reason why we purchase most of our food from them.. And there is one very major point in the climate comparing Canada and the USA. The climate in the USA has much longer warmer periods than in Canada with the result that Canada has months more cold weather and so the lifestyle in our climate is different.

Our front yard in March 2017 in North Bay, Ontario, Canada.

And when I say different I don't mean better or worse because one can have a lot of fun in Canada no matter where you are in it. But a lot of Canadians travel down to the warmer States in the USA in the winter months and we have the best neighbors in the world! Also the price of beer is cheaper in the USA than Canada

So at this point you will have a better understanding of how Canada compares with other countries and our neighbor to the south regarding real estate.

At this point we should have a good idea of where Canadian real estate is located and how large each province and territory is and where the majority of our population lives. What is strange is the population density and how it changes from each Province and

Territory and even stranger is looking at that density within areas of the province or territory because it is certainly not uniform. When you look at Toronto and see that the population density there is an amazing 4149.5 per square km and then when you look at the extremely high price of residential property in Toronto and yet see all the relatively empty land in the rest of the country you wonder who is managing real estate in Canada? Is somebody making a mistake? Looks like it!

In Canada we have three levels of government that manage crown lands and also provide rules and regulations and taxes and fees for services for freehold lands managed by the private sector. Each level of government collects taxes on real estate held by privately held freehold properties. They also collect fees for services. And as you might guess they wish to collect as much taxes and as many fees as the market will allow. As long as income climbs to allow the purchase and maintenance of real estate the public can afford to pay the costs associated with real estate. And what happens when people can't afford all the expenses associated with real estate?

People who once had no mortgages on their property go to their banker and take out a mortgage loan. And or they take out huge credit card and other types of loans paying their financial institutions several times the prime rate and they slowly go broke. And at some point they cannot afford to pay the mortgage payments and the other property expenses so they sell their real estate and rent an apartment instead. Personal wealth tends to go up and down.

UnREAL-ESTATE CANADA

Rich people from other countries see Canada as a great and safe place to invest their money so they come in and purchase real estate from Canadians. And at this point I think you will see what we are all up against. Real Estate is a complicated subject with many variables. There are trends as sales and prices go up and then down. There are trends in population density and trends in the overall economy including the world economy. Real estate is so complex that it is impossible to understand it all and make correct decisions on every issue. However when you have a good overall understanding of Real Estate in Canada you can greatly increase your chances of doing well and enjoying your life. And this is why I wrote this book! So let's continue on about more details in real estate and how you can make good decisions and greatly increase your chances of success.

Let's consider the population density per the larger cities in Canada and these are from the 2011 census. Here we have 33 cities in order of their population but check out their population density and think about that for a while.

Toronto (Ont.)	5,583,064	945.4
Montréal (Que.) †	3,824,221	898.1
Vancouver (B.C.)	2,313,328	802.5
Ottawa - Gatineau (Ont./Que.)	1,236,324	196.6
Calgary (Alta.)	1,214,839	237.9
Edmonton (Alta.)	1,159,869	123.0
Québec (Que.) †	765,706	228.6
Winnipeg (Man.) †	730,018	137.7
Hamilton (Ont.)	721,053	525.6
Kitchener - Cambridge - Waterloo	477,160	576.7
London (Ont.)	474,786	178.1
St. Catharines - Niagara (Ont.)	392,184	280.6
Halifax (N.S.)	390,328	71.0
Oshawa (Ont.)	356,177	394.2

Victoria (B.C.) †	344,615	495.0.
Windsor (Ont.)	319,246	312.3
Saskatoon (Sask.)	260,600	50.0
Regina (Sask.)	210,556	61.8
Sherbrooke (Que.)	201,890	138.3
St. John's (N.L.)	196,966	244.8
Barrie (Ont.)	187,013	208.3
Kelowna (B.C.)	179,839	61.9
Abbotsford - Mission (B.C.)	170,191	281.2
Greater Sudbury (Ont.)	160,770	47.1
Kingston (Ont.)	159,561	82.3
Saguenay (Que.)	157,790	61.5
Trois-Rivières (Que.)	151,773	145.8
Guelph (Ont.)	141,097	237.7
Moncton (N.B.)	138,644	57.6
Brantford (Ont.)	135,501	126.3
Saint John (N.B.)	127,761	38.0
Thunder Bay (Ont.)	121,596	47.6
Peterborough (Ont.)	118,975	79.0

The obvious question that I have is why on earth are our three levels of government in Canada, each of which employ very talented hard working people, not better managing the real estate in Canada to ensure that as many Canadians as possible can afford to gain freehold management of property? When you look at the actual numbers it is quite obvious that there is a problem in Canada with the management of our real estate. This book identifies these problems but we also wish to help you by suggesting the best approaches to dealing with real estate. Yes there are problems. Yes some people are making fortunes and yes we are doing some things right because we have one of the best countries in the world. But why is it with all the land that we have that millions of Canadians who cannot afford to purchase real estate and need to rent it? But the potential is there to solve these problems if we all try! Now let's consider details about real estate in Canada. And see what we can learn. Any why not have some fun doing it too!

Why on earth does Canada have dense traffic like this on the 401 highway near Toronto when we have so much nearly vacant land.

HOW CANADIAN REAL ESTATE REALLY WORKS

If you have a "lot of money" you can afford a very attractive home! If you don't you can look at a nice home that somebody else has and then try and figure out a way of buying one yourself.

If you make a good real estate deal you might have a nice place to live and you could end up with a large increase in your net asset value. There are a lot of really beautiful homes in Canada and the USA and some of them are breathtaking! Size is not the only factor and often you will find a very nice small house in a wonderful location that will work as well for you as a monster home in a very rich area. Again there are so many variables in real estate that we need to try and not over simplify suitable homes because too often if you consider all the information regarding the home you may arrive at a different decision regarding which one you would like the most.

Not all homes are big or in great condition but with a bit of effort you can still have fun!

But, if you make a bad deal you could end up with a huge financial loss and a very unpleasant place to live. So how does one learn about real estate? You can start by reading this book!

When we go to school we first learn the basics in the primary grades. Then it is on to high school where we learn even more. Following that we either go to work or head to college or University where we specialize in a given subject. Like how to spend a lot of time at he University Pub and still pass. One might think that since real estate is so important in our lives that we would learn something about it at school. Wrong!

I was lucky enough to attend school and graduate with a degree from a well respected Canadian university but during those years I received no education about real estate. Yes, I did take math and economics and science courses but not one course on real estate because there were no courses on that subject and at the time like my fellow students I saw no reason to study real estate anyway! So we all seem to approach our first real estate deal with absolutely no training or education on the subject. Even in subsequent deals we may not really understand what is going on. This book will change that! And looking back if I had better understood real estate I could have purchased a property while at university, rented some rooms out to pay for the expenses and mortgage and graduated with a pile of assets instead of normal student debt.

Canada is the second largest country in the world in terms of land mass. But we have a relatively small population of approximately 36.3 million which places us at the 38th most populated country in the world. Surprisingly, Canada is 10th in the world in Gross Domestic Product (GDP) so in comparison to other countries larger in population we are doing quite well financially. Approximately 90% of Canada's population is located in just a few communities in a small 100 mile wide band running along our southern border with the USA.

Another interesting fact is that the world population is growing and is now over 7.5 billion people. People from other countries see Canada as an excellent country to invest money in real estate because we live in a peaceful, successful country with huge amounts of available real estate that in several areas is going up in value at a better rate than many traditional investments. And an even more important factor is that Canada's government welcomes foreign investment and is quite happy to sell Canada to foreign interests with few if any restrictions. This is incredibly stupid but our governments have been doing it for decades. Even criminals see Canadian real estate as a potential location to launder money and covert their money into legal investments. There is even a Canadian term for it called "**snow washing**".

One might think that with all that land that real estate in Canada would be very affordable. And while it is affordable in lower populated areas it is also very expensive in more densely populated areas where most Canadians live and where foreigners have purchased Canadian property. A house on a large lot in Toronto or Vancouver or Montreal can cost over ten times the price of the same house on the same sized lot in parts of Northern Manitoba or other sparsely populated areas in other provinces.

And just because real estate in a higher priced area in Canada is much more expensive than real estate in other areas it does not mean that you will live a happier life in a more densely populated city. I have lived in a variety of areas in Canada with different densities. It is entirely possible to have just as much fun or even more fun in a more affordable area north of Canada's 100 mile population band. In the areas with more room, less traffic, larger properties you begin to realize that there are advantages that you seldom see mentioned in bigger cities. Canada is a fantastic place to live and there are so many choices that you really should try your best to see a few of them.

In some cases real estate in our Northern areas may involve large lots or even several acres of space. You may have a stream, a forest, a lake, land for growing crops or raising animals or land to start up manufacturing or commercial activities. In our case we have a family owned property that has been in our family for over half a century. The lot is relatively narrow at approx 50 feet but it is 650 feet long and contains a mix of lawn and forest and outcrops from the Canadian Shield and one can get a lot of joy from a lot like that. Many people have much larger lots involving over 100 acres and that is a lot of land to enjoy. So my main point is not to consider real estate from simply a financial perspective also consider it from an enjoyment perspective. So if you are in the lucky position of suddenly making a large amount of money on your property in a large Canadian city think about investing some of that money in a less densely populated area and having even more fun! In fact in the case of Toronto or Vancouver or Montreal this is what thousands of people are doing today.

There are lots of very interesting places to live in Canada like Wawa, Ontario- home of the largest goose in the world! If you have never visited Wawa yet be sure to place it on your bucket list! Wawa is fun!

There will be some people who will be quite upset with some of the facts I am sharing in this book. There are millions of Canadians associated with real estate from ownership to sales from construction to repair from banking to governments and taxation from advertising to legal issues from renting to owning to money laundering to crime. The list goes on. And when people from each area explain real estate information to you often it is to generate revenue for their own services. They honestly feel that their understanding of it based on their activities makes them an expert and while it does make them an expert in the area they work it the field is so huge that they are not experts in all aspects of real estate. It took me a few years of study to figure that one out! You really need to step back and see the big picture.

.

My suggestion is that before you enter the market to sell or purchase real estate please read this book first. Once you have a better understanding of how real estate in Canada really works you can then start asking the right questions, start better understanding what experts in the field are telling you and then be in a much better position to make the right decisions.

And remember that there is no such thing as perfection in attaining real estate knowledge. Yes it is possible to be an expert in some areas but when you have over 13.2 million residential homes in Canada in all sorts of locations with ever changing economic conditions from both internal and external sources in a world with over 7.5 billion humans in it can you really expert to be an expert in everything? Like me. Just kidding! Now for the good news! If you read this book and think about the ideas and facts that are presented and apply them your chances of obtaining a very good deal in real estate will be greatly increased. I think that your chances of success are high and imagine for a moment that you receive a handful of money from the facts you learned in this book. Best wishes for a good real estate deal and I hope that this book helps and saves you that handful of money! Or more. Maybe ten handfuls of money. Here I am holding $1500 to show you what it looks like. It looks nicer in your pocket than in somebody else's and that's another reason for reading this book!

Money has a certain feel to it. It is not like a credit or debit card or a cheque or money order. If you are looking at a used car or a boat where the seller is asking considerably more an offer of cash often results in a sale. Cash is magic in a way. You need to be careful with cash because there are folks out there that would quite cheerfully hit you over the head with a club to take it away from you. Criminals end up with lots of cash and somehow they need to transfer it into assets that appear honest and real estate is one asset they purchase!

REAL ESTATE - HOW IT REALLY WORKS

When we bought our first house we knew nothing about real estate. Through dumb luck we purchased our house at the bottom of the market in Victoria, British Columbia in a neighborhood where prices consistently go up. Previous to that purchase my wife and I had worked as professional real estate photographers in Calgary Alberta and we had the opportunity to photograph thousands of houses and meet many agents in the industry. We did that job on a part time basis in addition to our regular jobs for just over a year. This was our introduction to real estate.

As friends and family members purchased and sold their homes I became curious about real estate and the more I looked into it the more I became convinced that it was much more complicated than one might think when first looking at it. And it became obvious that a certain amount of dumbing down was going on in the market as individuals attempted to simplify what was happening and instead left the reader with an incomplete view of just how real estate worked.

I wrote this book to document my research and to share what I have learned. The surprising facts are that there are several players in the real estate market and each of them have vested interests in maintaining their positions and their income. There is also a fair amount of evil in the marketplace where the home owner ends up being the victim. Remember you make a profit in real estate when you sell a property for more than you have invested in it. And don't forget you need to adjust the totals for inflation because a dollar back in 1995 is no longer worth the same amount of money today. If you have a good understanding of just what is going on you also have a good chance of making a good profit on your real estate dealings.

This book will be of great use to the home buyer, the seller, the realtor and the real estate investor. It contains very useful information and a point of view that you will not find anywhere else. Although the book has been written from a Canadian perspective it will also be helpful in any real estate market. And if you are outside Canada and considering purchasing a property in Canada this book will give you an excellent insight as to what is really going on here and where the opportunities are.

I have divided the topic into logical chapters. As you read along you will begin to understand what the challenges and opportunities are. Please keep an open mind as you will encounter some ideas which at first might appear unusual or difficult to believe but which will begin to make sense as more examples are given.

And some chapters don't seem to be in the right place but what I have done on purpose is to try and mix up the viewpoints so that you won't look at real estate from the same direction all the time. It is a very complicated topic and you need to approach each decision point from several different directions. That sounds horrible but I am trying to share with you that if you look at everything from one direction and simplify things then your results might not work very well. Then you would blame me.

DEEP DARK SECRETS OF CANADIAN REAL ESTATE

When something is top secret a few people know about it but most people don't. So the people who know about it have an advantage over the others who don't have a clue.

Life is a one time gift that begins with birth and usually ends a relatively few years later with death -an event that is occasionally hastened by accident or health problems. During this process we humans progress through childhood, our teenage years, and maturity to our senior years and again to our eventual demise. A surprisingly important factor during our lives is the topic called real estate. And even more surprising is the fact that a lot of information regarding this topic is **Top Secret** and by that I mean that the majority of people are unaware of it.

UnREAL-ESTATE CANADA

During our early childhood we live in real estate controlled by our parents and as we age we may acquire control over real estate of our own. We usually start this process slowly by sort of owning our own bedroom. Some of us keep it very neat and well organized and others leave it a mess. Education is a key factor in raising children and teenagers and young adults. Here we try our best to ensure that our children have all the education they require to live successful lives.

Isn't it odd that Real Estate is not taught to our children as they grow up. We don't mention it in the primary grades or high school and even university. Despite the fact that we spend countless hours in our lives living in houses, apartments, condos, trailers, vessels etc. and despite the fact that much of the income we earn goes into the real estate that we live in – none of us have received anything about real estate from our education system. Real Estate remains a secret topic for most of us and then suddenly we act to acquire property ourselves. You can see what I am getting at now. I hope.

The premise of this book is that when it comes to real estate we need to have a good understanding of the topic and we need to start at square one because up until now we have never been properly introduced to the topic. The word stupid is a very sensitive word to most of us. When you know very little about a topic is it fair to be called stupid about it? I think it is. But some overly sensitive people will complain that calling somebody stupid is politically incorrect and that the word should never be used. I think they are stupid. I know what stupid is because over the years I have acted stupid myself. A few times.

I began to study real estate for this book four years ago. My background includes a University degree including studies in Economics, science, several years experience in financial management, accounting, banking, large and small business. I am one of those people who can think outside the box and keep their sense of humor. Early in my studies I began to realize that the topic was much more complex than I had originally thought. Then I realized that most people are operating on what can only be called simplified concepts about the topic. And this is where the idea of this book sprang up. I thought I could help! Like most Canadians I like to help!

In order to ensure that our knowledge about the state of Canada's economy was up to date we drove from North Bay, Ontario to Vancouver Island, British Columbia in 2016. Over the years I have visited most parts of Canada and we have lived in several geographical areas including our 40 foot sailboat on the Pacific Ocean on our West Coast, a motorhome and apartments and houses. We saw first hand real estate markets that were booming, steady, declining and changing and one thing in common was that wherever we went Canadians were happy, polite and friendly.

What follows is an introduction to Real Estate and the major factors which are involved in real estate transactions. The objective is to give you a much better understanding of the processes involved in buying and selling a home and other alternatives so that you can avoid mistakes and obtain the best deal.

UnREAL-ESTATE CANADA

THE HUMAN BRAIN and REAL ESTATE

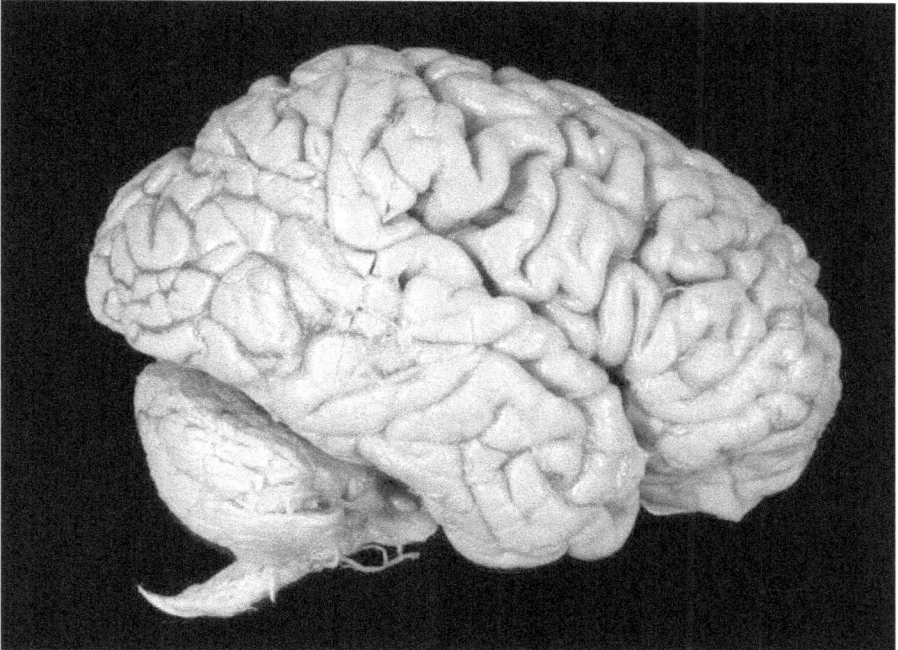

The human brain is probably the ugliest organ in the body as you can see here but without it life as we know it would not exist...Imagine the most attractive man or woman that you know and consider that their brain looks like this....

The Earth is populated by about 7.3 billion people. Each of us has a brain and each brain works slightly differently that is none of us have identical brains! The world is incredibly complicated and somehow the human brain must simplify perceptions. For example when snow falls we say "it is snowing". When it is raining we say "it is raining". We have simplified the process. In the case of snow, people living in the far north actually have well over 27 words to describe snow. There are also many words to describe rain.

The brain tends to think in what I will refer to as **subjective** terms. But we can also describe what is happening around us in **objective** terms. That is we can say that it is raining 50 mm of rain from the North West with a wind of 32 miles per hour. That gives us a more scientific description of the rain that is falling. There is much more information there than just saying "it is raining".

What I am trying to get across here is that our brains tend to simplify perceptions with subjective terms and when we get into trying to understand real estate we need to be careful that we look at it from a more objective viewpoint. Instead of saying "the house is big" lets try to understand how may square feet it is. What are the actual dimensions? What does a "big lot" mean?

If I was trying to sell you something I might say that the "yard is big" and I am trying to get across a subjective idea about size to you. But what you really want to know is how big? What are the dimensions? What is the area? Subjective terms tend to be relative because what is "big" to one person is "small" to another but if I tell you that the property is 50 feet wide and 300 feet deep then you actually know the size of the property in objective terms. An agent could tell you that the property has a "big yard" and then after you purchase it you may find out that your yard is actually the smallest yard on the street!

I tend to look at life from an objective viewpoint. Why? I have taken a lot of courses in science and that is how I think. I have had a lot of financial management jobs so again I think in terms of numbers not in terms of subjective terms like "expensive" or "under the market". But a lot of people think mainly in subjective terms. They may not be very good in Math and so everything gets simplified and terms like "good price" "fire sale" "excellent deal" etc are the terms they use to understand real estate. The danger of using mainly subjective terms in trying to understand real estate is that you will be taken advantage of and will get a bad deal.

And now for the final points on the human brain. One might think that if a person makes the wrong or a bad decision in real estate no matter who they are they are stupid. This could be true. But there are options for making a bad decision. A person can be unlucky. They could have made all the correct decisions and one month into the ownership of their new home there could be a small earthquake a couple of miles away that lets loose a major flood of water which pretty much destroys their property. So **luck** is a factor and it could be good luck or bad luck.

Another factor is being **naïve**. You could believe everything that was said about the property for sale and not think that you should confirm that the stated facts are true. You might not even get a home inspection not because you were stupid but because you believed everything the owner and the sales agent told you.

The other factor is that the person might be a **trusting person**. That is they trust everybody that tells them something that what they are saying is in fact true. That is close or a bit similar to being naïve.

So there you go. You can make a bad mistake in real estate by being unlucky, stupid, naïve or too trusting and consequently you can improve your odds by being smarter, confirming what people tell you and by not trusting everybody who tells you something. Except me.

I am trying to help you! I am not trying to make thousands of dollars off of your purchase or sale. But still as you read the book if you see something you are not sure about do some research on it. Don't go to a bank to ask them if they are honest and treat their customers well go to a discussion group where bank customers tell their stories or go to a correspondent's article on banks or review how the government is trying to control how banks operate.

And don't forget, the numbers I quote in the book change hourly and so today's numbers will be different but often the trends between the numbers stay the same. One example would be the percentage of GDP in Canada that is generated by Real Estate. I have seen estimates from 10.5 to almost 12 % and in both cases that placed Real Estate as the biggest source of GDP in Canada. When you are making a decision on real estate try and find out which direction the trends are going and at what rate as that could tell you a lot about what will happen next. .

EXPERTS

We can learn a lot from experts who understand a subject. And we can get confused by people who think they are an expert but don't really understand a subject.

Now for a deceptively simple topic that becomes worrisome almost immediately!

An expert is somebody who understands a given topic and who can be depended on to give good advice about that topic. Seems simple enough? But what if a person claimed to be an expert or believed they were an expert in a given topic and the reality is that they do not understand the topic and are in fact giving bad advice about that topic? Or what if the information they were giving was designed to help them and not you?

Let's say that you had a medical problem with your knee and so you mention it to your family Doctor. She asks you a couple of questions and then suggests you take Aspirin when your knee hurts. Then a couple of years later you realize that your knee hurts so much that you need to see your Doctor again. This time she refers you to an Orthopedic Specialist Doctor and She has an x-ray done on your knee and decides that your cartilage in your knee is worn out and you need a new artificial knee joint installed. What has just happened here? I use the knee joint thing because I have a right knee with worn out cartilage in it and I know how this patient would feel. This is an example of what happens when you receive an expert level of knowledge about something. And yes similar things can happen in other areas including mechanical repairs to your vehicle and yes you guessed it – Real Estate!

When I began researching this book I naturally looked for experts in the field. It took a while to realize that people claiming to be experts did not seem to fully understand all aspects of real estate and that in many cases the information they were giving was faulty or designed to help them and not you!

And I better explain that a bit. Yes the "experts" know their part of the real estate business very well and yes you can learn very useful facts from them but my point is that real estate is such a huge business that nobody can possibly be an expert in all parts of it so they tend to concentrate on the part of it that they work in.

Family members and friends will wish to help you with your real estate decisions. In some cases they may have purchased or sold real estate in the past and because of that they may feel that they have a better understanding of the topic than you do and that therefore they can give you advice. In fact they may have a better understanding of real estate than you do but my point here is that they are not "experts" in the field. So yes you should listen carefully to the advice that they give you because often they will give you some very useful information but you should also consider the points made in this book.

Men and Women are social animals and there are constant interactions between friends and acquaintances. There is nothing wrong with listening to or talking about real estate with a friend or acquaintance. At the same time if you wish to make the best decisions regarding real estate then you should have access to expert opinions from people who understand the topic and the situation that you find yourself in.

My suggestion is that nobody is an expert in all aspects of real estate. It is such a large and complex topic that you really need to consult with people who have expertise in sections of this topic.

Let me give you an example. When I went to University I took a course in computer programming and this was when programming was done with paper cards and main frames. This was in the 1970's a long time ago! You would wrap an elastic around the cards and then take them down to the computer centre where the main frame was located. There you would enter the cards into a card reader which would transfer information to the mainframe and cause it to perform certain functions. This was also the time that desktop computers called PC's were beginning to be introduced. It was possible during these times to have a expert level of knowledge about the entire computing industry. As an expert you could answer just about any question about computers and the programs that were available. But things quickly changed and then we had geometric growth in the number and types of computers and programs and suddenly it was impossible to be an expert in the entire field anymore. You could become an expert in a certain type of hardware or software but that was about the best you could do. The same sort of situation applies with real estate.

People with levels of expertise in real estate include realtors, lawyers, economists, bankers, Accountants, contractors, designers, tradesmen, town planers, and I am sure that there are others! You simply cannot expect one person to have a level of expertise in all aspects of real estate.

If you have unreasonable expectations you will just get angry when the information you receive is wrong!

And yet members of the public do have what I will call "unreasonable expectations" when it comes to assigning expert status in real estate. Many expect that Realtors are experts in all aspects of the field and can be depended on to give them the best advice. Others depend on friends and acquaintances and family members who have purchased real estate in the past to provide them with accurate expert level advice.

And this is where things become troubling. Have we accepted advice from others in the past expecting that they were giving us good advice when in fact it was wrong? Just who do we go to for expert advice?

I have identified areas of expertise. My suggestion would be to match these areas to the area of knowledge that you require advice on and start taking notes and doing your research.

Here is an example. Many years ago we purchased a house in Victoria BC. I was a little concerned about the traffic so contacted the local planning department. I received excellent advice advising me that the street was something called a "secondary arterial" and that traffic would gradually increase over time. We owned the home for over ten years and that is precisely what the traffic did. The advice was free, it was accurate and very useful. I had approached a person who was an expert in the area that I needed information about and he gave me that information.

Remember, people are sensitive beings. If they feel that they are experts in a field when in fact they are not you should not challenge them on it. That will only make them angry with you. Be polite, listen to what they have to say and be sure to obtain advice from experts in the particular segment of real estate that you are enquiring about. I used medicine as an example because they have many specialties in that field of study too. And it is a real challenge for the person asked the question to admit that they cannot answer it and that you really should see "an expert" in that area.

Some people will understandably claim expert status when they encounter a bit of luck in real estate for example when they happen to buy at the bottom of the market just prior to it rising substantially. Were they experts or just lucky? If you do as they suggest will you be lucky too? Or is the market moving in the opposite direction?

People that like you will want to help you. They will have the best of intentions. You need to be sensitive to this while still keeping your radar up to identify information which may not be true. Real estate is complex, the stakes are high in that the financial transactions will be some of the biggest in your lifetime and making a mistake could result in a financial disaster that will affect the rest of your life. Good luck!

HOW TO SIMPLIFY REAL ESTATE TRANSACTIONS

If you can't explain it **simply**, you don't understand it well enough.

— Albert Einstein

Albert came up with a simple formula $E=mc^2$ which shows how Energy is equal to the mass of an item multiplied by the speed of light squared. Imagine if Mr. Einstein had concentrated on real estate instead of physics.

If you are a buyer or a seller you first need to determine why you wish to buy or sell. Think about it. Be sure you are making the best decision because once you make it a series of events will happen and there will be certain results and you need to be sure that those results will be to your advantage. In some cases other people want you to proceed and it is because of the advantages that they will achieve not what will happen to your situation.

Next concentrate on the asking price and the offer price and what you would accept as a selling or buying price. And that is just the start. You also need to find out a lot of information about the property itself and your particular needs. But first let's consider price. In each case the buyer and the seller will have a range of prices and if the range overlaps there is a zone in which a sale or purchase could take place.

Normally what happens is that the seller starts the process by listing the home with an agent or putting up a sale sign themselves. Sometimes the process is started when there is a knock at the owner's door and a Real Estate Agent asks them if they are interested in selling because they have a buyer who wishes to purchase their property. And when the owner decides to sell their property an asking price needs to be determined. The prospective buyer looks at the property and comes to a decision on whether they wish to own the property because it meets their needs. Then they come up with a price to offer the seller.

When the seller is presented with the offer the seller must make a **decision**. Do they accept the offer or do they counter with a lower price? If they accept the offer the sale proceeds. If they return the offer with a lower acceptable price the buyer must now consider if they will pay that price. The buyer may repeat the process and either offer the person the same price or a higher price or they may offer the reduced price the seller has requested. The process could be and often is repeated.

As you can see the process can be quite stressful. For both parties this is likely one of the largest transactions they have had in their lives. A lot is at stake. The buyer wants the property and will be thinking about living there and all the enjoyment they could have there. The seller wants to sell and they realize that if the property is sold they possibly could be totally out of debt and perhaps even have some capital to use on other projects.

Real estate deals do cause stress. Unfortunately.

The resistance in both parties is there. The buyer wants to get the property at the lowest price they can get it at and the seller wants the highest price they can get for it. And now something unexpected happens.

The real estate agent only makes money IF there is a sale. They must have a sale. So what they try and do is apply force and tricks and whatever is necessary to talk both seller and buyer into the deal. But remember they are doing this for themselves because if there is no sale they do not get paid. If the seller gets less than they want for the property the real estate agent still gets paid. If the buyer pays more money for the property than they want to the real estate agent still gets paid! This is a very important point.

The real estate agent has been wearing his or her friendly hat. They have been polite and helpful and very friendly. But now he is putting on the Closer's Hat. And the behavior of the Real Estate Agent may change! Or not. But remember the objective now is to close the deal. In my mind this is just like flipping a switch to turn on or off a light. The change in behavior can be sudden and unexpected. And you might not even notice that there was a change until after the sale was completed! Then it suddenly hits you what your Agent did to complete the sale. And on one hand you could say that was their job to complete the sale and on the other you might realize that despite the fact the sale was completed you may have lost some money in the process.

CAN YOU REALLY OWN REAL ESTATE?

From our earliest years we are convinced that we can own things we like. We try our best to protect them and prevent others from taking them away. But eventually somebody gets them!

One of the main concepts of real estate is that you can **own** it. Let's consider that for a moment. Can you really own real estate? Remember we started with talking about the planet Earth and made the point that real estate was part of it. So do you think that you can really own part of the planet Earth or is this entire process a bit of a joke? The Earth has been here for millions of years and you will be here for the blink of an eye in comparison. Are you really into blinking ownership?

To begin, let's consider how mother nature treats land ownership. Each acre of land is full of life from tiny insects to frogs and snakes, small and big animals and birds. Do they own the land? Freddie frog may have taken up residence in a small pond. He may live there for several months thinking that it is his pond. Then suddenly Betty bird has him for lunch. The bird might think that she is in control of the land when one day she swoops down for another frog and a Sidney snake grabs her. Ronnie rabbit might have his own hole and thinks that he owns it until Francine fox has him for lunch. The point here is that in nature there is no thing called "land ownership". A species may be dominate in an area but not for long. Control over the land is always being passed around.

With humans we seem to have a different concept of land ownership. In North America the concept is that you can own your land all you need is a legal deed to it. People will work like dogs for decades to pay off mortgages on land so that they can own it. But if they miss two or three municipal tax payments on the land the city will confiscate it and use the proceeds to pay off the tax owing. So did they really own it?

The concept of land ownership can get quite ridiculous. In Canada if somebody steps on your land you can have them charged with trespass. In some States in the USA you can shoot somebody trespassing on your land. People put up no trespass signs, they erect fences and even install cameras, guard dogs and alarms to prevent others from stepping on their land. And some people step on their land anyways!

My point here is that a main premise in real estate is that you can own your land. Trillions of dollars are exchanged in the process to establish ownership and express the value of land. Do you really own it? The life cycle of a human is a mere blink of the eye in the history of the planet. Does a rabbit own the forest? Does a fish own the sea? Does a bird own the sky? Do you really own your real estate? Do you own this book? If you paid for it or if a nice person gave it to you as a gift then you do own it! So relax about the book.

I think that it is more accurate to say that humans can to a certain degree **control** real estate. That is you can control access to your yard and home. You can do this as long as you pay taxes and there are no floods or fires. You can have your name placed on a property ownership list which is maintained by a government office. You can sell that control or ownership to another person.

This concept of control rather than ownership will incense some people. They will scream at you and say that they OWN the property. Fine. That is their point of view. What I am trying to do here is to give you an option on how to understand owning property. It is a very interesting concept when you start to think about it.

WHAT DO YOU NEED YOUR PROPERTY FOR?

A basic question in real estate and one which does not get asked as much as it should is .."What do you need your property for?" Are you going to use it to raise a family, keep a horse, your retirement, as a home base while you travel, a revenue source, a home for your elderly parents? Do you want to run a business in your home? Do you want to have shop facilities to do mechanical work? Are you looking for a safe investment so that you can build up your equity and leave something in your estate for your kids? Do you want a low maintenance home in a low tax area? What do you want? Do you want to live in an upscale residence close to your business associates and friends?

I ask this question because one property cannot do all things and if you purchase a property ignoring what you want to use it for you will just be frustrated. So the best approach is to think about what you really want the property for and then decide if you can afford what you want or do you need to make some reductions? And when you look at a property you need to consider the list of things that you want it for and decide if the property meets those needs.

Have you ever wondered how many people have purchased property and then decided that it does not meet their requirements and so go out and sell the property they purchased and then buy new property? This is a very expensive process. Occasionally in the case of rising prices it might generate profits and increases in property value but in cases where the prices are steady or falling the cost to do this will result in a loss of asset value. So my point is that it would be wise to carefully consider what your property requirements are before you enter the real estate market and start spending your money.

ARE YOU BUYING A PROPERTY OR GOING INTO DEBT?

What if you got a note like this? How would you feel?

Often people remark that they "bought a house". But what does that really mean? Let's say that the house was $850,000. But they didn't have $850,000 they had $50.000 so they got a mortgage for $800,000. Now on one hand they "own the house" but on the other they owe $800,000 on a mortgage. And the mortgage includes interest so if they make payments over 30 years (360 payments) they may pay $533,772.90 or more for interest for a total of $1,333,772.90 for the $850,000 house. But it gets worse. If you are in the 15% tax bracket then you also need to pay $200,065.94 taxes on the money you use for interest and mortgage payments. And every year you pay city taxes and various other costs like water and sewer and gas and things. It is a bit different if you have $850,000 of spare money in the bank and you write a cheque for the property. In that case you are transferring one asset to another and in times of rising real estate prices you would very likely increase the value of your assets faster in real estate than letting the loot sit in the bank.

My point here is that if you look at all the taxes and other expenses that you need to pay when you have a mortgage that your so called purchase of this property is really just jumping into a cesspool of **debt**. Unless of course the property is going up in value quickly. In which case you could make more money than in other investments even if you purchased a rental property and let it remain unoccupied for several months. In fact in 2016/17 this is precisely what investors were doing in the Toronto real estate market! So here we are with a rental shortage and yet thousands of properties are left unoccupied. This is incredibly stupid from the perspective of a person desperately looking for a place to rent and being unable to find one and it shows how our three levels of government seem to not understand the dangers of allowing people to invest in real estate in a rising market while leaving the property empty. Why do they leave the property empty? Simple they want to sell it and they don't want to incur any expenses giving their renters notices or preparing the rental units for sale.

There are facts that your Real Estate Agent, banker, lawyer won't tell you. Because if they told you then you wouldn't likely purchase the property and they wouldn't make any money from you. The media won't tell you because they make lots of money from real estate ads. And I will take one more run at this topic just to make sure that I have made my point about buying vs going into debt.

When you buy something you take an asset like cash and you give it to the person selling the item. What you have done is taken one asset and effectively converted it into another asset. You don't have the money anymore but you now own whatever you purchased. Now let's consider a house. If the house is $500,000 and you have that in your bank and you write the seller a cheque for $500,000 then you own the house. But what if you only have $50,000 in the bank and you needed to obtain a mortgage on the house for $450,000. This time around are you really buying the house? No. You are going into debt for $450,000 and in order to pay it off over 30 years and 360 payments you need to earn the money and pay taxes on your earnings and then you need to pay interest to the mortgage holder in addition to the amounts placed on principle.

And what really frustrates me is that people will claim that they "**just bought the house**". They didn't buy the house they went into debt and should the market value not keep up with inflation or should there be a sudden drop in the value of the house then they could have an upside down mortgage where they owe the bank more money than the house is worth. I think that another term should be used when a mortgage is obtained to purchase a house. Lets call it "going into debt" Do the math and you will be horrified how much money that house will actually cost you in taxes and interest and all the other costs of home ownership.

So there I have just told you some facts about purchasing a home that no Real Estate broker or Banker or Lawyer or House Inspector or Government Employee would ever tell you. And they will all be mad at me for telling you this.

Humans sometimes express their opinions by getting mad an emotional term and that often happens in real estate and other places too! So how does one react to a mad man or a mad woman? Do you get mad yourself?

President Trump is a good example of a very successful individual who made billions in business and in a very hard fought election was elected to the most powerful position in the world. Millions of people love him and millions don't. Many people are earning lots of money picking on him. The different attitudes show us how the public reacts in different ways to the same situation. Real estate is like that too!

REVENUE POTENTIAL

When considering a property very few people tend to consider its potential to generate income. Let's consider a property with a full basement. It is usually possible to design in the components that would be required to rent out the basement as a separate suite. This could generate a significant amount of revenue for you. You may not need the revenue now. But what happens when you retire? What happens when you lose your job? How about unexpected expenses?

Homes which are 1000 or less square feet are difficult but not impossible to include a revenue producing space in. But houses of 1500 square feet up are increasingly easy to ensure that there is a suitable space for possible future revenue.

Having a potential revenue producing room also increases the value of your home when the time comes to sell it.

A separate living space also allows you to host friends and visitors and family members coming back to the home for visits or whatever. In today's economy youth unemployment is high and it is not unusual to welcome your adult children back as they recover from a bad economy or work on their education or save up for a property of their own.

Now it doesn't mean that there actually needs to be a separate suite built into your home just that the potential for having one without major additional building is a good idea. We have friends who have a modest sized two story home with a basement. The basement has a separate suite built in including a bedroom, bathroom and shower and a separate entrance which also leads into the main home. The home is perfect for visitors and would also work well for student accommodation. I would say that three are three levels of revenue potential in a property.

Lets start with the initial level. Even in a relatively small property if you had a separate bedroom it would be possible to rent that bedroom out to a student. The student would still need to share certain part of the property like the bathroom and kitchen and perhaps even the living room and laundry but in theory if you found an appropriate student that would be an initial way of earning some additional income from your property.

Now let's go to the second level. Here you would have separate quarters for the person renting the space and they would have their own entrance, their own washroom and access to either their own or shared laundry facilities. You would need about 500 or 600 square feet for a minimum sized second suite and possibly more but there are certain advantages here. You could charge a higher rent than just for one room and the renter would be separated from having access to your space. You could also use the space for seasonal renting rather than having a renter there all year. And if you traveled on longer vacations or would be away for a few days it would be helpful to have a person in your building looking after things. I think myself that this is the preferred level.

But you would also have an advanced level of rentals too. For example let's say that you purchased a four plex apartment building with two floors and two units on each floor. You kept one unit for yourself and rented out the other three. With a unit like this it could be possible that the rent would cover ALL the expenses associated with the building and that you could enjoy two things –free rent for yourself and a possible increase in property value over time. There may even be tax advantages as the expenses associated with maintaining the building could be helping to reduce the taxes you would normally pay so it may be possible to reduce your taxes on your overall income by managing a rental building.

And from a potential revenue perspective there is a very important point about basements in homes that you might like to purchase. Unfortunately home builders will make basements that are horrible. Why? Because they want to save money. So although a home might have a so called basement it may not really be a basement.

Take a look at the height of the basement. I have seen some basements where the height is less than six feet. So if you finished the ceiling your head would bump into it. Why isn't it two feet higher? Money is the reason. The builder saved a few hundred or thousand dollars by placing in a sub standard basement. Or they used a substandard floor that cracked or leaked. Don't purchase that house thinking that you can use the basement. The cost to add the required two feet to the height of the basement would be tens of thousands of dollars and a huge amount of work would be required.

It is so frustrating to see a substandard basement. My advice is to just stay away from them!

THE CONDO or APARTMENT RIP OFF

Have you ever considered the differences between a condo and an apartment? If you were a developer with access to several million dollars of financing which type of investment would you prefer? If you wanted to live in the dwelling which one would you prefer?

In any business transaction the main objective is to generate wealth in a short period of time which means that the transaction must result in a profit. The profit represents the new wealth. If your transactions did not generate wealth but instead caused a loss then over time you would destroy your wealth be out of business and end up living in poverty.

There are many ways to generate a profit. You can manufacture items and sell them at a higher price than what they cost to make. You can provide a service and charge for it more than it cost you to supply it. Or you can engage in activity where debt is transferred from you to another party and no exchange of goods or services takes place. In other words you can rip people off. And on that point let me explain to you why I suggest that a Condo is often a rip off when compared to an apartment. And sometimes, in a rising market it is a good idea! So again we have a level of complexity here. Wouldn't it be nice if everything was simple?

When you rent an apartment it is usually done on a monthly basis often with an annual lease where you agree to keep the apartment for a year. Your landlord provides the financing for the apartment building, pays for the building insurance and pays the building taxes.

They ensure that common areas are kept clean and that maintenance is done. The landlord also takes all the risk during downturns in the real estate market. Basically all you need to do is pay your rent on a monthly basis and look after the interior of your apartment. Although you have no ownership rights you do have a right to live in the apartment for as long as the lease lasts as long as you obey reasonable rules and as long as you pay your rent. The Landlord makes a profit every year of ownership and may make a profit or loss when the building is sold.

Now let us consider Condos. The developer starts selling condo units off prior to the completion of the building. They obtain their profit almost immediately. The condo owners take on all responsibility for their units, for the common spaces and for the insurance and taxes. They also take on all risks associated with real estate fluctuations. So you can begin to see what is happening here. Is it a good thing or a bad thing or does the damn thing vary with changing real estate values? Unfortunately the answer is yes to each situation.

And let us consider the concept of ownership and condo's. Does one really own a condo? Or could it be reasonably argued that ownership is in fact shared with other condo owners in the complex? If there are ten levels in a complex then don't you really own only a miniscule of the underlying lot size? That is you don't own 10% of it you may only own 1% or even less of the land your condo sits above.

The bottom line is that a condo is a simple rip off of the public where all the risks and costs of maintaining an apartment building are transferred to the condo owner so that the condo developer can maximize their profits and minimize the time required to generate wealth on their investment.

And before some readers gasp in horror let me say that this ONLY applies when the real estate value of a condo property is stagnant and not keeping up with inflation OR when the market is falling. The only time where a condo investment generates wealth for the condo owner is when real estate is increasing in value. And those could be very good times and we see them in Toronto in 2017 where condo owners have made huge increases in asset values of their property.

During times when the cycle is headed down the loss of equity will be added to all the costs of ownership and there will be no advantage to the condo owner over living in an apartment. In fact during those times the condo investment will be worse than renting an apartment. Because not only do they have all the real costs of maintaining the condo but they are also incurring all the potential costs of a downturn in the real estate market where their asset value for their condo is going down several thousand dollars a year. If you added that potential loss to the actual funds spent monthly to maintain the condo you could be looking at double or triple the rent of a similar sized apartment if the condo owner sold during this period of downturn..

If you are considering a condo purchase think again. Is the market going up or down and what are the chances of it going down during your ownership? Would an apartment be a better way to go?

From a builder's perspective in early 2017 in Toronto all you need to do is place a sign on a lot saying that you are building a condo there and you will receive hundreds of requests from interested prospective buyers. Condo building is a very efficient method of turning real estate in to excellent profits very quickly. As long as the market continues to go up rapidly.

There is one obvious question here with condos and apartments and houses. If the average Canadian family income is now around 70K then the average Canadian cannot afford a house or a condo so they would need an apartment. But if the builder makes more money from a condo why would they want to build an affordable apartment and so where do the people with average or below salaries live? One might think that our three levels of government just might be managing this issue well. Are they? As I am completing this book I see that the Mayor of Toronto and the Finance Ministers of Ontario and Canada are meeting to see if they can somehow solve the hideous rental availability problem in Toronto without harming the value of properties owned by citizens who have made fortunes in asset value thanks to rising markets.

In Toronto the market has gone up over 33% in one 12 month period. And I don't blame the market I blame the three levels of government in Canada that have allowed the market to do this. Clearly the rules and regulations that government is supposed to manage were not there and this is why the market is in such a mess. Yes it is great to see all those home owner millionaires but how about the average Canadians who are now looking for a place to live? Is it great for them too? Nope.

WHY IS REAL ESTATE SO EXPENSIVE?

I have approached this topic from a Canadian perspective although the comments will also apply to most other countries. Basic economics tells us that when the supply of an item is less than the demand for it the price goes up. When the price goes up the demand goes down and some form of equilibrium is reached.

When you look at Canada and note the huge amount of land compared to the relatively small population you might think that because the supply appears large and the demand for it relatively small that prices would be low. And when you look at the United States with ten times the Canadian population you might think that because demand is high and supply smaller than in Canada that prices might be higher than Canadian prices.

And here we run into the problem of oversimplification of a complex problem. There are other factors at work here. In Canada nearly all of the land is **Crown Land** legally owned by the Crown and managed by the provincial and federal government. In the USA nearly all the land is privately owned land.

In Canada nearly 90% of the population lives in a band of land 100 miles wide sitting on the US border and within this band the population is concentrated in just a few areas. In the USA the population is more widely distributed although there are also areas where it is concentrated.

What this means is that the standard rules of economics relating to supply and demand and price still apply however different numbers are encountered in different markets. You cannot apply the same numbers from a Toronto or Vancouver market to one in Northern Canada or in rural areas. This makes things much more complicated and accounts for the often confusing information on prices that our media reports. In fact one market may be going up while another goes down or sideways and yet another is stagnant and not even keeping up with annual inflation. This fact makes it difficult to identify trends that are applicable across the country.

For both buyer and seller it is important to know if the local market is rising or falling or staying the same. For example in a rising market it is much safer to purchase a home from a buyer's perspective because they know that prices are increasing and if they keep the home for a few months or years they will gain additional equity and or turn a profit if they sell. But in a falling market the great danger to a buyer is that the prices will continue to fall after they purchase the property and they will lose equity. In a falling market there is a tendency for lower offers to be tendered and in a rising market often higher offers are tendered.

From the seller's point of view in a rising market there might not be the same pressure to sell because they realize that the longer they keep the property the more it will be worth. There will be a tendency to not consider low ball or lower offers and there would likely be a tendency to want to get a bidding war going on the property where possibly more than the asking price will be offered.

UnREAL-ESTATE CANADA

Now here is a description of why real estate in certain parts of Canada is so expensive. I have made the point that in Canada there are certain desirable areas where our population is concentrated. There are large population densities in these areas. So you have a limited supply of land and a large demand. Since demand is greater than supply the basic laws of economics state that the prices will go up. Usually what happens is that over time the prices trend upwards at a certain rate each year. So you may have a 10% or more increase in the more desirable areas while at the same time there may only a 3 or 4 % increase or even a decrease in less desirable areas. Think about that fact. And remember one more important factor and that is **inflation**.

Every year inflation has been around 2% sometimes a bit less. You can check it all out on line at the **Bank of Canada inflation calculator**. And you may be surprised because if you thought your land had gone up 2% per year and you held it for then years then you may think that you just made a 20% profit on your investment. This simply is not true. Because the actual value of a dollar changes every year by the amount of inflation you may discover that what you thought was a 20% profit which say could be $200,000 on a Toronto property was in fact a zero increase and you made absolutely no profit on it when you adjusted your sale price for inflation.

And just to make this clear a dollar is not a constant value item. It changes in value every year based on the annual inflation rate. That is so confusing to so many people. Let me give you an example. While at University in the early 1970's I worked an afternoon shift at a tool manufacturing plant and earned about

$14.25 an hour with the incentive offered. So if in 2017 somebody tells me that they got a job for $14.25 an hour I would certainly not say "Hey that's what I made at University!" It turns out that the money per hour I was making back then is worth $85.70 in 2017 dollars. And so my point here is that you need to be careful when calculating your profit or loss on a real estate deal because you absolutely need to enter the differences in the value of a dollar first. Note that the tax department doesn't look at it this way. To them a dollar is a dollar. Why? Because to them if your dollar amount ten years after the purchase is higher than the original dollar amount then you get charged taxes on the so called profit you made on the sale. But it might not have been a profit at all in real dollar terms. Oh I find that so frustrating but as you can see inflation is not that difficult to calculate so please remember to do it with your real estate deals.

Let me give you an example. Let's say that you purchased a property in Toronto in 1980 for $100,000 and in 2017 you sold it for $300,000 so you bragged to your friends that you "made a $200,000 profit. Then one of your friends asks you to read this book where we advise you to check out the Bank of Canada inflation calculator which shows that $100,000 in 1980 is now worth $306,619.39 so you actually LOST $6,619.39 plus any additional costs you paid associated with the sale like the Agent's commission and lawyers fees and moving expenses etc etc. So suddenly your emotions of happiness and glee change to shock and horror. Sorry about that but I really want to help you better understand real estate. Now you hate me.

If you have an area that is trending up from year to year you have a potential area to invest your available money in. So in some situations you can actually make more money investing in real estate than you can investing in the stock market or operating a small business.

But remember just because a market is trending up and people are making excellent revenue in it by selling their properties it does NOT mean that the same will happen in all markets. In fact in some markets where the values are not keeping up with inflation or are sinking in value you could easily lose money if you purchased a house then sold it a couple of years later.

And there is one really important factor to consider if you are purchasing real estate for mainly investment purposes. In certain markets housing bubbles are forming and prices seem extremely high two or three or four or even more time the price of a house in less desirable locations. When there is a housing bubble with greatly inflated prices at some point the bubble bursts and the housing prices reduce by 20 ,30 or even 40 or more percent. That could represent a disastrous loss of your investment if you had to sell. It might represent a loss of all the equity you had in the property.

So in summary there are two reasons why some real estate is very expensive. One reason might be that there is limited supply and greater demand and together with this reason you may be in a market where several investors are purchasing property to take advantage of the trending upward prices.

EMOTIONS

Sometimes we get angry in real estate deals.

Selling or buying real estate can be a very emotional event. It is essentially a business transaction. The buyer and the seller arrive at a price that both agree upon and the sale and purchase is consummated. Let's consider how emotions make their way into this process.

First of all emotions are feelings such as love and hate, joy and sadness, fear and anger. If a buyer gives you a low ball offer you may lose your temper and tell him to go screw himself. You may use other words.

Words that rhyme with truck. A buyer may get a wonderful deal and be filled with happiness. It gets complicated.

The buyer will tend to be happier the less he or she pays for a property and the seller will be happier the more they receive for a property. The buyer will be sad and angry the more they pay for a property and the seller will be sad and angry as they receive less money for the property.

The seller will tend to be fearful when they refuse an offer and counter with a new offer. They are fearful that they will loose the offer. The buyer will suffer feelings of greed as they wish to keep as much of their equity as they can.

The main point here is that the entire process of buying and selling properties is emotional. The danger is that emotions will get in the way of making a sound business decision. If for example a seller is insulted by a low ball offer and simply refuses it they are allowing their emotions to rule them. Perhaps the better approach would have been to counter offer at a more reasonable price.

The advantage of using a realtor is that they soak up quite a bit of the emotion or at least act as a buffer between buyer and seller. And when emotions do start to run the realtor can be there to try and divert them from preventing the sale. I don't know how they handle it. I have known some excellent real estate agents over the years and have seen them perform and they impressed me. I wonder if they take drugs or alcohol to relax? Can you imagine how your guts would feel if you presented a million dollar offer to a seller which would have generate a $50,000 commission for you and suddenly the Seller tells you they changed their mind and are not selling? And you wanted to purchase a new car because the engine on your old one just quit. Are we talking stress here? Oh yes!

I think that it is very difficult but not impossible to push away one's emotions during a real estate transaction and concentrate on the business aspects of the deal. It would require a conscious effort to do so. Then, after the deal is concluded, let the emotions run!

Here is the problem. Some people are much more emotional than others. They would find it very difficult if not impossible to control emotions and concentrate entirely on the financial aspects of the sale. After the sale is concluded they may harbor residual emotions which could last for years. If you are like this I would recommend that you seriously consider using the services of a realtor and make your best attempt to mute your emotions during the sale. And having said that I think that it is perfectly natural that a forced sale or a sale of a family property with lots of memories may generate emotions many years after the event.

Let us consider just what an emotion is. It is a feeling. Typical emotions are being Happy or Sad being Angry or Nervous. But the feeling also influences your behavior. For example if you are angry you may not be able to successfully negotiate a deal with somebody. Let's say that you are a buyer and you offered a seller $200,000 for a property they were asking $350,000 for. They told you to "fuck off" and you get angry and tell them the same. And no deal occurs because your emotions are controlling your behavior. My point here is that emotions affect both the buyer and the seller and even the real estate agent.

Often when humans discover a problem or potential problem they also come up with a simple solution. When I tell you that emotions play a part in real estate deals you may then decide to not display any emotions and thus avoid any possible negative effects. That could be wrong.

All that I am saying is that emotions are a natural component of any human behavior. The best approach is to use emotions to help gain your objective. Let's look at some examples.

When you wish to sell a property you may talk with a Real Estate Agent and make a decision to use or not use their services. Think about this. And think about emotions. It is very likely that the Agent will be very friendly to you. They will attempt to establish a friendly relationship with you. They will listen to you, smile, offer useful advice. But they will also have a contract ready with a pen. Why?

If the Real Estate Agent obtains a signed contract from you to sell your property they immediately increase their chances of making a commission on any sale. So that signed contract could be worth thousands of dollars to them. When this approach is used the seller is impressed. They appreciate the friendly emotions offered and they tend to reciprocate. They might tell stories about the property and the Agent will be both very interested and very helpful.

In a Real Estate deal the first step is to decide that you wish to sell your property. The second step is to list it with a Real Estate Agent. The first objective of the Agent is to convince you to sign the sales contract. For a moment lets consider what happens when you sign that agreement.

As the listing agent the real estate agent can take that signed contract back to the office and then go on vacation. Why? Because they have done their jobs as listing agents and they will qualify for a portion of the commission when and if the property sells. Another agent from that real estate office may be the one who arranges the sale of your property or it may even be another agent from another real estate company. They also receive a portion of the sales commission.

I suggest that your best approach is to first realize what is going on and why the Agent is approaching you in a friendly way. And there is no reason why you cannot be friendly back to the agent. However you MUST realize that you are entering a business deal. So simply being friendly is not the best approach.

Each contract has certain terms like the length of time the contract is valid for. The Agent will want a long time because the longer the better as it increases the possibility that a sale will occur. The Agent will also wish to obtain a good commission rate on the sale. There is usually some flexibility there.

There is nothing wrong with being friendly. However you as a seller must realize that there is just one objective that the Agent has and that is to obtain your signature on the Sales contract. So they are using emotions to establish a business deal. And for a moment let's consider a business deal.

UnREAL-ESTATE CANADA

When somebody buys something from someone there needs to be an agreement on the price. The seller needs to set the price at a level that enough buyers will purchase the items so that they can sell enough of them to make a reasonable profit and cover their expenses.

And this can become complicated! For example a Real Estate company could obtain a listing and sell the property the next day! Or they may never sell the property or they may be able to sell it during the final week of the listing agreement. So in some cases the Real Estate Company may have invested considerable time and money into the sale and in other cases almost no expenses were encountered.

At this point let's remember one fact about the Real Estate business. This is not a simple job and people in this industry work very hard to do their jobs. The average income for a Real Estate Agent is quite low. Yes there are Agents who make very good salaries and yes during good times and rising prices and large volumes business is good. But all emotions aside the Real Estate Agent is providing you with a service and that service is definitely worth some money. But there are three main objectives here – your sale, the purchase by the buyer and the commission made by the Real Estate company. Each one of these three objectives wishes to maximize the deal to their advantage. So imagine three people around a desk all trying to come to a deal. And imagine the emotions that will flow. Happy, Sad, Nervous, Anger, etc etc.

There are times in this process that my suggestion would be to allow your emotions to run! For example let's stay you sold your property for $50,000 more than your asking price. The deal was successfully completed.

You received the payment and it is sitting in your bank. Celebrate! Don't worry about controlling your emotions. If you are happy give your agent an unexpected gift. Give them a Tim's Card for $200 and a Movie card for $200 and a thank you card. Give the person who purchased your property a nice gift when they move in. Take $1000 from that 50 extra thousand you received and convert it into gifts for the people that made it happen. Have a happy day/week or month! Enjoy yourself!

Now let's consider other emotions like ....Anger. Let's say that as a buyer you offer the seller an offer that is 25% lower than their asking price. Let's say the seller is angry with you and sends you a rude message on your offer. What do you do? Do you get mad too?

No you don't. The best approach is to control your emotions. Don't get mad. If you do get mad and refuse to make any more offers and you really want the property you won't get it. Nor will the seller get a sale from you. In reality I doubt the Agent would show you the rude comments on the offer anyway. They would more likely just tell you that the offer was not accepted and suggest that you increase it. Why? Because without a sale the Agent receives no money for their work. They may be feeling emotions too!

One question that might come up is how does a Real Estate Agent deal with your emotions to obtain a sale? If for example you are mad at the offer what would they do? If they agree with you then you may stay angry with the offer. And there would be no sale. So possibly they could make a bit of a joke about it to try and reduce your anger and then offer an alternative price that if you accept might result in a sale. Now who are they working for? The answer is simple.

The Agent is really working for you to sell the property, for themselves to collect the commission and for the buyer to identify an offer that will be accepted. My opinion is that there is a hierarchy here with the Agent being number one, the buyer being number two and the seller being number three. In other words the Agent's main objective is to collect their commission on the sale. If there is no sale there is no commission and only expenses.

So let's get back to emotions again. And how does the seller, the buyer and the Real Estate Agent best handle emotions? I have a theory. Eliminate the emotions until after the sale is completed. Treat it for what it is. A business deal. Assets are being transferred from one person to another. One person is obtaining a property and the other two persons are obtaining money. You can be polite but you don't need to be friendly or happy or angry or sad or nervous etc.

In a rising market you may receive an early offer for your property at or very close to your asking price. Then you may receive additional offers at amounts greater than your asking price. What should you do? The obvious answer is that you should accept the best offer. However here is the problem. The nature of the offers might be different. Some may just offer you the asking amount with no other conditions in a very short period of time. Others may offer you more but the offer may be over a longer period of time with specific conditions such as a home inspection. Now what if the home inspection uncovers some work that needs to be done that you may or may not be aware of? Possibly the person making the offer would modify it to reduce the offer by the amount required to do the work. Or depending on the work the person could cancel their offer. Or possibly the offer would be based on obtaining the mortgage funds and their bank might refuse so again the offer could be cancelled. So it does get complicated and keeping emotions out of it helps. Look at the risk. Look at the way the market is moving. Is there a pending crash on the way? Take everything into consideration then make your decision.

You thought I might end it here about emotions eh? Well you see there is an issue. It is possible to use emotions and obtain a sale. What if the seller was angry all the time. What if when an offer was submitted the seller just said nasty things about it? How would this effect the Real Estate Agent?

Consider for a moment that you are the Real Estate Agent. You have an offer ready for your customer. But your customer is angry. They see the offer and say nasty angry things about it. And even worse the seller accuses you of not doing your job very well. What are you going to do? You have several thousand dollars sitting on just one action a signature from the seller. But they aren't happy! Now you feel stressed. And the stress may cause you to do something to try and make the offer better. You might reduce your commission! Possibly that would make the seller happy enough to sign the offer and accept it. You would not like the seller. In fact you would likely hate them because it could very likely mean the loss of half of your commission. But you are desperate for sales. And so you make the offer and the seller is still mad at you and refuses to sign then offer. Now your only option is to go back to the buyer and see if you can obtain a better offer. Thankfully your buyer does make a bigger offer.

You take the new offer to your seller and again they seem angry. So in desperation you again add your reduction in commission to the deal. The seller again tells you that they are not happy with the offer and that you should have done a better job. Now you have a problem because now emotions are flowing. You hate the seller. But again if you don't get a sale here you make no money and now you may even get a negative letter to your employer. So you go back to the buyer and find out that they are really very interested in purchasing the property and that they will in fact pay the full asking price. You are relieved and take the signed offer over to the buyer.

But the buyer doesn't like the offer even though it is the amount they asked for. And they are still not happy with you! You are suffering from stress and unhappiness and anger. You would love to tell the seller to fuck off and punch him and leave and never talk to him again and maybe even get a new job. So you apologize to the seller and tell them that you greatly regret not being able to obtain this offer before but you have it now and you think it is an accomplishment to obtain the asking price especially when the seller has made two previous lower offers. To your surprise the seller asks for the offer, looks at it and signs it and slaps you on the back and says "well done" with a big smile on their face. Suddenly your emotions change. You are relieved and your stress level is down and you have just made a $15,000 commission.

Then you go to your car, phone the buyer and tell them the offer has been accepted. Then you take a second look at the signature on the offer and realize that the seller has signed it as "Donald Duck". You are now furious. And you get a call from your office telling you that the seller has just cancelled the contract with your Real Estate Agency. They also want to talk to you because the seller has had some complaints about your service.

Here we have an example of emotions. Can you imagine for a moment how terrible you would feel if YOU were the real estate agent in this situation. Your emotions would be so strong that you might wish to invest in a bottle of booze or some sort of drug. How anyone could go through something like that and not be angry and stressed out?

This example is a bit far fetched perhaps but it does show you the advantages of NOT allowing your emotions to enter a real estate deal. I mean that was my objective but to be honest I was getting stressed just telling the story!

If you are a buyer don't "fall in love" with a property before you own it. If you are a seller don't get angry with a lack of offers until you get one that you like! If you are a real estate agent don't get upset with either buyers or sellers. Relax. The deal will either go or not. If it goes through you will make a commission and if it doesn't you won't.

Another thought here to help you reduce the emotional component. If you think about it there really is no such thing as ownership of real estate. Why? Because the real estate will be there for decades and decades but you won't. At some point you will die or get sick and need to go to a nursing home or you may need to move to another city. And if you really think that you own that property think of what would happen if you didn't pay the taxes on it for three years. Think of what would happen if a large fire tore through your neighborhood. Think of what would happen if some horrible weather like a tornado or hurricane or flood ruined your property. So what do you really own now?

The reality is that millions of people do not own property and they simply rent it from others. At first the level of home ownership in Canada and the USA seems high at around 70% of the population but only about 30% or so actually own their homes without a mortgage. So when you step back and consider it all many more people have mortgages or no home compared to the slim minority that own their homes without a mortgage' I won't quote the numbers as I have not been able to confirm them from multiple sources but it most certainly appears that the majority of homes owned by Americans and Canadians also have mortgages against them. And because of the failing economy in the last few years it appears that the trend in 2017 is for a larger percentage of home owners to have mortgages and a growing number of people renting their property rather than owning it.

TROLLS AND HATERS AND EMOTIONS AND REAL ESTATE

Some people are never happy. There are some people who hate everything. I call them **Trolls** and or **Haters**. My guess is that they represent between 20 and 35% of our society. In social media today if you put a comment about anything online someone will say something nasty about it. As a Publisher I learned early that trolls and haters exist and there is nothing that you can do about it. So ignore them and carry on and enjoy life. Or you can hide in a corner and never say anything but that is not much fun. There will be a political motivation or a gender motivation or whatever but for some reason or another some people will whine and complain and say nasty things. So let's consider Real Estate.

Let's say that a Real Estate agent works hard to sell your home and they succeed. But the home is sold at $10,000 less than your asking price. Nevertheless you got the majority of funds you were asking for and many would say you got a good price. If you were a Troll or Hater you would immediately complain to your friends and others about how your real estate agent screwed up and didn't do their job. Now my point here is that if you step back and look at the deal from a distance you will see that it was a fair deal and that the

Agent did in fact do a good job. Perhaps they talked with over 40 potential buyers and perhaps there were good reasons why most of the people didn't want your property. There is no law that you can't say what you want to say. But if you take the Troll or Hater approach in a real estate deal you will cause harm to the Agent and you will also share incorrect information with anyone that you complain and whine to about the transaction. As an example what if you placed your property for sale and your Agent phones you the next day with an offer for the amount you were asking? If you accept the offer then in one day your Agent will make thousands of dollars. Is that fair?

Absolutely not! But the problem is that this is the way the real estate market works. This is not the Agent's fault. What you could do is accept the offer with the provision that the commission would be reduced by two percent. That would be $2000 per every $100,000 in the selling price. In Toronto this would be $20,000 on a one million dollar home. But this would be a huge problem for the Agent because they would need to confirm the reduction with their office. If the listing agent was the one with the offer you might get an agreement but if another selling agent appeared with the offer then this would affect the amount of commission to the listing and selling agent.

It can get a little sticky here. You did sign the contract agreeing to a stated commission of say 5% and they did get the price you wanted. But now from a business perspective you may have an opportunity to save $20,000 in expenses. $20,000 is a lot of money. You could purchase a nice boat, go on a nice vacation, purchase a lot of new furniture some new computers or give a nice gift to your kids. But from the perspective of your Real Estate Agent you have just ripped them off. If you were in that position what would you think? So I think that there is a personal decision here however there is also a business opportunity with reasonably low risk to save yourself $20,000 which I might add is a lot less than you paid for this book!

And on that point what if you read this book, applied one of the several concepts presented and saved yourself $100,000.00 or even more. Wouldn't it be a nice idea to send your Author a small gift? Just a thought. My final point here is that we are all trolls and haters at times during our lives. Sometimes we all have bad days. But if you find yourself being angry most of the time and not smiling very much and feeling stressed and unhappy then try and relax. Look at the sunny side of life. There is a tremendous amount of potential fun and enjoyment in real estate in Canada and many other countries on our planet. Yes there are challenges and yes sometimes finances are a problem. My parents lived through the depression in Canada and told me some very scary stories. And in 2017 despite the fact that as I write this conditions are pretty good we just don't know for sure what will happen next. So have fun and enjoy every day!

UNREASONABLE EXPECTATIONS

You wanted a dark blue hull and this yacht is all the same colour
.

Today's consumer has watched a lot of TV where designers spend thousands staging a home for sale, where bunches of flowers and freshly baked goods are available and where the entire home has been repainted, decluttered and cleaned to a high standard. These people have high and often unreasonable expectations when they view a home. For some reason women seem to express their frustrations more in this area than most men. They simply cannot live in the home because the kitchen is dated or the wrong color or both. Or perhaps they were looking for an "open concept" and the home was divided into good sized rooms which would prevent them from spying on the kids as they played or keeping track of their guests as they cooked or whatever.

My point here is that you will encounter people with unreasonable expectations and there is little if anything you can do about it. This is how they were trained. They simply cannot help it.

I find that watching the Home and Garden TV shows about real estate to be very entertaining. Not only is the property that they show very interesting but so are the reactions from prospective buyers also very interesting. Some of the buyers seem to be friendly people who you might like to have a beer or coffee with and talk about real estate and the property they purchased or built. But others seem to be unreasonable whiners that are not very likable. And one of the points I get upset with is the comments on kitchen design and open concept. But actually I think this is why their shows are so popular because you tend to get involved with the viewers. People love to react to other people an to views and events. It's normal and it is fun. Usually.

Let's consider just what **open concept** really is. I think it is a clever term that builders and sellers wish to associate with a positive thought. But is it really a positive component? From a builder's perspective an open concept structure has fewer walls in it so less structure and material is required so the cost to manufacture it is lower. But from a users perspective there are fewer private spaces where you can do something different from what other people in the room are doing. For example you could have an office in one room where you conduct business. You could have a spare bedroom where you have guests who visit. You could have a space for watching TV or listening to a stereo or painting pictures or doing whatever you want to do. Yes an open concept is attractive at times but after seeing thousands of houses of all types I would not pick an open concept house myself. Why? You ask.

One of the biggest advantages of having separate spaces is that you can do something different in each. You could have a spare room that you convert into a library and have a comfortable chair and a suitable light to sit down and read a good Abook. Like this one. You could think about it as you read and not be distracted by somebody watching TV or cooking or whatever. Or you could have a room where you keep some exercise equipment and you could get some healthy exercise again while others are doing something else. And you could be working on a project that leaves a bit of a mess and then just shut the door and travel to other parts of the house.

But if you have one big open space there is no privacy and some dummies are even having washrooms without doors on them! Open Concept! No thanks!

GOOD AND EVIL AND REAL ESTATE

You might say that life is the study of opposites. Humans perceive light and dark, big and small, anger and joy, love and hate, cold and hot, expensive and cheap, fast and slow and so on. Many of these opposites also apply in real estate. The one that we will consider now is good and evil.

Let's consider a home that is on the market. You check it over and it seems to meet nearly all of your expectations. But your real estate agent seems worried. He really didn't want to show you the home but you had insisted. And when you tell him that you want to put in an offer he takes you aside and tells you that he needs to talk to you.

"You don't really want that house" he says. Then he goes on to tell you that it was the home of a murderer. The home had been a crime scene and police had dug up sections of the basement and back yard. Suddenly you have completely lost interest in the home. This is an example of how evil can influence real estate transactions and also how your real estate agent can really help you..

Good can be involved too! A contractor could build a home for his daughter and spare no expense or effort to make it an ideal quality built home.

As you might expect evil will cause more risk to the new homeowner than good. You could encounter a case where a member of the construction crew was unhappy with his employer and decides to get even before he quits. So he sabotages the building of the home by purposely building in problems. It seems unlikely that something like this would happen. And yet we all know that employees are not always happy many with good reasons. They didn't get paid or they didn't get along well with the foreman. Or whatever and they are not happy. And so evil emerges.

What if the builder decided not to build to the standard that he was paid for? He wanted to make a bigger profit on your job so that he could cover some financial problems he had from a previous house. So he cut corners and took your materials off the job site and placed them in his garage. Again evil is emerging.

The bottom line is that there are evil people in the world and sometimes even good people act in an evil way. You simply cannot trust people to do what they say they are going to do or what they have been paid to do. If you paid for a 6" thick slab for your patio measure it after construction to ensure that you actually got a 6" slab. If you got a four inch slab you got ripped off because you paid for that additional concrete which was likely used on another job.

When a home is built the foundation is a absolutely critical step. Usually a sub contractor will be hired by your General Contractor and they will come in and complete the foundation. Go out and measure the darn thing before the contractor goes to the next step and has a crew working on framing the floor and walls. Is the foundation the right thickness? Are the walls level at the top? Are the walls at 90 degrees to the floor slab? Was the foundation properly reinforced before the cement was poured? Was the correct grade of cement used? Was the temperature suitable for curing the foundation? If there are problems with the foundation you will have problems with the home so it is wise to spend time ensuring that the jobs are done properly.

But here is a problem. In manufacturing we have the concept of quality control and workers independent from the production workers will routinely test products to ensure that they meet or exceed the minimum quality standards for that product. If a problem is identified the cause is fixed very rapidly so that more substandard products will not be produced. The substandard products are taken out and not included in the inventory of products placed for sale.

In home construction only a partial quality control system is in place. The building inspector will inspect certain key components of the house and the General Contractor will help to set a standard but the reality is that it is possible to produce substandard housing that may not meet building codes. This is evil emerging again.

I would like to see a final inspection report covering the major components of the home the foundation, plumbing, electrical, framing, roof, windows and finish. The inspection report would grade the home A, B, C and D where D is a fail, C is average, B is good and A is above average. The inspection report would be done by a completely independent body.

At this point in time we do not have that type of report. Consequently we have evil in home construction and houses which are potential money pits where extra repairs and maintenance will be required due to faulty construction and poor materials. .

When you purchase a home you do not receive any guarantee. This seems odd to me. If I buy a new car for $30,000 I get a power train guarantee with it. If I buy a half million dollar home I may get nothing. This is a reflection of the problems in the industry. This is a reflection of the evil in the industry that nobody wants to talk about. It is one of the deep dark secrets of Real Estate.

And we better inform you about something that most Canadians are not aware of and that is construction site or **job site theft**. This is not a little problem in Canada in 2017 and some in the insurance industry are calling it a problem of epidemic proportions. In Toronto alone there is over 12 million dollars of job site theft each year and in Canada the total is over 46 million. Insurance companies have paid so much out for job site theft than in many cases they are reluctant to insure contractors for theft. On average over 3.3% of home sites are experiencing thefts each year. The theft could involve vehicles, equipment, tools, materials or household contents.

So despite the fact that Realtors have a code of conduct, that there are disclosure statements the seller signs off, the fact that a building inspector has approved the structure and qualified trades have built it and lawyers have charged you to complete the sale you are still faced with the problem of evil. Maybe nobody noticed that old rotting steel oil tank and the fact that tons of soil in your yard are contaminated. Good luck!

COMMERCIAL REAL ESTATE IN CANADA

Let's start by remembering that there are three basic types of real estate –**residential**, **commercial** and **industrial**. This chapter will focus on Commercial Real Estate. Canadians might think that since Commercial real estate is important and that the three levels of government in Canada –municipal, provincial and federal are actively managing it so that it works in the best interests of all Canadians. Nice thought. But they would be wrong. Our three levels of government have completely fucked up the management of commercial real estate in Canada. I guess that I should have used a politically correct term but what the hell there are some outrageous things going on in commercial real estate in Canada and it is time to spill the beans.

For example let's consider who purchased the majority of commercial real estate in Canada in 2016. Who do you think is buying Canada? In the first six months of 2016 two billion dollars of Canadian commercial real estate was sold. 65.4% of that real estate was purchased by China. The big purchase was the Bentall Centre in Vancouver which was purchased for over one billion dollars. This is a 1.5 million square foot office and shop complex in downtown Vancouver. It is now owned by the **Anbang Group**. This group also owns **Cedar Tree Investment Canada Inc**. which has also just purchased a majority ownership in **Retirement Concepts** which owns 24 retirement homes in Canada mostly in BC and also owns several properties that are available for expansion. It is interesting to note that Anbang Group's purchase of Retirement Concepts required Federal government approval and in 2017 they approved the sale. Why did they approve the sale you ask? Mr. Trudeau is concerned that there is not enough investment money in Canada and has opened to doors to China to buy Canada. He has also opened the doors again to China to again purchase petroleum resources in western Canada similar to the Nexen Petroleum purchase approved by Mr. Harper. After allowing that I think that Mr. Harper realized that he screwed up so he prevented further purchases by China and then Mr. Trudeau again allowed China to purchase Canadian Petroleum resources. I am sorry but I find it very difficult to be polite when I see such incredible stupidity where Canada is allowing foreign countries to purchase Canadian resources. The example I use is Norway the country that has over 1.2 trillion dollars in the bank from petroleum sales and Canada had a 1.2 trillion dollar federal and provincial debt when Mr. Trudeau took over and Canada has exported more petroleum products than Norway! Talk about UnReal-Estate Canada that is one of many examples. .

I could go on about commercial real estate in Canada but one could write several books about this topic. In my opinion Commercial property in Canada should remain under Canadian ownership as a minimum majority ownership. So I would support the concept of up to a 49% ownership of commercial real estate by a foreign company but the 51% or more must remain in the ownership of a Canadian owned company not a company located in Canada owned by foreign interests.

Here is the problem. Commercial real estate's main objective is to generate a profit. That profit will flow to the owners of the real estate. If the owners are in foreign countries then the profits will flow out of Canada to those countries and the whole idea of generating a profit in Canada for Canadian interests is ruined. What you are actually doing in allowing foreign countries to purchase commercial real estate in Canada is selling Canada to foreign countries. Imagine working all your life then going to a retirement home subsidized with tax dollars from other Canadians and the profits from your stay in that retirement home go to the owners in China. And this is just one example. Imagine for a moment how much of Canada's commercial real estate is owned by foreign countries and how much of Canada isn't really Canada anymore.

And I have nothing against China. They have one of the biggest manufacturing industries on the planet. They are intelligent. They work very hard. They invest their money very intelligently. They have done very well in the last few decades. We could learn a lot from them. But selling Canada to China is not wise. Yes we should do business with China but if we sell Canada to China then China will be doing business with itself. The companies in Canada that China trades with will be owned by China. All the wealth generated by the trade will go back to China. And it is up to our three levels of government to control Canadian real estate so that it stays Canadian.

AGE

This chart pretty much sums up the average life. Life could end at any age but on average it looks something like this. So as you can see your ownership or rental of real estate only lasts a few decades. So have some fun!

Age is a topic that you might find very strange to find in a book about real estate. I can tell you that your Author is 68 years old. I do have an understanding about age and life and real estate. So I will share it. And I think that you may we surprised with some of the facts raised.

Let's start off with your early years. For the first nine months you begin with developing into a baby that is then brought into the outside world instead of being a part of your Mothers body.

Then you start to grow and learn basic human behavior like how to go to the bathroom and how to talk and how to move around. A few years pass and you go to kindergarten and grade one. You continue to grow and finish primary school and then usually high school and sometimes you go on to College or University but the point here is that until this time you normally remain in the same home that your family is in and as far as real estate goes they are usually paying all the expenses and often you get your own room free!

So now we look at your life as you enter your second decade. At this point you likely will live in your own space and it could be a house, apartment or condo. It would be likely that you would rent it but it is possible that with the assistance of your family you could purchase it. I think based on my observations that rentals are more likely. And someplace in your second decade of life in your 20's you would likely find a job or perhaps continue on in school.

So now we are looking at your third decade. You are in your 30's and at this stage it is possible that you will enter into a purchase of some real estate if your have managed to find a decent job. If you are having problems finding a decent job you may still be obtaining your living quarters via rent. And there are some interesting things happening in 2017 with people in their third decade of life . Many fall into the descriptive term of **Millennial** or a person born in the late 1960s to the late 1970's and early 1980's. They are also called **Generation Y**. The big event was the downturn of the economy in 2008 which resulted in a lot of unemployment. Sometimes this group moved back to their parent's homes. On the positive side they have a much better understanding of communication, media and digital technology and so when it comes to real estate they are in a better position to research the information they need to make a good decision on real estate. Because of the high prices of real estate in large hot spot cities like Toronto and Vancouver they are often purchasing property in the outskirts of these areas.

Now on to the fourth decade of life. In 2017 people who were born around 1977 would also be members of the **X Generation** who were born from approximately the late 1960's to the early 1980s. Now here is the problem. If you are in your fourth generation of life and are aged 40 to 49 years old do you really wish to purchase real estate. I suspect that Real Estate Agents will go ballistic when I ask this question and I agree that there may be more than one answer. But consider this. If you are that age and you wish to enter into a mortgage for some real estate the mortgage normally is set for 30 years so that when you pay it off you will be somewhere between 70 and 79 years old. But often people retire when they approach 60 or 65. I retired at 53 from a regular job and switched over to my private businesses which I still enjoy. But the problem is how are you going to make your mortgage payments if you are retired and are on a reduced income? If somehow you were fairly well off and money wasn't a problem then there would be nothing to worry about. But for millions of Canadians this could be a problem. I found an age distribution table that indicated that there were 4.8 million Canadians between the ages of 45 and 54. I would suggest that if you are in your forth decade that you do some research about how many people in your age range have mortgages or own real estate. My main thought here is that if you are in your forth decade and you do not own real estate yet and you do not have a large amount of wealth to purchase real estate than the idea of getting into a 30 year mortgage would ONLY make sense IF **the real estate was going up at a faster rate than inflation** and ownership would provide you with a better return on your available assets than anything else. But here is the warning. If the market collapses any wealth you have could be lost and you would be facing a financial disaster. So my suggestion would be to not purchase real estate if you are in your fourth decade. You are too old.

And now let's go to the fifth decade. If you were born between approximately 1958 and 1967 then in 2017 you would be a half century old and would be in your 50th decade of life. If you just started out with a mortgage at your age you would be looking at 30 years to pay it off at a regular payment schedule of 360 payments and so you would be between 80 and 89 when it was paid off. The obvious question is why bother? And the alternatives are similar to those in their forth decade of life. Yes if the prices are rising and if you have the funds then not a problem but otherwise what is the point? Look for an apartment or trailer instead or find a liveaboard boat like we once owned and enjoy life instead of spending all your money on a mortgage that you will likely never pay off anyway.

That takes us up to the sixth decade of your life and that's the decade I am in so can speak with some more knowledge on this one. A 30 year mortgage would place you at age 90 to 99 when you paid off your mortgage and here is the problem. The average life span of a Canadian is **81.24 years**. So on average you will be dead before your mortgage is paid off. Yes you could be lucky but think about it. If the real estate prices are steady or falling in value and you can come up with a reason why you should purchase a house and get a 30 year mortgage to pay it off please let me know what that reason is. I am curious and perhaps I have missed something. There is no point to it. Find an apartment or an old age home and enjoy your remaining years of life. Have some fun. Don't spend all your available funds on a mortgage!

And that takes us to the remaining decades of your life. You are now an old fart. Who knows when the lights will all go out? But it will happen and there is no escape. Do you really wish to purchase real estate? Perhaps you have a ton of money. In that case go ahead. Do whatever you want to do that will make you happy. But if you don't have a ton of money and you are dependent on the Canada Pension Plan and the old age pension and perhaps pensions you earned from employment then why on earth would you wish to take your limited available funds and dump them into a mortgage with all the interest and taxes and fees for services that you need to pay on a real estate property?

Now lets look at this age issue from another perspective because one point I have made in this book is that real estate is a very complex subject. There is a factor that is fair to say is independent of age and that is **wealth**. If a person is wealthy then really age does not matter. And they could be using real estate for speculation that is to generate more asset value in a rising market. Or they could be involved in actually providing mortgages so that when the market crashes they will gain ownership of the properties they have provided mortgages for. In other words they could be simply using real estate to have fun investing their wealth to make more wealth. They may own multiple residential properties and they may be investing in outlying areas from our hot spot cities like Toronto and Vancouver with the objective of making even more money as average Canadians are excluded from expensive residential areas so they move to the outlying areas which the rich folks already have investments in. So on one hand I am saying that there is a relationship between the number of decades of life you are living in and the real estate you should or not invest in and on the other hand I am admitting that the situation is entirely different for wealthy folks.

Now one might think that since our three levels of government are responsible for managing the real estate in Canada and setting up the rules and regulations that they might get together and try and ensure that since Canada has such a massive amount of available land that there would be a way for ALL Canadians to share that land at a reasonable and affordable cost. Why does an average house in Toronto cost ten or more times than exactly the same house on exactly the same lot size in many other areas of Canada outside the major population band?

So I hope that our leaders and employees in our governments will read this book and consider better ways to manage Canada's real estate. These are intelligent, honest, hard working people and I am sure that if they tried as a team they could come up with some solutions, But if they continue on operating in three separate sections and don't work together we could be headed for a terrible crash in the real estate market in Canada and disaster for Canadians who cannot afford a place to live and work and enjoy life.

And perhaps others in the Real Estate Market could participate in these changes. We have over 110,000 Realtors in Canada who are knowledgeable about Canadian real estate who could help. We also have Lawyers who fully understand the existing rules and regulations and laws regarding real estate. And we have owners and potential buyers who share that interest and so we have the potential knowledge and people to solve all the problems Canada faces in real estate today. But sitting back and doing nothing will achieve the same. Nothing.

FOLLOW THE MONEY

We published a book on how business really works in Canada (and the USA and other countries too) and a key point in the 420 pages of **Your Very First Billion** was that if you wish to understand a financial transaction you must "follow the money". So let's do that in a typical Real Estate deal.

Let's say that you actually own your home and it is mortgage free. You place it for sale with a real estate agent for an asking price of $600,000.00. Let's say that the Agent brings you an offer to purchase for $600,000 and you accept it. Here is where the money goes:

Purchase $600,000.00 deposited to your bank account.

Real Estate fee of 5% in Ontario would be $30,000.00

Real Estate fee of 7% on first $100,000.00 and 3% on remainder in BC = $22,000.00

Lawyer's fees of $1000.00 for the seller. (It could be lower or higher)

These numbers are approximate. It is possible you may be able to negotiate slightly better terms or the expenses could be higher if there are issues with the property. But the bottom line here is that as a seller of a property you own without a mortgage your costs will be in the $23,000.00 to $31,000.00 range if you sell it via a Real Estate Agent.

If the home was your principal residence then the profit you made on it is not taxable. Which is very interesting. Because in some markets home values have doubled in the last ten years but you don't need to pay a cent of taxes on that. But if you had that money in a bank account and you were paid interest you would need to pay taxes on the interest you made. And to make it even more interesting as we all know if you look at the actual value of money over the years it changes with inflation. Check out the **Bank of Canada Inflation calculator** to find out how much it changes. Strangely Revenue Canada makes no changes based on inflation on any profit you make on a secondary home property that was not your principal residence. It sounds a bit goofy and it is. But that is another story.

So anyway from a sellers perspective we have shown you how following your money works with a person selling their primary residence.

Now let's look at the situation from the point of view of the purchaser.

Purchase price	$600,000
Down Payment	$60,000
Mortgage	$540,000
Lawyer's fees	$2500
Home Inspection	$500
Property Survey	$1000
Property Valuation fee	$200
Prov Land Transfer tax	$6000

Municipal land transfer tax	$5500
Title Insurance	$250
Insurance on Mortgage	$540
Misc. other expenses	$1000
Interest year one on mortgage	$21,600
Plus municipal taxes	$8,000

Year One expenses approx $47,200 plus any painting and repairs required. Let's call it $50,000.

So the cash flow for the purchase for the first year was the $60,000 down payment and the $50,000 misc. payments for a total cash flow out of $110,000 oh and I forgot the mortgage payments which would be about $2578.04 a month at 4% for a total annual cost of $30,936.48 and so your total cash flowing out for year one with your down payment for your home purchase would be $140,936.48

Now I will ask you a couple of questions here. Do you think that your Real Estate Agent, your Bank, your Lawyer or anyone will tell you what your first year costs are going to be when you purchase your home? If you divided that huge total by 12 to see how much on average it would cost you per month for the first year it would come to a staggering $11,744.71 per month!!!!

The only sane reason for making a purchase like this would be if the real estate market was rising quickly.

In Toronto the average house prices went up approx 22% from 2015 to 2016 In one 12 month period they went up over 33%. That is insane.

So if this home was located there and if the home was purchased in 2016 the value of the home would increase from $600,000 to $732,000 for an increase of $132,000 and this would be fabulous because your costs that year to acquire the property were approximately $140,936.48 a difference of only $8936.00 So while you wouldn't see any net increase in your assets the first year in the second year IF the rate stayed the same you would make something in the $90,000.00 range in increase asset value. I say something like because that would be the ballpark amount which would change with the actual increase in value and the actual expenses you incurred.

So what does this all mean? We have followed the money. And now we understand it ?

Not really because there is one thing that we don't know. When will the market crash? And it will. Bankers and Real Estate companies and the Governments are predicting large changes in value downward in 2017. And that could be a disaster! Because the sudden drop in asset value would be added to the other expenses you have owning the house and very quickly your down payment asset value would disappear and those funds would be gone if you had to sell the property.

So on one hand we have a happy story as far as asset values go and on the other we have a pending financial disaster and the loss of tens of thousands of dollars in asset value. Perhaps hundreds of thousands of dollars of losses.

So what does this mean? It means that when people who are going to buy property start to think of the risk they will become increasingly reluctant to get into the market. This will cause the sales volumes to decrease. This will result in prices going down by those with high debt loads in an attempt to prevent a disaster. And when this happens and the market begins to fall even more people will be very reluctant to get into it.

This is not a happy story at this point. This is very serious stuff. And the story gets worse.

We are going to follow the money again. That darn money. The number of households in Canada is approximately 13,320,600 with a population of 32,856,975 which means that on average 2.5 people live in each household. So the ballpark figure for the value of all those households is likely about 3.3 trillion dollars. And what is a trillion dollars?

Fist of all you need to know what a million dollars is like. The average value of a home in Toronto is now over one million dollars! If you pick up a one hundred dollar bill and then make up a pack of 100 of them you have a total of $10,000. Now if you make up 100 packets of 100$ bills you have one million dollars. Actually you could carry that around in a large grocery bag.

So what does a billion look like then? Imagine a standard sized fully loaded pallet of $100 bills a full 100,000 thousand of those packets of 100 bills each and that is one billion dollars. So we now approach the trillion. You need 100,000 billion dollars which is an absolutely huge amount of money.

UnREAL-ESTATE CANADA

Now step back and consider this. Our total real estate value for households in Canada is about 3.3 trillion dollars. Just think of the amount of loss the value of that real estate went down even 1% in one year. Think of what could happen if the value went up by 1%. Even small increases or decreases can mean huge amounts of money in our total real estate market. And since government taxes are related to the value of the property that means if the property values went up so would the taxes and if they went down so would the taxes.

My suggestion would be that because of the size of the real estate market it is basically impossible to understand it all. How does one manage an industry that is beyond human understanding? The answer is that they don't and this is the major reason why our governments at the municipal, provincial and federal levels have never been able to efficiently manage real estate. Each level of government looks at real estate as a source of tax money and as a place to charge fees for services. As a result huge amounts of money are flowing from the owners of real estate to governments every year. This raises the question of who really owns that 3.3 trillion or so of real estate in Canada? And that is just the household real estate. Let's say that trillions of dollars of real estate exist in various formats in Canada from household to industrial to natural resources to farms to empty land owned by the government. Now that I have prepared you for it I will tell you something about real estate in Canada that you very likely didn't know.

Only about 11% of the land in Canada is privately owned! The rest or 89% of Canada is called Crown Lands and is 41% owned by the Federal government and 48% owned by the Provincial government.

You may be shocked to learn who owns the land in the USA. There private ownership is over 3 times that in Canada at 39.8% and public ownership is at 60.2%. When you review the ownership in each state there are huge variations in who owns the land as an example in Texas 95.8% of the land is privately owned and in Arkansas the opposite occurs with 95.8% of the land being government owned.

You may think that with this information you better understand real estate in Canada. Wrong. Let's consider land ownership again in Canada. I have told you that 89% of Canada is Crown Lands owned by the government. So one might think that applies to the area you live in. Nope. In fact the Federal government only owns about 4% of land in Canadian provinces. They own most of the land in Canadian territories like the Yukon, Northwest Territories and Nunavut. And it gets even more complicated thus proving my point that land ownership is so vast a topic that it would be impossible for anyone to understand it very well.

We now know who owns the land. More or less. But are we referring to the surface only? What if you owned an acre of land and suddenly when you were drilling for water you hit oil instead. Do you own the subsurface rights too? In some areas of the country you might and in other areas the Province or the Federal government might own it. And how about First Nations lands? Canada signed 11 contracts with our First Nations. There were no Indian wars like in the USA. So who owns that land?

UnREAL-ESTATE CANADA

I will end this chapter now. My main point is that you will never understand land ownership when it comes to real estate in Canada. Is private ownership a real factor in Canada? Do you really own the land if our Governments collects so much taxes on it every year? And so many fees for services?

Here is the problem. In Canada taxes and fees for services are so high that if you do own property a large proportion of your income goes to our governments in the form of taxes and fees for services. Should your income decrease you will reach a point where you can no longer pay the fees for services and all the taxes and you would need to sell your property. And when you do that you will need to pay off all the debts associated with your property such as the balance of mortgages you may own on it. And when you purchase a property there are huge amounts of additional expenses associated with the sale. If the property value goes up significantly every year then there is a change that after two or three years that the net asset value of your property will increase. BUT if the land prices start to tumble you are in a dreadful position. Your net asset value will decrease to the point where instead of an asset you have a debt which will grow as property values decrease.

At this point in this chapter my best advice to you is to open a bottle of good quality wine and sit in a nice comfortable chair with the TV and radio off and the lights dimmed. Drink the bottle of wine. Possibly share it with your partner. Then go to sleep and forget Real Estate for a day. Because I have told you facts that nobody else will ever tell you and now you understand what is really going on in Canadian Real Estate and as you can see it is not the story that your Bankers, Real Estate Agents, Media, Government, Lawyers, Home inspectors, and anyone else associated with real estate will tell you. And they are not trying to hide these facts from you.

Real Estate is so complex that each group mentioned concentrates their efforts on only certain aspects of it. They are hard working, honest, friendly people who are convinced that they are helping you and they are experts in their fields. This is how they earn their money and this is how they support their families. I approach the subject of real estate from a different perspective.

What I am doing is sharing reality with you regarding real estate in Canada. It may also apply to other countries too! I am not saying that those involved in real estate are evil. I am not saying that they are ripping you off. I am providing you with factual information based on the real world that will allow you to better understand what you face in real estate and how best you can act to live a happy life.

And if you think that every thing I have said in this book is incorrect you are right. I was just kidding. Not. You have no idea how much I would have liked to be kidding you. But I am sharing with you what I have learned about real estate in Canada. There are good things, bad things, fun things, scary things, shocking things and just about every time of thing you can think about lurking in real estate. And the more you know the better off you are to participate in this activity.

THE CANADIAN GDP WHERE DOES IT COME FROM EH?

You might wonder where the Gross Domestic Products are actually produced in the Canadian economy and here is a list from 2012. Notice that Real Estate is the biggest source of Canadian GDP which is very surprising given that our three levels of government are not managing it very well. :

- **12.34 Real estate and rental and leasing**
- 10.86 Manufacturing
- 07.96 Mining, quarrying and oil or gas extraction
- 07.03 Health care and social assistance
- 06.90 Public administration
- 06.55 Finance and insurance
- 05.41 Wholesale trade
- 05.41 Retail trade
- 05.38 Educational services
- 05.21 Professional scientific and technical services
- 04.20 Transportation and warehousing
- 03.31 Information and cultural industries
- 02.58 Administrative and support, waste management and remediation services
- 02.46 Utilities
- 02.10 Accommodation and food services
- 02.04 Other services (except public administration)
- 01.59 Agriculture, forestry, fishing and hunting
- 00.76 Management of companies and enterprises

- 00.75 Arts, entertainment and recreation

CANADIAN BANKS

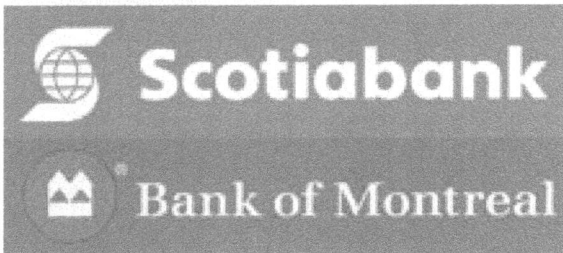

Canadian Banks are very interesting businesses. Many years ago when I was between Universities I worked for a bank and rose to the level of a Branch Accountant. Back then I learned some interesting things about banking and since then I have noticed several developments especially in the area of technology. At one time banks were not computerized and accounts and books had to be balanced at the end of each day. After I left banks brought in computers and started opening up bank machines which replaced a lot of staff. And after that one could do a lot of banking without even visiting a bank by doing it on line. You can transfer money electronically, pay bills on line and check your account balances without visiting a bank. So there were changes in the amount of actual contact between a banker and their client. In the good ole days our Manager kept some alcohol in his office and when a customer came over to sign some demand notes for his business he might be offered a drink and the door to the Manager's office would be closed.

I started to notice that Bank Managers would provide services to customers not to help the customer but to maximize profits for the bank. The first time I saw this I was a bit shocked and even now I remember the incident. I informed our Bank Manager that one of our customers had a large deposit in their savings account and was not earning a very high interest rate and that we should tell her to take some of that $300,000 she had and place it in a certificate of deposit which paid higher rates. The Manager stared at me in anger and said NO and not to mention it to the customer. The customer was an older lady who was basically being ripped off by the bank. I was not impressed and was glad to return to University a few months later.

And today I see reports that our Canadian Banks are ripping off their customers even more than I noticed back almost fifty years ago. Clearly Canada has a problem with Banks and just as clearly there needs to be some changes. If you are interested in the topic check out recent findings about Canadian banks and how they are ripping off their customers. And I will say one more thing and that is the bankers that I worked with were honest hard working people and it is not their fault. And bankers are always underpaid at the branch level. The fault lies with the senior management of banks. The main objective of senior management in Canadian banks is to make a profit so that they can receive a higher wage and obtain bonus payments. In the case of real estate mortgages Canada needs to set new rules and regulations regarding how they are administered and offered. I have no problem with a bank making a fair profit on a mortgage but they are making much more than fair profits. The Canada Bank Act and the Bank of Canada and the Minister of Finance are the main players in government in banking in Canada.

The Bank Act is so complicated that the Banks have been able to pretty much do what they wanted to do with few actual controls to protect their customer's best interests. As a result the banks charge a huge amount more than say the overnight bank rate on loans and credit cards and mortgages and they sneak in all sorts of fees for services to boost their profits. Consequently if you need money the Canadian banks will screw you and if you have money and wish to invest it in Canadian banks they will screw you again. Owning some of the bank stock is one way to participate in the huge amount of revenue Canadian banks make from their clients every year. The government is very reluctant to exert controls on banks because their concern is that it will harm the economy But the reality is that because Canadian banks charge so much interest and so many fees for services that it is almost impossible to operate a business in Canada and make any money. And when it comes to real estate deals Check it out. Review the prime rate, the bank mortgage rate, their savings account rates and their credit cards and other account rates and service charges. And after you do that you will understand that Canadian banks are ripping you off all the time and the

Canadian government is doing nothing to stop it. And in 2017 we are seeing Canadian banks closing branches an and dismissing staff and automating as many processes as they can. They are even converting full time staff to part time staff. To be honest I am glad that I left my bank job when I was in my 20's and went back to University. Banks have excellent hard working staff and they are screwing them too!

HOME EQUITY REVERSE MORTGAGE LOANS

Let me start off this chapter by saying that I personally think that **reverse mortgage** loans are very cleverly advertised. But from a financial perspective when you review the actual numbers there are serious problems and I wonder if they are a reflection of the huge errors our governments are making in Canadian Real Estate. The CBC runs thousands of ads for the company that provides Reverse mortgage loans and so it participates in the clever advertising campaign and the company appears to be growing steadily. Lets start by looking at what a reverse mortgage loan really is.

First of all psychology is used to present this method in a positive emotional sense. I have a degree in psychology and understand what they are doing. I also have worked in management positions in Banking and Government so understand finance and accounting too. For example the term "reverse mortgage" sounds positive in comparison to the term "mortgage" which sounds negative. So one term would make you happy and the other would make you sad. But in fact both are the same -they are a mortgage it is only the method of payment which differs.

And there is one fact about he two types of mortgages which is not mentioned in the description and that is the fact that the interest rate on a so called reverse mortgage loan is not only much higher than a traditional mortgage it is also compounding the interest that is added in every year. So while in a traditional mortgage your interest rate stays the same in a so called reverse mortgage the interest rate rises annually because you are paying interest on the interest. It is not a reverse mortgage it is really a delayed payment higher interest mortgage and if the government told them they had to change the name to make it more accurate they would have fewer people applying for it.

So sit down and relax because I am going to suggest to you why your governments are allowing this business to make money like this. This process actually saves the government money! By selling your house to the mortgage company you generate cash and then you don't require as much government assistance so government costs are lower. So that is how I look at it. Now let's consider other aspects of this process.

If you are an older homeowner who is retired and no longer working then unless you have a source of income coming in every month with the rising prices in Canada you will reach a point where you no longer have enough money to meet those expenses. And so what happens if you need a new roof or some home repairs or if you wish to go on a vacation or help your kids?

If you visit your bank they would be reluctant to give you a loan because of your age, your lack of income and your potential inability of making payments on the loan. A bank has certain standards and it is not that they don't wish to make money from you it is that they have certain ethical rules they must follow under the Bank Act.

UnREAL-ESTATE CANADA

In Canada a company called HomEquity Bank began to give reverse mortgages to home owners. It was formed by Mr. William Turner in Vancouver in 1986 and was called the Canadian Home Income Plan Corporation and in 2002 it was publicly traded on the Toronto Stock Exchange as the Hom Equity Income Trust. In 2012 the company was sold to Birch Hill Equity Partners a privately owned partnership and in 2014 the Chip Home Income Plan was changed to the Chip Reverse Mortgage. In 2017 **HomEquity Bank** began a "partnership" with the famous and very popular Canadian skater Kurt Browning a person with a very strong positive reputation with Canadians.

HomEquity Bank claims to be "helping" seniors by providing funds for them based on their ownership of their homes and notes that it will not be necessary to pay off the loans until the owners move out of their homes or sell it or croak. We all love Kurt Browning and we all love helping senior citizens so what this business is clearly doing is using positive emotions to sell their services. They also place thousands of ads on the CBC to ensure that Canadians are aware of their product. But what are these folks really doing? If they are really "helping seniors" we would all support them.

If you went to your bank and requested a loan and owned your home and had some income coming in the bank would likely give you a loan at a low interest rate. But if you purchase a reverse mortgage from HomEquity Bank your interest rates are significantly higher and because you are not making payments your interest gets added to the principal of your loan and your interest charged goes even higher.

 So the question now is are your really helping senior citizens if you charge them more for a mortgage than a bank would charge? I will let you answer that question. You have convinced the seniors with millions of dollars of advertising and with help the wonderful Kurt Browing that you are helping them. I have always liked Kurt who is a fantastic Canadian skater and I have always respected Bankers but my suggestion here is to actually look at the numbers and are there alternatives with better numbers?

Yes there are. Go to a bank. If you require $5000 ask for a loan for $10,000 and place $5000 in a savings account then arrange for loan payments to be taken out of the savings account. The interest on the savings account will reduce the interest on your loan and you will not be required to make any payments until the funds in our savings account are used up. And you still own your home –all of it.

Lets look at the interest costs. A home mortgage interest rate as I write this in early 2017 is 2.99% and a home equity reverse mortgage is 5.5% and that is a difference of 2.6% which would be equal to $2600 extra dollars interest on a $100,000 loan for one years interest. Are you being helped by paying more interest?

And what happens in a falling market? And at this point in time it is clear that Canada will have a falling market in real estate because the markets in Vancouver and Toronto have hit all time highs. Get some paper and a calculator and do the math on what happens to your property and mortgage in a falling market.

I would like to give you more information about reverse mortgages and alternatives like a **HELOC** a Home Equity Line of Credit but it would take several chapters to explain all the details. I suggest that your review the information on the Government of Canada website about Reverse Mortgages and about Borrowing Against Home Equity and there is one warning. The Government site is what we call "politically correct" so there is this level of civility plastered over the facts. But if you read the points made carefully and make some notes it is clear that there are serious problems with home equity reverse mortgages and only one company in Canada provides this type of mortgage and that is HomEquity Bank. Personally I would not recommend them but that is your decision and my suggestion would be to simply do the math and forget all the positive advertisement and come up with a decision based on the numbers. .

Being an ex banker myself I always thought that the main purpose of a bank is to serve their customers best needs and in doing so collect a fair return. I think that charging customers more than the market should charge them is something that Finance Companies were once noted for and more recently cash loans companies and Banks were not. There was a time that you could trust your bank and the people who worked there. And now it seems times are changing. So take care!

If you are at the point in your life where you can no longer afford to maintain your real estate property or afford other living expenses then there are several much more logical and better alternatives than obtaining a reverse mortgage rip off. What are they?

You could sell your property and move to a more affordable property and keep the majority of your home equity instead of allowing a mortgage company to capture it. You could either purchase another property of less value and less cost to maintain or you could rent a property and still have enough money for other purposes. The bottom line is that it is incredibly dumb to attempt to maintain ownership of your property by using a home equity mortgage because what you are doing is allowing a business to take over your property and pay much more interest on the process than a bank would charge you for a normal mortgage payment.

If you have already done this and are furious with me for telling you this information then I am sorry. I am sorry for you. And I am angry with our three levels of government who failed miserably to manage Canadian real estate and allowed this to happen. The Federal government has reduced the percentage of the value of the property that can be subject to home equity mortgages from 80% to 55% which was a small step in the right direction but in my opinion they should reduce that number to zero. And the mortgage rates they charge should not be any more than the mortgage rates charged in traditional mortgages.

Real Estate generates more GDP in Canada than any other financial activity. It is a multi multi billion dollar activity and if you wish to participate in it you need to do so with people that you trust and you also need to review the numbers and treat it as a business deal. People who provide services in real estate do so to generate revenue and profits and your objective is to limit costs and improve your net asset value. There are folks who provide an honest service that can help you and folks who you need to be very careful with.

UnREAL-ESTATE CANADA

You only have one life so try your best and have fun! And remember in Canada we have over one million Canadians who are worth over one million dollars. I think that if all Canadians read this book the number would be a lot higher!

QUALITY CONSTRUCTION

It takes lots of skill and labor to make a concrete block foundation but actually a poured concrete foundation reinforced with steel is a much better foundation that results in a stronger and drier basement and a better longer lasting support for your home.

When a structure is built it can be built to the local building code, to a level below the code or at a level above the code. You would be making a grave mistake if you only considered the building code when assessing the quality of construction. The design and finish are also critically important.

So what I am saying here is that you can have a house built to code which looks ugly and which is poorly designed and you won't enjoy it and it will likely be difficult to sell. Your home inspector should be able to uncover problems where the home was not built to code. But it is unlikely that he or she will be able to identify shortcomings in design and finish.

When a structure is built you might expect professional carpenters, electricians and plumbers to do all the work. You might expect that they are all professionals and have their papers that and that they are licensed. Unfortunately, this is not the case. There are a few reasons why the person actually doing the job is unqualified. There may not be a qualified professional available – they might be finishing up on another job. It is possible that an apprentice will be doing the work and his or her background can vary considerably. Some are excellent others are just starting out, some are poor. Also there may be a funding problem. It could be that the agreed amount has proved too small because of problems encountered on the job. In a reno perhaps additional problems are uncovered when walls or floor coverings are removed. In new construction perhaps there is a soil problem or a water table is higher than planned or the weather is not cooperating. So the general contractor needs to cut costs in order to bring the job in on budget.

In my mind there is nothing worse that encountering a job that somebody was paid good money to complete and it was done incorrectly and needs to be redone. Grrrrrrrrrrrrrr. But it happens. Ideally you will encounter great work done by professional tradesmen that stands the test of time and that requires no additional repairs or reworking. And there are lots of excellent tradesmen out there.

In fact it might not be a tradesman that did the work. It could have been a homeowner or his or her friend that did it. Or perhaps the father in law or brother did the work. They had never done it before but offered to help. And they botched it.

When you do a job once for the first time you learn how to do it correctly for the next time. You may not have the correct tools or equipment and you tend to make mistakes. A professional tradesman knows exactly how to do a job and has the tools and equipment to do it properly and usually they do the job quickly too.

There are people out there who are brilliant when it comes to construction. They do perfect work. I have a brother in law like that! His house is perfect. Every job he has done in it exceeded any construction standard. I have known several tradesmen over the years who do this type of work. Occasionally on TV you see them there too and Mike Holmes comes to mind. He does fantastic work. There are several others who also are excellent builders and you should watch them on Home and Gardens TV. Once a high standard is set and achieved it becomes a source of joy for as long as you own the home. And then the next owner loves it too! And the opposite occurs with sub standard construction. Let me give you an example.

When a contractor is building a home on a concrete block foundation each concrete block needs to be carefully set in place. Each one is normally just over 8" high and the foundation height and thus the basement or crawl space in the home is established by how many layers of concrete blocks are laid. Now let's consider a crawl space with say a clearance of about three feet. What if you made it one block higher? That is another 8 inches or so. How about two blocks higher? That would raise your crawl space from about three feet to over four feet . But it would be so much easier to access that crawl space if you had the room to move around and having had homes with crawl spaces I can tell you that I hate having to crawl around where you can barely move.

And consider the next step where instead of a crawl space you build a basement. Again the number of layers of concrete foundation blocks are critical if the contractor uses concrete blocks instead of poured concrete.. You could make the basement only six feet high in which case if you wanted to add a ceiling at some point your head would hit it. But this is exactly what some builders do to save money.

I think that building codes should prevent builders from building homes with narrow crawl spaces and low basements. Yes prices would increase slightly but the resulting houses would be significantly more practical and useable. So if you are looking at a home with a narrow crawl space or a basement that is too low don't buy it. You will end up regretting it. As a general rule I think that the foundation of a house is much more important than prospective home buyers seem to think. They need to be built to a high quality standard and if they are not the house and homeowner will suffer. And yes there are real challenges here to do that job. The weather is sometimes lousy too wet or too cold and sometimes the water table is too close to the surface or the soil is not very stable or there could be other problems. But your entire house is built on the foundation and if your foundation is not up to a very good quality standard you are screwed. So to speak. And if you think that this is not a problem in Canada think again. There are differences in the quality of cement, the thickness of cement, the reinforcements in cement and the skill used in building the foundations. Some companies do an excellent job and others do a terrible job.

You may be curious as to why I have an interest in cement. At one time I owned a 36 foot Ferro cement sailboat a vessel made out of layers of steel reinforcement and cement. I do understand more about cement than the average person and I know there are strong points and weak points. To give you an example there are still ferro cement boats out there on the Ocean today that my good friend the late John Samson built in the 1970's. So these vessels are approaching half a century of use. And yet some ferro cement vessels built by amateurs that sank when they were first launched because they weren't built very well. And in the case of houses with cement foundations I have seen too many over the years where the foundations were cracking where the basements were leaking where the supports for the joists were not sufficient. And I have also seen reinforced poured cement foundations with no problems that were built to a high standard.

Humans tend to learn more as they age. So when a person in their early twenties looks at a property with an objective of judging the build quality you might expect them not to notice some things which a person twice their age might notice based on their experience. So if you are new to real estate it helps if you have others to give you guidance. A fresh coat of paint and some clever staging can hide a lot of faults.

BUILDING TO MINIMUM CODE?

When houses are built the builders have various objectives. First of all they need to make a profit. And in Canada this is much more difficult that one might hope. When a builder hires staff or arranges for subcontractors not only must he pay for the wage for the workers but also for the additional health and employment benefits that they receive. The builder must also obtain staff who can do the job well and on time. But what happens when there are supplier shortages or bad weather (which we have a lot of) and costs start climbing? What happens when the home owner starts requesting additional details or special fittings? What happens when the bank starts increasing the interest rate that the builder pays on his outstanding debts? What happens when other builders offer a similar product for less money?

What happens is that the builder starts to cut corners and reduce his costs. Instead of hiring fully qualified trades people he hires people who are just learning the trade and suddenly your home becomes a classroom for them where they make mistakes. The builder then uses cheaper materials and suddenly you have a problem. While some of the material may look fine it usually does not have the wear ability of the better grades of material. As an example they may install a Chinese made plastic sump pump with a one year guarantee rather than a cast iron one made in the USA that may outlast you.

There are thousands of houses out there that have been built to minimum standards or even below minimum standards. If you purchase one of them you will have continual expenses maintaining and repairing them.

I think it would we wise to sit down with your home inspector and let them know that a quality build is important to you and that they should report any item which is under code or where the construction was not done correctly.

In Canada we have a huge quality problem when it comes to house construction. It is one of the dark secrets of real estate here. Lots of people with vested interests will be angered by this statement. We have home inspectors not doing their jobs, building inspectors who miss things, trades people who do substandard work and contractors who are desperately trying to stay in business

It is not uncommon for a contractor to declare bankruptcy not pay the sub trades then arrange for associates or family members to purchase court ordered sales at fire sale prices. They then start up again under another name. And to be fair in Canada we also have companies that build quality structures efficiently. I have seen them. At University I got a part time job with one of them and I was impressed. So if you can find a company with an excellent reputation for quality construction go with them rather that a company that doesn't have that reputation. Yes price is important but if your property starts to break down just after a few months of service have you really saved any money? Nope.

STRUCTURE

Some homes are very attractive in an area with very attractive other homes and there is a feeling of uniformity or perhaps adherence to a high standard. The homes are normally designed by architects and usually they all seem to fit together forming a community of very desirable and very expensive homes.

A key component of a home is it's structure. The finish might be gone or the wrong colour and that is a relatively inexpensive problem to fix. But if there is a problem with the structure which is normally invisible to the eye –then you have a problem.

One problem is that the structure may be difficult to see as it is covered by finishes such as plaster, linoleum, wall board, paint, siding, etc. If you smell rot or mold or see surfaces sagging or cracking then you need to inspect the underlying structure to find out what is going on.

In the original construction sometimes mistakes are made. The crew could be new or the weather could be bad or they may be experiencing a personnel problem.

Or maybe too many jobs were attempted that day. There are lots of reasons why jobs are not done right. If you purchase the property you may need to redo the work that is faulty. If this is all built into your offer then no problem but if the structural problems become visible after you purchase the home you have an expensive problem to fix. It may not be an impossible problem to fix.

Here is an example of a problem that would be very difficult and expensive to fix. Lets say that in an attempt to save some nails for a building project at home a contractor skimped on the number of nails used to fasten 2X4's to upper and lower plates. He managed to save two nails for every 2X4 that he installed in your new home. He ended up with an entire big box of nails which he then used to build his garage and you paid for them.

HOME INSPECTORS

This is *another* sensitive topic. Why? Because there are a lot of variables here. There are different types of home inspections. There are different types of home inspectors. Sometimes bribes or perhaps the more politically correct term "gifts" are given to modify the results of the inspection and to generate more business. Sometimes the home inspector does an excellent job and they save you grief and money. And other times a home inspector makes a mistake and causes you grief and extra costs. And to be fair many other occupations have similar problems. Accounting and Medicine comes to mind.

In medicine in Canada there are two basic types of annual checkups an annual checkup which reviews your health status with a series of blood tests and other tests and an annual review whch is less expensive and which involves a series of questions and fewer actual tests. In Accounting we have thousands of excellent people working with financial jobs and some have passed professional standards and some have not. And not all professional Accountants are the same. So let's review home inspectors.

The first obvious question is how much does a home inspection cost? In Canada there is no standard fee for a home inspection. The estimates I have see indicate that a home inspection will take between 2.5 to three hours plus transportation to and from the site. Let's call that at least half a day. That might be accurate but I doubt it. My guess is that the total time to request, arrange a time, make the inspection, do the report and collect the fees would be more like one working day. Yes it could be a bit less for a small property of approximately 1000 square feet but I will stay with the one day estimate. So what would that cost?

If you were doing a home inspection you would need a portable computer, some electronic measuring devices and possibly some other equipment and my guess is that you would require that plus your transportation and a cell phone. Most of that gear would last several years but lets just say that your total cost for equipment would be $50,000 and after three years the value of the equipment would be approximately $20,000 so your equipment costs could be about $10,000 a year. If you did one home inspection per day and there were say 250 inspections per year your actual costs might be in the $40 -$50 range per inspection and your labour costs would be say $30 an hour so one might think that a reasonable cost for a home inspection might be about $240 labor and $30 for equipment for a total of about $270.

When I checked the home inspection costs in Canada they varied from $199.00 to $500 plus tax and additional fees for crawl spaces and other items. If the home inspector was able to do two quick home inspections per day then a very low $199 fee might make sense because that would cover their costs and labor. But as you can see this is not a high paying job. And the fees are taxable so the government makes money on each home inspection for doing nothing than putting it's hand out to the home inspector to collect a portion of the funds he has charged you.

In Canada there are no national standards approved by our governments for home inspectors and each province has their own rules most of them having no rules on home inspectors. There is a national organization called the **CAHPI** - Canadian Association of Home and Property Inspectors that is attempting to set standards and qualifications and rules of conduct. There is also the NHICC the National Home Inspector Certification Council. And so while there are attempts to establish standards and requirements and controls over home inspectors in Canada I feel the best way to describe the correct situation in 2017 is to say that we aren't there yet.

.So what does one do when they want a Home Inspection? The best advice that I can give you is to ask around and see if you can identify a good home inspector at a reasonable cost given the size and complexity of the property you want inspected. And here are more problems. Occasionally the home inspector suggested by the buyer's agent receives "gifts" from the agent and unfortunately this also applies to home inspectors suggested by the sellers agent. They receive gifts or you could call them bribes if you wish to give a report that puts the agent in the best position. They may wish to hide or show defects. And to be fair that gift may be simply more business so there is a great difficulty in identifying any illegal activity here. What is wrong with giving more business to a person who does a good job? Yes something would be wrong with giving more business to an inspector who gives inaccurate inspections so that you can make more money.

But in many cases the home inspection was excellent and the home inspector was honest and accurate.   But now you know! And now I am sure some Home Inspectors will hate me.

My objective here is to provide an accurate report on how real estate property in Canada is purchased and sold and how people participating in this process can obtain the best results and wherever possible avoid problems that exist in the business.   So if you are a good home inspector who does a good job for a fair price and provides an honest and accurate report to the buyer or seller then there is no problem. If you are doing something else then there is a problem. And perhaps I should mention one more problem.

In order to provide a home inspection service a home inspector must pay fees to a lot of people who only boost up their costs. One example is sales tax. That is a federal and provincial open hand. Another are business licenses and that is a municipal open hand. Then we have insurance in case the home inspector makes a mistake and gets charged. And then there is the sales tax on all the supplies and equipment the home inspector uses. And add any annual fees to home inspector organizations and the costs associated with certification and you have a situation where a simple two or three hour inspection comes with significant costs for offering the service.

Is there a solution here? Yes. We have three levels of government in Canada and they are not doing their job in managing real estate in Canada. They need to get together and set standards Canada wide for home inspections and the people who do them and they even need to set the costs of an inspection. If they don't get together we will continue to have the same problems that we have now in Home Inspections in Canada. Given that Canada is now 150 years old in 2017 one might think that a relatively simple problem could have been solved by now. Nope. And we have some excellent, hard working people in the civil service so what is the problem?

IS YOUR HOME MADE IN CHINA???

This is a sensitive topic. I will start by saying that I love Chinese food, I have Chinese friends and Canadians with Chinese roots have made excellent hard working, productive Canadians I also respect the accomplishments of China of which there are many.

The main problem with China is that they produce low quality cheaply priced consumer goods based on some of the lowest labour rates on the planet and some of the worst working conditions. One of the reasons they do this is that the buyer will demand a lower price and in order to give them goods at that price the Chinese will lower the quality. As a result they have taken over a large percentage of world manufacturing and have put manufacturing in North America out of business.

One might argue that China is simply working hard and prospering and to a degree that is entirely correct. But for hundreds of years countries built up trade based upon not only the price but the quality of their products. The knife stamped Sheffield England, the Hudson' Bay Blanket, the Chevrolet, The Volkswagen all are products where the consumer can trust that there is quality and good service can be expected. "China" stamped on a product is usually an indicator that it is cheaply made and that you shouldn't expect good wear from it.

UnREAL-ESTATE CANADA

Do you really want your house made from components made in China. Chinese nails, fixtures, flooring, paint, wallboard, siding. Etc?

I was shocked when I learned that there is only one major supplier of nails that manufactures them in North America – Maze Nails of Illinois. They produce a high quality product made from recycled steel and treated with a double hot dipped zinc treatment. A person would be a fool not to insist that these nails were used in construction of their home and instead allow their contractor to build their homes with made in china nails. But if you don't know about it then why would you insist that North American nails be used?

It gets worse. Between 2001 and 2007 huge amounts of defective drywall made in China were imported into Canada and the USA. The hundreds of millions of sheets were applied in new construction and renovations in over 100,000 homes in 14 states with 40,000 homes in Florida being affected. In addition 929,000 square metres of defective drywall was imported into Canada and applied to homes in the BC lower mainland the Prairie provinces and Ontario in the Toronto region . What does this bad drywall do you say? It generates toxic hydrogen sulphide , sulpher dioxide and other gases which all cause health problems. The ONLY way to solve the problem is to gut the home, remove ALL the drywall and rebuild. So this is a huge expense.

Now let's say that your home has the defective Chinese drywall in it and you place it for sale. Are you going to make that declaration? If you do your home is worth nothing and it may bankrupt you and your family. Chinese drywall is one of the deep dark secrets of real estate. But now you know about it.

One of the problems in detecting Chinese products is that often a North American brand name or trade name will be used to disguise the fact the product is actually made in China.

Manufactures must make a profit on their products or they will go out of business. As labor and environmental costs and taxes go up the margin in their good which includes their profit goes down. When a Chinese manufacturer approaches them and suggests that they can increase their margin significantly by moving production to China the manufacturer is caught between a rock and a hard place. If they keep manufacturing in North America eventually they will go out of business but if they move it to China they will continue to generate healthy margins and good profits. And senior executives in companies are given bonuses if they can generate good profits.

Our retailers support manufacturing in China. In the USA most products that Wal-Mart sells are from China and in Canada most products sold by Canadian Tire are from China. The last thing the retailers want to do is advertise the fact that certain items are made in the USA or Canada. Then the public might expect that other items should be made in North America too. So the retailers sell items via "house brands" where they use a North American sounding name to sell goods actually made in China.

The bottom line is that many components in your home may be made in China and may be of inferior quality compared to North American or European made products. What does one do?

Don't purchase a home with Chinese drywall in it is a good start. And when you find a home with lots of made in China fixtures and fittings be sure the price reflects the lower quality items. You will have a problem knowing if the nails were made in China but if they were they are not up to the quality of North American nail makers. That means they will corrode faster and be weaker than quality nails. And you are screwed. So in some cases you can act to protect yourself and in others there is little that you can do.

In the case of new home construction it would be a good idea to specify with your builder that ALL components are to be made in North America. If you can confirm that this was done it will increase the value of your home compared to a home made with Chinese components. The reason for this is that there will be a market out there who will want this type of home and quality of build. It will likely cost you 5% more to build the home but you should get that and possibly more back when you sell.

Will the quality problem in China ever be solved? Japan had a similar problem and they solved it and now made in Japan means you very likely will obtain a quality product. Made in Germany is almost a guarantee that the product will be superior. As I write this in 2017 I think it is possible that quality in China will continue to improve at that at some point in the future it may reach acceptable standards. For example I have noticed quality improvements with certain tools and China does make a lot of quality electronic items. But until that time the message is clear that if you encounter made in China products in home construction be careful.

EVERY PROPERTY HAS PROBLEMS

Cougars are very attractive animals except that they will attack people and eat them! If you live on Vancouver Island and other parts of BC you need to watch out for them. They also like pets and kids! Yes they are cute.

Humans are not perfect. They make mistakes. When they build things they make mistakes. Some people make mistakes more than others. Now consider a house. You begin with a lot, dig a foundation, erect the framing, install plumbing and electrical and finish the home. At each step you can make mistakes.

When considering a home the buyer needs to identify what is wrong with the home. It will not be perfect but all mistakes are relative. A home inspector can help but remember everyone makes mistakes including the home inspector.

Most but not all mistakes can be corrected. Mistakes reduce the value of the home. If you can identify the problems before you purchase the home it may be possible to negotiate with the seller for them to make the repairs or accept an offer less than the asking price.

Sometimes a property has problems due to natural aging. After a while paint wears out. Wood trim sometimes rots. Foundations sometime crack or leak. Roofs only last a while and then the shingles need to be replaced.

And at this point I will caution you. The human brain must deal with an extremely complex world and one way that it does this is to simplify what it sees. For example you may look at a property and say "I like it!" But think it over. While you may like some things like the design or color or landscaping or furniture or whatever there may be several things that you don't like. Possibly the furnace is on its last legs. Maybe the roof is getting close to the time it needs replacing. In other words you may be fixating on one factor and ignoring the others. And if you purchase the house the other factors may prove very unsatisfactory to you! I think that I have an answer!

When you look at a property become very analytical instead of just being subjective. Convert various facts about the house into numbers. So a living room is not "big" it is 20 by 30 feet. The roof is not in "good condition" it is 12 years old and will likely need replacement in 4 years. The yard is not "big" it is 50 feet by 300 feet. And when the Agent is showing you the home don't let them describe it in subjective terms. Ask them for the numbers and take notes. That may shock them but suddenly you are in control. Ask them things like how deep is the water table in the yard? They may hate you for the questions but you will still establish control over the viewing.

OPEN CONCEPT

Today the public is being taught that homes should be designed using something called an open concept. That is instead of having smaller rooms the walls come down to reveal a large space. At first this might seem like a wonderful idea –but is it?

There are advantages to having many separate living spaces. You can use them as bedrooms, studies, offices, dining rooms, games rooms, whatever. You can close the door to them and enjoy a level of privacy. You can have a stronger structure with more load bearing walls.

Yet the design shows on TV constantly refer to "open concept" and they never list the advantages of other designs. So when a prospective home buyer is asked what they are looking for the first thing that comes out of their mouths is "open concept" They must have it. And think about the psychology of the term for a moment. "Open" is a positive sounding term. "Concept" is also positive and refers to an idea so when you join the term together you have a positive sounding term which generates a positive reaction from the person hearing the term.

I have lived in homes with open concept and those without it. In the case of dining rooms I much prefer having a separate dining room to having a table in a corner of an open concept space. In the open space often the living room furniture, food prep area, and even the entrance way are all visible as you try and enjoy and concentrate on your meals. Suddenly you lose the advantage of having a separate enclosed space to enjoy your meals and socialize with your family. Instead you have people wolfing down food while sitting on the couch watching TV.

I see the lack of an open concept to be a potential advantage to the buyer looking for a livable home at a lower price. I also see it as a potential advantage to a homeowner who can then explain the advantages of the non open concept approach to prospective buyers.

Usually a home without the open concept design will have a hallway or two to make the rooms accessible. An argument might be that the space used for the hallways is better used as living space in an open concept home. I don't accept that argument because I think that the hallway remains a living space in a home.

The only way that you can truly understand the differences between open concept and separate rooms is to live in both for a while. Then I am convinced that you will see what I mean. You will say "Ron you are so smart and helpful" I will say " Yes I am!" But pushing that all aside consider the advantages of each type of construction the more traditional interiors with interior walls and separate spaces and that big open space type of design. Make a list. Think it over and you decide.

SAFE ROOMS AND SAFES

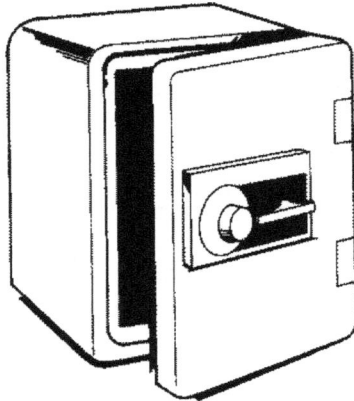

A safe offers one additional level of security for your valuables that a criminal wants to steal. Yes any safe can be broken into however the level of difficulty is higher and as the weight of the safe increases so does the difficulty in stealing it. They can toss a five pound safe into their backpack but a 200 pound safe will likely stay where you left it!

A determined thief will usually be able to break into your home. He or she will then have access to anything that is lying around. The criminal can take a back pack and start quickly dumping stuff that can be sold into it. There is nothing much you can do about it. In Canada there is a residential break in every 90 seconds and 80% of them are during daylight hours by amateur burglars. The entrance is normally via the basement entrance or first floor door or window.

But what about your high grade stuff. Your important jewelry, your passport and high value items.

When you live in a home there are three basic risks to consider: Fire, Weather and Crime. Fire could originate in your neighbors home, your home or even from a local arsonist. To protect yourself against fire you need a method to escape, smoke alarms, and a method of putting out fires. We have all heard of people who have died in houses equipped with smoke alarms because the battery went dead or they deactivated them because they went off during cooking. The solution is pretty simple. Change your batteries on a regular basis and don't use dollar store batteries use a quality brand name battery. I knew a person who died in a fire because they didn't have a battery in their smoke detector. A terrible and completely preventable loss.

In the case of weather your main problem is wind. Wind will take down trees and cause items to fly through the air as dangerous projectiles. As the wind gets stronger it can remove roofs and destroy buildings. You need to look at the trees on your property and your neighbor's property. What would happen if the wind knocked them down on your house? In some cases the trees are relatively small and even if they are knocked down onto the house not much should happen. But in other cases a large tree could break right through your roof and end up crushing you in your bed. Not good. You might decide to prune or take down large trees which threaten your house. In some cases with large trees there are issues here as you would need to get a professional in to do the work and it could cost you several thousand dollars. In other cases you might be able to do the work yourself with your chainsaw or a neighbor might do it for a case of beer or whatever.

Crime is a more complicated matter. There is no way that an average home can be made burglar proof in that a determined burglar will find a way to break in while you are away or when you are sleeping. Yes you can have an alarm system. They can disarm that. Yes you can have movement activated cameras which will record the crooks when they break in. But they can be in and out in a matter of minutes before the police can arrive.

Another problem is that the homeowner does not know what the motive of the criminal is. On one hand if the criminal just wants to steal things for resale one could argue that in the scheme of things this is not the end of the world. I mean so what if you lose a bit of your stuff even the stuff you like. Unfortunately the criminal could have darker objectives in that for whatever reason they might wish to harm you and or your family to the point of even killing you.

So let us consider the situation where a criminal(s) break into your main entrance while you and the family are watching TV. One moment you are there with your family and seconds later the crooks have joined you and they are armed and dangerous. The best way to prevent this situation from occurring is to ensure that your entrance doors are strong enough to resist a person from breaking them down. This is going to cost you several thousand dollars. This is the reason that it is seldom done. Most doors are so flimsy that you can kick them in or just place your shoulder on them and push them in.

Strong doors will slow the criminals down and give you a few seconds to react. There should be at least one room in your home that can be considered a safe room. Here the doors will be strong enough to prevent a determined crook from breaking them down. And you should have weapons in the safe room to protect yourself should the criminal succeed in breaking down the door. Imagine for a moment that you are in the safe room with your family and the crooks start to try and break in. If you have a military background you know what you need to do. If not you may not understand what is going on. Let me tell you. The bad guys are trying to break the door down and attack you. They may be trying to kill or injure you. You have a choice. Canadians are by nature a friendly people. But have you ever watched an adult Canadian hockey game where a fight starts? Canadians stop being friendly when the fight starts. And this is what you need to do if you are attacked by criminals. You need to defend yourself. Think how you will do that in your home. Have a plan.

And I would like to explain one fact about security. You can have what are called "levels of security". For example you can have a lock on your doors. But locks can be broken rather easily. That is level one. Then you can have alarm systems. That would be level 2. You can have local or wired alarm systems that are monitored by an alarm company. You can have locks on inside doors for example on your office door inside your home. That would be level 3. And you can have concealed spaces for certain items that are difficult to find and that is level 4. You can also have various types of safes from small to large. A thief may simply pick up a small safe and steal it. But picking up a safe that weighs a hundred pounds is a different story and so that could provide another level of security. There are several different levels of security for safes and actually it would be silly to purchase one that you could easily carry away and some are about the size of small fishing tackle boxes! There should be a relationship between the value of the items you place in the safes and the security level of the safes, For example if the valuables that you place inside your safe are under $500 it would be silly to purchase an expensive safe and if the value was over several thousand dollars it would be silly to purchase a cheap one. Talk to you local lock shop that sells safes and see what they suggest and often they have used safes which can be purchased at very fair prices. In some cases you can also secure the safe inside your building so you can place another level of security on it. You could for example bolt it to the floor. But remember every safe can be broken into eventually and since most break ins are done by amateur crooks it is unlikely they will be able to get into a good quality safe.

The safe room mentioned earlier could provide one more level of security. Security cameras located outside the home can provide an excellent level of security and today you can get a connection to them on your cell phone.

There should be a relation between the threat in the area that you live in and the items that you have in your home. It would be kind of pointless to put in a $2000 digital camera security system to protect $500 worth of used furniture in your residence and perhaps an eight year old computer with Microsoft XP on it. Phone or visit your local police station and find out what sort of crime is going on in your area. Do a bit of research. Step outside and look over your home and decide where the dangers are. And remember that every 90 seconds in Canada there is a burglary. So in the time it takes to watch a good TV program there would be on average about 40 break ins across Canada but that is an average and in crime ridden areas there might be a higher risk. Let's say that you leave a new lawnmower in your back yard and you come back after going shopping to find out that it is gone. You paid almost $400 for it. Your home insurance has a $500 exemption. If you had placed it under lock it would still be there. All you would need to do is buy and wire cable or chain and a $2 lock from the dollar store and secure it to something in your yard. If you had done that and invested about $5 in the problem you would have saved a $400 loss.

Crooks often cruise around in a car or van looking for opportunities or they may even drive by on a bike with a back pack on. If they see that your car is not there they may cruise into your drive way and run up to the back door and use a screw driver or their shoulder to break into your back door. They can rush through your home stuffing goodies into their back pack and be out and gone in less that two or three minutes. They might be wearing gloves so that no fingerprints will be left. They may even open your fridge and stuff some food into their pack. They are out there and so you need to establish a reasonable level of security for your home to protect yourself. I suggest that you visit the stats can site online and check out crime stats and trends. It is a little shocking and remember that not all crimes are reported but it will give you a better idea of what you are up against.

CRIME

As you know there are certain laws and regulations in our society and as you also know there are people who break these laws with the main objective of making some money. We have crime everywhere. We are not talking about a multi million dollar activity. In the USA recent estimates indicate that over 700 billion dollars of crime exists every year and in Canada estimates are that 70 billion dollars of crime occurs every year. To give you an idea of how significant that number is of all the provinces in Canada only Ontario has a larger annual budget than the amount of annual criminal activity in Canada and so there is more criminal activity in Canada than in any of the budgets for the 9 other provinces in Canada.

When we try and understand how significant crime is in our society we look at stats from our police forces but there is a problem with this approach. Our police are brave, hard working, honest people who place their lives on the line every time they put on their uniforms. When there is an emergency they are called it to help and every day is a busy day for them. Stats Can is an excellent source to become better aware of just what is happening with crime and police in Canada. In May of 2015 they reported that there were 68,777 police in Canada and in 2013 the amount spent on police services was 13.6 billion dollars. The number of police per 100,000 is 194 however many provinces are reducing that to 150 and we are lower in police officers per 100,000 Canadians than 11 other countries in the world. You really should look at the stats. And they just cover reported crimes.

And here is a much much bigger problem. And yes it does relate to real estate in Canada. Not all crimes committed are reported to the police as they only deal with criminal code offenses. What if a crime is committed and it is not reported to the police? It will not appear in records of criminal activity but it still exists. And what if a behavior is actually not ethical but it does not break a law in the criminal code? Now we are getting into the real problem regarding crime and real estate. Every day Canadians behave in unethical ways. They lie, cheat, don't tell you the information that you really need to know. Even large companies will pursue marketing techniques of questionable status. They will do things to make you wish to purchase their products even when they know that their products have problems. We often see this in vehicle sales.

A car company may be aware of the fact that there is a problem with a vehicle they produce but instead of fixing the problem they sell it anyway. For example what if a car had a design that caused the passenger compartment to crumple in a certain type of accident. The honest thing to do would be to stop selling the car and buy back the ones that they sold. But car companies do not operate like that. And as a result we have some cars that are more dangerous than others in collisions. There was one company that had a gas tank located too close to the rear that caught fire during a rear end accident and the company sold that car for years. But do similar things happen in real estate? Yes they do!

Consider for a moment the amount of crime that takes place in home construction in Canada. Over 64 million dollars of tools, equipment and supplies are stolen from homes under construction and homes being updated or repaired every year. Over 3.3% of these homes are subject to crime. Insurance companies are now reluctant to provide insurance for contractors to cover this expense. Who are committing the crimes? In some cases it is the employees of the contractor, in others the subcontractor and in others criminals will enter a property and steal metals, tools, equipment and building supplies. I will show you some examples which I know will make you uncomfortable but you need to know what is really going on.

Let's say that you hire a contractor to do some major updates to your home. He charges you for $2000 worth of lumber and plywood. When the job is finished there is some lumber that was not required. Your contractor places 4 sheets of plywood in his truck and takes it home to place in his garage. Who pays for that plywood? How about the Electrician who installs an electrical panel in your home? The kit for the panel comes with 20 circuit breakers but you only needed 15. Your electrician places 5 circuit breakers in his truck and drives home with them. Those are your circuit beakers and he just ripped you off. The list goes on and on. An none of these criminal acts are reported to the police and none appear in crime stats. One more example.

I purchased a house and before picking a lawyer asked what it would cost for their services. They told me. So I hired them and when I got the bill it was $500 higher than the bill they quoted me. I was furious and disputed the bill and they lowered it back to the level they originally quoted me and you could tell they weren't happy. So even Lawyers are involved in questionable behaviors and I have no problems with lawyers. They are great people and they do an excellent job. So lets continue on with crime...

In the world there is nearly 2 trillion dollars of crime every year and this does not include money laundering which is when the proceeds of crime are invested back into legal activities such as real estate. But often criminal events occur without us noticing them. So let's look at crime and real estate. And I warn you that after you read this chapter you will be a little upset. So perhaps just read it in sections take a rest and have a beer and watch some TV and go for a walk. Then come back and keep on reading. You are going to learn things about real estate and Crime that you likely did not know but you should know if you are getting into the real estate market. So here goes.

Money Laundering

You probably have heard of the phrase "dirty money" before. That's when you make money from a crime. Now you have the cash sitting in front of you. It is **dirty money**. How do you place that money into an asset that everyone will consider to be a clean asset or how do you **launder** the money? In Canada we have had a multi billion dollar drug industry for decades. The government and the police are aware of it but they have not placed enough resources on the problem to stop it. And I think that one concern is that because crime is a multi billion dollar industry and because so many people are dependent on it for a income that the government is reluctant to stop it. I also suspect that cash payments are being made so that there is added reluctance to stop the drug activity. A recent change at the federal level seems to be an attempt to legalize marijuana in the next few years so that the government can control it and take the cash and potential taxes away from organized crime.

Consider for a moment what organized crime must do when cash is accumulated. If they just keep it in a box there is no growth of capital and in fact with inflation at 2% per year for every million dollars they have they would lose $20,000.00 in purchasing power. In fact they would lose more that that! If they purchased real estate and real estate was increasing in value at 6% per year after you account for inflation the crooks would be $80,000.00 ahead. In Toronto and Vancouver the prices of real estate are skyrocketing and in early 2017 they would make much more than just 6%. And that is just on the rising asset value of the property. But what if they also rented out the property! They could be even more ahead. For every million dollar real estate investment they could generate and additional $50,000 or more in rent. Now they would normally need to pay taxes on that rental income right? But what if they mortgaged the property and started paying interest payments on the mortgage? That would greatly reduce the taxes and they could use the money from the mortgage to purchase another property! And so on.

And so as you once you launder money you can invest the money into an asset that appears to be a perfectly legitimate legal asset and you can use it to generate more revenue and enjoy the increases in rising real estate asset values.

Now here comes the big question. It could very well be that money laundering in Canada is not a multi million dollar activity it is much more likely to be a multi billion dollar activity. And if you are investing billions of dollars into Canadian real estate do you think that organized crime might have some professional Real Estate Agents working with or for them? Well the story gets worse. It gets much worse.

Not only is organized crime in Canada involved in money laundering but organized crime and terrorists in other countries are also engaged in money laundering in Canada and taking advantage and also participating in the large increases in value of real estate in Vancouver and Toronto. They are taking money obtained by criminal activities and laundering that many through companies and bank accounts and converting the funds into Canadian real estate. And this should shock you because if you look at the amount of money laundering in the world it is NOT a multi billion dollar activity it is in the 3 to 4 trillion dollar level and that is a staggering amount of money. And billions of dollars gets funneled into Canada in the form of money laundering. Canada as of 2017 has not placed sufficient resources on the problem to stop or control it and as a result money laundering in Canada is occurring in an uncontrolled way. You won't read about it in our media nor will you hear a political party in Canada talking about it but the reality is that money laundering in Canada is a common activity in the billions of dollars and real estate is a way that layering and money laundering occurs in Canada.

So how is this being done? You begin by placing the funds in a country and this is called **placement**. Then you do something called **layering** which makes auditing where the funds actually came from very difficult. You can start with a legally incorporated company. The next step is **integration** where you place the laundered funds back into a legitimate business. Then you can deposit cash into bank accounts for that company. Then you can use cheques from that company to transfer funds to lawyer's offices and the lawyer and real estate agent can participate in a property purchase. And suddenly you have a legal company that is now the owner for several real estate properties. You could incorporate a new company or you could purchase an existing company. You could even use two companies one outside the country and one in Canada. And just to scare you a bit more money laundering crime money does not need to be placed into just residential real estate. It can be and it is placed into industrial and commercial real estate too.

Conducting business in Canada is difficult and as we show in our book **Your Very First Billion** when you start a business in Canada over 80% of them are out of business by year five. But if you have a business with rising valued real estate property in it the story is different. This is why when criminals launder money in Canada they may decide not to start up manufacturing plants or resource companies they simply purchase rising real estate. Then when the real estate stops increasing in value or starts to fall they may place their money in other types of real estate where they can make a profit too.

Ok at this point I have given you an introduction into money laundering in Canada now I am going to give you some warnings about how you can recognize it. Let's say that you are in a nice residential area in Canada. A house in your neighborhood is sold it is a large home capable of housing several people. Then let's say you meet the owner. The owner is very pleasant and is involved in business and advises you that they will be moving to other business locations that they have during the year and that they will be staying in that house for several months each year. You are impressed because they are nice and because they have a business and because they have other residences too. What is really going on here?

It is possible that there is nothing going on here and that the purchase was perfectly legal and that the people are very nice and good business people and you think that it is a positive purchase for your neighborhood. That situation is possible. But here is another situation which is also possible given that you are living in an area with a rising real estate asset value. Perhaps you are seeing money laundering in action. Perhaps the funds used to purchase this property came from crime. The new neighbor that you talked to is simply integrating laundered funds into a legal asset in society. They didn't purchase the house to live in it. They purchased it because it was increasing in value at a rate of 15% per year and that covers all their costs of keeping it and also generates an increase in value every year at a higher rate than they can get at a bank.

Canada does not have a clue how to manage and prevent money laundering. They have not placed enough resources on preventing it. It is raging away in Canada. Other countries have placed controls on money laundering. In Switzerland they have placed restraints on people from outside their country who try to purchase land in one of their 36 Cantons. In Hong Kong there are restraints against any foreign purchases of property unless the person is a full time resident of Hong Kong. In Australia they have controls on what type of property a foreign buyer can purchase and they limit that to new homes and apartments. But in Canada there are almost no controls and so money is being laundered purchasing homes and condos in Toronto and Vancouver.

Now here is the problem. Home prices in Vancouver are now over 1 million dollars and in Toronto they also recently went over one million dollars but the average or median income in both cities is in the mid 70k range so the average Canadian can not buy a property in either Vancouver or Toronto but the people laundering money there are purchasing property and continuing to push property prices up! And our government is doing nothing to solve the problem.

So how does this affect you? If you don't live in the Toronto or Vancouver area it might not affect you much if you are trying to sell or purchase your real estate. If you do live in those areas it may affect you. In fact if you are a seller it is possible that you may obtain an excellent price from somebody trying to launder money in Canada. Which countries are laundering money in Canada? China, India, Iran, and anywhere else where there are criminals with lots of money. Remember criminals in the world raise over 2 trillion dollars of money every year.

Where is crime located? Near the property you wish to purchase? Who do you think will tell you if the property you are considering purchasing is in a safe area from crime? Will the owner give you a warning??

I don't think so. Will the selling agent for the Real Estate company warn you? Nope! Will anybody warn you? Probably not.

My suggestion is that when you are considering purchasing property in a neighborhood that you also do some research. Check out the local police force, the crime stats from Stats Canada, the presence of any gangs in the area and so on. It would also be wise to investigate just what is happening on the racial front. By that I mean that certain races in Canada tend to congregate in specific locations and while I am not saying that you should avoid certain races I am saying that you should be aware of what is happening because it is possible that there will be a link between who is buying and selling property and their race. If you feel more comfortable using another word that word is demographics. Let me give you an example.

One Canadian joke is "what is the river that separates China and India? Answer – The Fraser River! This joke was developed because the dominant race living in Richmond is from China and the dominant race living in Surrey is from India. The dominant race will impact things like schools, restaurants, stores, churches and so on. If that is not a problem for you then no problem. But if you are from another race and wish to live in an area where more people from your race live then this could be a problem both for purchasing and selling a property. I am not saying that Canadians are racist but it is very clear that in Canada one way that races get along reasonably well with each other is that they often reside in neighborhoods where their races tend to congregate. Yes there is a level of typical political correctness about the words race and religion in Canada and so some topics are not openly discussed but "demogaphics" are a crucial factor in the purchase and sale of real estate in Canada.

And before we end this chapter on crime I better introduce the topic of organized crime. We could say that there are three levels of criminal activity. The introductory level were most people make some criminal activity in their lives, the amateur level were a start up criminal operates by themselves and commits small crimes like house and car break ins and organized crime where very significant amounts of criminal activity takes place. All forms of crime are dangerous to you but organized crime is something that you need to be aware of.

First of all you really need to respect organized crime. These folks are not amateurs. They are professional criminals. I am not suggesting that you need to agree with them. I am saying that you need to respect them. In organized crime there are levels. At the intro levels the criminal does not make very much money but as they go up in levels they make more and when they get into the senior levels they make very good incomes.

And here is one problem. Organized crime participates in real estate investments. If for some reason they want your property they will do whatever is necessary to obtain it. They may offer you a reasonable offer. You can decline it. They may or may not increase their offer to an offer higher than the actual value of the property. And of course you can decline that. They may murder you. And his is where I am trying to make a point. You need to be aware that organized crime exists in Canada and conducts billions of dollars of business each year. You also need to be aware they do not follow the same rules that others in real estate follow. I would love to share a solution with you but here is the problem.

Organized crime has occurred in Canada for a long long time. It is a multi billion dollar industry. Our police do not have the resources to fight and destroy organized crime so it will continue. I suggest that you research the **mafia**, the **hells angels** and other major organized crimes in Canada so that you better understand what is really going on. And remember that in some crime groups you are not a full member until you have murdered somebody. All I can say is respect them. They have been here for a long time and they will be here in the future. And there is a huge difference between some amateur criminal who breaks into your home and stuffs things into their back packs and organized crime.

Let me tell you a story. In the 1990's in Victoria BC I was considering purchasing a warehouse that a friend had built. It was a two story structure with 1500 square feet on the ground floor. I placed an offer it and then another issue came up and I was unable to purchase it. Somebody else purchased it and converted it to a grow op. Then they got caught. To this day I wish I had purchased the warehouse. But looking back I came head to head with organized crime and they won. It would have been an ideal location for one of my honest businesses and it would have produced positive results but instead it was a grow op. I don't even like to think about it because it pisses me off. But that is the story. So if you come into contact with organized crime remember that these folks are professional criminals and you need to be careful.

MAKING AN OFFER

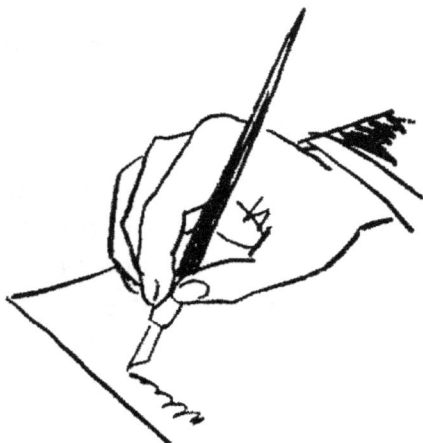

When you are buying a house you have several options when you make an offer. You can offer what the person is asking for the house. You can offer more. You can offer a bit less or you could go for a low ball offer and offer significantly less. So you have basically four choices and with the low ball offer you have a few options there too. Also what you should attempt to do is find out WHY is the owner trying to sell the property? If you know why that might allow you to make a better offer. There could be a divorce occurring and possibly both parties just want to get out of the house. There could be a need to move to another city or move to an old age home. There could be many reasons so it is very wise to find out why they want to sell. Here is what will likely happen with the different types of offers.

In the case of the significant low ball offer the one that is 25% under the asking price or even more this will normally make the seller angry with you and usually you will receive either an alternate price or you won't get any reaction or your seller will just say no. In terms of emotions it is likely the owner will get mad with you and would love to tell you to "fuck off" in fact they may say that to your agent. Also there may be other reactions depending on how long the property was on the market and which direction the market is going. If the property has been on the market for several months and or if the market is clearly not going up and may be falling then there may be some interest in your offer but I still think there would be anger and frustration.

If you offer is lower but still a reasonable offer say a 10% reduction then it is likely that the seller will consider it. They may suggest a counter offer to you say 5% from the asking price. In a market that is clearly rising they may not show much interest because they know that there will be more offers coming. But there is a chance that they will consider and possibly accept your offer.

If your offer is at 15% below the asking price that is becoming a large deduction. In the case of a $500,000.00 property that would represent a $75,000.00 reduction from the listed price. The owner might come back at you with say a price of $475,000.00 or more. Who knows?

When setting the offer price don't go by percentage points alone go by the closest best sounding price for example $449,000 sounds less than $450,000.00 but there is only a $1000.00 difference. Write down a few numbers close to the amount you wish to offer then pick the one that looks like the best offer.

I advise you to eliminate emotions when you make a low ball offer. It is very likely the seller will be mad at you. They may just say NO! Or they may counter with another offer from the full asking price to an amount a bit less. At this point you have your offer in and you are going to step two the negotiations. If you don't like the counter and you probably won't revise your offer and place some conditions in it like obtaining a credit for the repairs required and the furniture and other useful equipment on the property. They may have a good ride on lawn mower or a boat or a snow blower or something that you may need to purchase in the future. So you could increase your offer slightly but have that increase offset by the other benefits you are obtaining from the equipment. You have a choice. You can place another offer in with those equipment and furniture qualifications or you can stop. Then wait a month or two and if the property is not sold make another offer still a low ball offer but at this point the seller might be more interested in your offer. Don't tell the seller that is all you can afford and don't insult the property but you could include items related to the repairs required. The bottom line here is that you want to keep it non emotional if possible. And your success or failure will also be determined by the nature of the market. Is it a buyers market or a sellers market? If values are going up it is a sellers market and it is unlikely that your low ball offer will be accepted. But if it is a buyer's market and the prices are going down then the longer the property is on the market the greater your chances are of having a low ball offer that will be accepted.

Note that you can also improve your offer by not requiring a home inspection or a mortgage approval and by setting a shorter or longer acceptance period. It could be that the seller wants to stay in the house for a few months until they find a replacement place to live. Not a problem. And that would be an incentive because if they take a low ball offer and still have to move out in a short period of time that may prove difficult especially if one of the reasons they are selling are weak finances. Consider that you may allow the seller to continue living in the home for say 3 to six months and that could be a relatively small expense for you but a huge advantage for them.

REAL ESTATE AGENTS AND OFFERS

Now remember that the higher the price the more commission that the listing agent and selling agent and their real estate companies make. So they would all prefer the highest sale price possible. BUT if there is no sale this also means that nobody makes any commission.

So we have two objectives but clearly one objective the actual **sale** is more important to the Real Estate Agents. But if you are the seller or buyer you both have opposite objectives. As the seller you want the highest price for your property even if it comes with a higher commission and if you are the buyer you want the lowest price for the sale. So you can appreciate that there is a level of complexity here. It is not "simple". Although from another point of view all three individuals want the same thing – a sale. It is just the nature of the sale that is different.

And there is one more aspect to a sale that you need to be aware of and that is **timing.** Both Agents will want the real estate sale to occur as quickly as possible. Yes they would love the amount to be as high as possible because the higher the price the more commission both agents are paid. But ANY commission is better than no commission and in terms of priority it is fair to say that both agents would be happier if the sale was sooner even if the price was lower. Think about the significance of this for a minute because when you understand it you will have a better plan to negotiate the purchase or sale.

But what is simple here is that you are NOT all three people -you are just one of them. So although you need to be aware of the objectives of the other two you need to concentrate on achieving **your** objective.

And as I have said a few times there is a level of complexity here! And there is a type of contest going on. Remember that the Real Estate Agent is a professional in Real estate and you are not. They can be a great source of useful information. However they have objectives and the main one is to obtain a sale and so you should be ready to react properly to any subtle or obvious pressure to achieve their goals.

Remember these are hard working people who don't make a penny until there is a sale and even when there is a sale they don't get all the commission. In fact with some real estate companies the Agent may be required to give between 30 and 50% of his commission to the company and if they are performing only one function as the listing agent or selling agent they only are assigned half the commission so the actual amount that goes in their pockets after paying other commissions and expenses and then taxes could be a surprisingly small portion of the commission that the seller pays.

My advice is to be friendly but also be **business like** and concentrate on the business aspect of this deal. And that refers to the dollars and cents and the dates and the terms and stuff like that. Put on your business cap! You are making the decisions!

THE OPEN HOUSE -GOOD OR BAD OR WHAT?

Ok you are the seller and your Agent arranges an open house for your property. They place signs in your neighborhood and you prepare your property for inspection and then you go someplace and wait. Go and have a coffee. It usually lasts two hours sometimes more if there are a lot of visitors. Now before I tell you something that will likely surprise and disappoint you lets consider what you could do to prepare for the open house.

1. First of all make sure everything is clean and tidy.
2. Place some flowers and or a plate full of cookies out for visitors. Consider having coffee available too. I know this is a bit strange (OK very strange!) but you might also consider having a decanter of red wine available and a cheese plate. That would likely cost about $100 if you placed say three bottles in the fridge and got a decent cheese plate and some cookies but it might cause the visitors to linger a bit, discuss the property a bit and leave them with a good and positive memory of the visit. They might also

think you were a bit strange so there is a risk. And if you are selling an inexpensive property skip the quality wine and consider getting a jug of the cheap stuff.

3. Consider hiring a staging company to move in some good looking furniture and make the property look even better than it does normally. If you have worn out old furniture the newer better quality furniture will appeal to the higher end of the market of viewers. Yes it will cost you a few hundred dollars but if it results in a sale it might be worth it too. But remember usually an Open House does not result in a sale.

4. Make sure that you take a digital photo of each room showing the contents. The photos may help with future advertising but the best reason for doing this will be told to you now.

5. And remember there are two types of open houses one for the public and one where just other real agents are invited. If you have one just for real estate agents that would be likely for a more expensive property and I can't see a logical reason for having an agent only party for lower priced properties.

The Bad

Open houses sometimes result in visitors coming over to steal items from your home. They could come over as a couple and while one person is talking to the Real Estate Agent the other one could be pocketing your valuables. In an open house anybody can come it and criminals understand this is an opportunity to enter a home without having to break into it. That's bad. Reduce your risks by locking up any valuables.

There is an annoying problem with open houses and that is the weather. Let's say it is raining and the ground outside is wet and possibly muddy. Some people will go to the open house and then walk around your home in their muddy shoes and if you have carpeting or expensive rugs they can make a real mess. And it could be expensive to clean. Often open houses require that you take your shoes off but sometimes during the summer people wear sandals so they then walk around your house with smelly dirty feet. Yuck! It is possible to purchase some cloth foot protectors and keep a box by the door but then people look kind of silly walking around in them and that might affect the image your house makes in their minds. So my point here is that the weather is an issue for open houses.

Some open houses are very crowded and dozens of people will visit which is good and some attract almost no visitors which is not good unless one of them purchases your house! If there are a lot of people it is difficult for the Agent to remain in contact with everyone and especially if there is a back yard to inspect and different floors and large numbers of rooms. Be sure that there is a good flyer describing the home with pictures that the viewer can take with them.

There is another fact about open houses which may be negative. If there is a problem in your area like noisy kids, noisy traffic, loud noise, smoke from a local factory, or smells and traffic from a local restaurant or other business then people who visit your open house will see this and be left with a negative opinion. You may be able to hide some of these events by picking a good day and time.

I remember going to an open house on Vancouver Island A few years ago and the new homes were very nice and everything looked very good but then we got a very strong wiff of smoke from a local mill and during the day the wind changed directions so at certain times you didn't notice it as much. My eyes hurt and I started to cough and I realized at the time that I simply could not live there for that reason. The pollution from the mill was horrible. I am sure they must have fixed it by now but back then it was one good example of how an otherwise good bit of real estate had a huge problem. So it is a good idea to check out things like smells and noise and traffic and stuff like that when you visit an open house.

The main advantage of an open house is often not for the seller but instead for the Real Estate Agent because they can make contacts with potential buyers and then show them other properties so that they can earn the buyers agent commission. At times where this is the main objective a broker may even charge the home owner a marketing fee between say $50.00 and $500 depending on the value of the property and yes while there are expenses associated with an Open house normally these expenses are covered by the broker from any commission they make on a sale. But when they know or strongly suspect might be a better description that the price is too high or that the chances of a sale from the open house are very low and the main advantage to them would be finding new customers then some brokers may wish to charge that fee. In a way it makes sense because if the expectations for price are too high from the owner then the chances of actually getting a sale are very slim. But in another way usually an open house only assists in the marketing of the property and only a small percentage say under 10% of the visitors actually end up purchasing the house after seeing it. I suppose the seller could negotiate with the broker over the fee as to weather it would be charged or not and if charged how much it might be and why. In the scheme of things the fee is a relatively small amount and the danger here is that it would also generate ill feelings between the broker and the seller so I would consider the advantages and disadvantages here before raising the issue. For example in some cases the Broker will purchase a plate of cookies or some flowers or some folders to assist in the open house and may obtain the services of a helper. Each case might be a bit different so think about it first!

But there is another advantage to the seller because the Open House is actually a marketing tool that will inform more of the public that your house is for sale. And if they visit or even see the signs they will likely tell their friends. Open houses seldom result in an offer although in a sellers market when prices are going up they can generate multiple offers. But the Real Estate Agent has a great advantage here because you are paying all the expenses and they are being introduced to prospective buyers who may be looking for other houses and the Agent can show them. I can't give you a percentage of open houses where a sale results because there are too many factors at work here. I have seen quotes as low as 2% being the actual sales resulting from an open house but I suspect that amount does not also include the effect marketing will have on the buyers in the market. Your price, other properties in the area, their prices, the weather, the market conditions, the time on the market, the local economy and so on are all factors. But I think it is fair to say that usually or in a relatively small number of cases does a sale result from an open house. But here is the problem. While usually a direct sale does not occur sometimes it does! And sometimes the marketing from the sale generates a viewing from a friend of one of the people who went to your open house. And if it does the open house would have been worth it!

Here is the danger when it comes to open houses. People naturally tend to simplify facts. They may just say " An open house won't result in a sale" or they might say "an open house only helps the real estate agent" or they will say "somebody will steal something" or they will say "staging a house is too expensive and is a waste of money" or something else. And here is the problem. A portion of what they are saying might be true. But the situation is more complex than a simple statement will describe.

The reality is that your Agent wants to earn a commission and wants to sell your home and the open house may generate a sale directly or it may generate a sale by marketing the fact that your home is for sale. So if somebody spouts off one of these simple facts smile and agree and carry on. And have the open house anyway!

Buying the House

At this point let's say that you are ready to make an offer on the property. It could be house, an apartment, a condo or a farm or whatever but you have found something you like and think that you can afford so you wish to make an offer. You have considered the best approach for the offer based on many factors and you have sat down with some paper and pens and a calculator and have it all figured out. So here is what comes next:

You going to enter the legal world and your offer is a legal document that once you sign and release you are required by law to follow.

First consider if you wish to make the offer **conditional** and if you do consider what those conditions will be. Some conditions are items like – approval of your mortgage application, a home inspection, any items in the home that must be included, the time that the offer is in effect, the date of sale.

The offer will include your name and address and the name and address of the owner, the offer price, the deposit amount that you will include, the closing date for the sale, the possession date which would normally be between 30 and 90 days from the date of the offer, the date and time the offer ends. You would also ask for a copy of the **land survey** for the property.

Your lawyer will review your offer to ensure that it is legally correct and then your realtor will deliver it to the seller.

Now things get interesting. The seller can either accept the offer or reject it or make a **counter offer**. The seller may change the offer amount and closing dates. And it is possible that offers and counter offers can go back and forth several times. At the last transfer a decision is made to either purchase the property at an agreed price and terms or not. If the offer is not accepted that is the end of this story.

But if the offer is now accepted here is what happens next and remember there could be some variations but here are the main points:

When the offer closes your mortgage holder will transfer funds to your lawyer and you will also give your lawyer a certified check for the down payment. Your lawyer will after paying all outstanding accounts transfer the money to the seller's lawyer and will register the home in your name give you the deed to the property and give you the keys.

At this point there is a **transition** in ownership and you need to be sure that you have the property covered by insurance and secured. You don't want the seller to move out then some kids break in before you move in and destroy the place. That would be bad.

And there is another issue with offers. What if you are a seller for example and your Agent advises you that they have an offer on your property. You review it and it looks interesting and you consider returning a counter offer on it raising price slightly. But now something new happens. Your broker advises you that two more people would like to make an offer. You have this one offer in progress. Should you allow bidders to make another offer or refuse until you have finished negotiating with this offer? Some Brokers will not allow another offer to be considered and some will but will also advise the new bidders that there is an offer in progress. And consider what could happen.

You could accept the first offer which might be conditional on obtaining mortgage funds. Then you are advised that the approved mortgage funds are not sufficient to allow the bidder to pay your full price. Now what do you do? Do you allow other bidders to place their bids? Do you reject the first bid because they were unable to make the mortgage condition? Do you allow them more time to try and find another source of mortgage funds? You have a bit of a problem here but an obvious approach would appear to be to allow new bids in.

Remember that if you ask for advice from your Broker their main objective is to get a sale because without a sale they don't make a penny. But your objective is to obtain a sale with the **best terms** and the **best price**. And when there are several variables it is difficult to give a simple yes or no answer as what to do. So think it over. But remember the longer you wait to make a decision the more people will walk away. My point here is that this is not a time to take days to make a decision you should make in hours or even minutes The reality is that it is a better idea to accept offers even with an offer in progress as long as you tell the person that there is an offer in progress then inform them as soon as possible on the status of the offer should it be accepted.

The End and the Beginning

Now here is a problem. You have just purchased the property and you have the keys and all the bills are paid and the seller has moved out and you are happy. You got the house for the price you were willing to pay. Now it is possible that the seller is not happy. Perhaps you got their house because they needed to sell because of financial problems and as a result they had to sell it to you for less money that they thought it was worth. So they don't like you. They feel that you ripped them off. So we have an end and a beginning here. You have a decision to make.

An effort can be made to establish a friendship with the sellers or you can ignore them. I think that there may be advantages to establishing a friendship with the sellers. And with the real estate agents who participated in the sale and were paid a commission for it. After all you all have something in common the property itself and you all participated in a challenging business deal.

It is possible that you are friendly by nature and so being friendly to the seller and Agents would not be very difficult and it is also possible that you are not friendly by nature and tend to be quiet and so it would be a bit difficult to establish a friendship. My main suggestion here is that friendship is something to consider and yes there could be advantages. Let's say that you receive mail for the previous owner. Yes you could simply place **return to sende**r on the envelope and place it into the post office. Or you could forward it to the seller by placing it in an envelope and mailing it to them. Include a brief note. Yes that will cost you a few dollars but compared to the value of the purchase that is not a lot of money and it would be nice thing to do. If they are in town possibly you could give them a call. You don't need to be really friendly if you don't want to you can be polite. I think that it is something to consider and again yes there may be variables here where possibly it is not appropriate but I have found over the years that if you are friendly usually you receive a friendly response. For example if you are sitting on a bus or a coffee shop and you say something to a person sitting close to you often you get a friendly response. If you are waiting in a line and again you say something to the people ahead of you or waiting behind you again you often get a friendly response and a friendly conversation can start. But if you say nothing than often nothing will happen.

It is something to consider. And yes possibly there is a small risk but usually if you are friendly you have more fun and a more positive time and that is what life is all about. You never know when the big day will come when your heart will stop and you will as we ex Navy people say "cross the bar" so my advice is to try and have fun!

A Better Understanding of Real Estate People

You are entering a business deal. You sign the contract and your Agents collect a commission. No sale – No pay. Things can get tense. Your deal may be their pay to purchase food and family expenses for the next month!

If you are going to purchase or sell real estate you really should better understand the people who work in the Real Estate Sales. If you don't understand what is going on you could lose money and if you do understand them you could get better deals and possibly even make money. And even in bad times when you may lose anyway a good level of understanding may limit that loss. So let's take a look at the activity we refer to as Real Estate sales.

UnREAL-ESTATE CANADA

First of all let's consider the fact that Real Estate people interact with all types of people who own and wish to purchase real estate or wish to sell services to assist these sales or those who wish to engage in some form of criminal act in real estate. To do this a Real Estate worker needs to have good social skills. They need to present themselves in a way that attracts people. This could mean dress, appearance, memberships in social and sports groups, long work days, communications equipment and ability to work efficiently and other factors. But for a moment let's remember what a Real Estate worker does.

When you are in the real estate occupation you have two main jobs to do. You assist in the **listing** of property for sale and the actual **sale** of that property to a buyer. And this is where all your income comes from only if there is a sale. So you could obtain a listing for a property but if there is no sale there is no income for you. So clearly the most important activity is the real estate sale. One could argue that the listing is just as important but my point is that while a listing is very important if there is no sale there is no payment to those working in real estate.

When you look at all ten provinces in Canada you may be surprised at how many Realtors we have. There are over 108,700 realtors or one for every 245 Canadians over the age of 19. On average a Realtor might make about $60,000 a year in commission income. There are some who will make a fortune and others that won't make anything and the state of the economy in real estate is a big factor. The more property values increase the larger the commissions on their sale and the more people are interested in trying to list and sell real estate. Some people are just starting out and have their initial training but have few if any sales. Others have established a successful career and some are now office managers in real estate companies. So in other words the abilities and experience of each sales person are not the same. You should research who you are dealing with. How long have they been working in Real Estate. See if you can find out how well they are doing with sales and I know that might be difficult. See if you can talk to any people who have worked with them.

Now think about this. You are dealing with people that ONLY make money if they get a sale or purchase of property. So right away you must realize that there is pressure here to make that happen. There are certain rules those in the field must follow or they may be fined or warned or even lose their license. But how would you feel if you had a family of two young children and living expenses to meet and sales were down and competition up and you had very little credit left and no money in the bank to meet your expenses. There would be a great pressure on you to do whatever was necessary to obtain a listing and sales.

Now think about that. And the amount of stress on a person working in real estate can be quite intense and the high level of competition only makes that stress worse. Imagine how you would feel if you were interviewed by a prospective client who had a very attractive property of high value and they decided after talking to you that they wanted you as their agent and they signed a sales agreement with you. Imagine how wonderful you would feel knowing that there was a $50,000.00 pending commission here if you were able to also sell the property as a selling agent. Yes you would have some expenses and yes your real estate office would want a split of your commission from 30 to possibly 50% of what you made BUT this is still a lot of money. You know the house is in demand and you know that the price is reasonable for the market so you are pretty convinced that you will make some very good money on the sale. You go home and your spouse asks you if there is any available money for food and some expenses that are coming up and you say things are looking good. Now your family is happy too. Not only that your boss is happy because she was going to call you in to have a discussion about your lack of sales and listings for the last two months and she was considering giving you an ultimatum regarding your employment with the firm. She was getting desperate too because another real estate office had opened in the area and sales and listings were down significantly for her office and trouble was looming. Nice story eh? Now let's look at it again.

You visit the person who wants to place their very nice house on the market. They ask you a few questions and you think that you gave the right answer. During the conversation they asked which church you went to which you thought at the time was a bit odd but you quickly told them and then other questions were asked and you thought the meeting went well and it ended on a hand shake and the owner said they would let you know. And so you went home happy and to your office the next day happy. You were waiting for the message that you were going to be the listing agent! But later that afternoon you got a polite e-mail telling you that a decision had been made for the listing and that the owner had chosen the real estate office across the street from your location but they thanked you.

You find out later that the owner was not a member of the same church that you were and that they preferred to deal with members of their own church and own racial background. You are now devastated. You have failed. You must tell your spouse and Office manager that the listing has fallen through. Nobody is happy. A cloud of depression engulfs you. You are very sad and also very angry. And later that day as you drive by the property you see it. A for sale sign from the company across the street from yours. Your only chance now is to try and sell the property as the buying agent. Your commission will be half of what it could have been if you had done both jobs. And so you start to work phoning everyone you know who may be interested in the property. You work all night up to 10:30 phoning several people and two of them express an interest in seeing the property. There is now a glimmer of hope. The next day in the morning you contact the listing agent and tell them you have two people who wish to see the property. Then you get shocked. The listing agent tells you that there is an offer in on the property now and a visit can only be arranged after a decision is made on the offer. When you drive home that day you see a SOLD sign on the real estate sign.

Now how do you think the poor Real Estate Agent would feel if this second story occurred? It would be a disaster for them. How do you think the property owner would feel? They would be very happy because a fellow member of their church with a surname that was one of their race had sold the property in one day at the asking price and at terms they agreed to.

Sometimes when you tell a story the people you tell it to get wound up in it too. And this story has two possible endings. But is it just a story or is it a real description of what happens on a regular basis in the Real Estate world? And now do you better understand what the people working in Real Estate are up against? Because now we are going back to the real world in an area I will call the dark zone where real estate employees bend and break the rules and use techniques that are either questionable and unethical or even illegal to obtain listings and get sales. If you are a real estate worker and you read this you may be upset. You may not act like this yourself or you may know fellow workers that have done these things or you likely will not want your customers to be aware of what is really going on. Not all the time. But sometimes!

And how much does a Real Estate Agent really make? In rapidly rising markets like say Toronto or Vancouver some properties go on the market and sell in three days or less. How much work is involved? But what if the property takes months to sell and dozens of potential buyers are shown the property? What does the Agent make then? And why should the buyer's agent need to work like a dog while the sellers agent only needs to get the property listed? Lots of questions and lots of answers. I have seen some real estate agents become millionaires and others go broke. I have seen people in the industry say that on average in an average market a Real Estate Agent makes $20 an hour. But others in rising markets have made thousands of dollars an hour. My point here is that due to the rules and the nature of the business and how Realtors are paid the concept of an "average income" or "average hourly rate" is meaningless compared to other occupations where there actually is an average hourly rate. So don't be too quick to state that Realtors are over or under paid.

Setting the Listing Price.

A real estate agent will usually have a good understanding of what your property is worth on the market. You may not have this same understanding and there are three basic opinions you could have. You might think the property is worth less than it really is, or you may think the property is worth close to what it really is or you might think that the property is worth more than it really is. And yes there are variations.

You could be close or out a bit or a lot. So let's consider this. If you are under the market and are willing to list the property at that price it would make the property a lot easier to sell but the commission would be less. Lets say that it was 10% under the market and the price you wanted was $500,000.00 The actual value was very close to $550,000.00 If the property was listed at the market price and if it sold at that price then the agent would make $2500 less commission which of course would need to be split between them and the buyers agent and the real estate offices but the bottom line is that the net commission to the listing agent would fall by approximately $625.00. Nevertheless they would receive the commission on the sale at or around $500,000.00. This seems fairly easy to understand but it might get a bit more complicated. Here is why.

If the listing agent listed your property at $50,000 less that the market value this should generate more interest from potential buyers. It may be possible that the listing agent would know a potential buyer who may purchase the property at that lower price or even give a lower offer on it and be able to purchase it. Now it gets really complicated. If the listing agent can also act as the buying agent they can double their commission. This is all perfectly legal. So even though the property owner is getting less than they could for the sale the Real estate agent is getting more commission for the sale. And this is all legal. But think about it. Should the agent have told the owner that they were setting the price too low? .

There is a phrase in the real estate market called **"don't know don't tell"** and it refers to cases where the Agent actually knows about something that the property owner should know but they don't tell them. You may feel that the broker working for you should give you their full disclosure about any information on the property that you should be aware of. But very often if an agent knows something negative about the property that may prevent you from purchasing it they often tend to say nothing. Some agents will tell you everything they know about the property which is good. Again this is legal although it certainly is on the line in my mind because the Agent is making a commission from the seller and therefore should be working on the seller's behalf but instead was working for themselves.. But they are working for themselves because they are not your employees they are your agents providing you with a service. And you might think that this is the end of the story. Wrong. It gets even worse. And we go in activity which breaks the rules set up by real estate organizations and possibly even the law!

Let's say that we have a rising market. Let's say the property owner is desperate for a sale and for various reasons just wants to get out of their house. Perhaps a spouse has died. Perhaps a break up of the marriage or a transfer of a job or something has happened and the owner just wants out as fast as possible and is willing to sell the property well under the actual market value. Here is what could happen. The Real estate agent could phone a business friend with access to a large amount of money and get them to make an offer on the property at a reduced price from the listing price. This is done and the friend of the agent now owns the property. The Agent has done both jobs listing and selling agent. So they get both commissions.   But a few months later the friend of the agent calls them up and places the property back on the market. The Agent manages to sell the property. The agent collects another double commission from the sale and the friend makes a $100,000 profit which they split with the agent. And this payment may be in cash as a gift. No taxes! So on one property the Agent has made the equivalent of over three full commissions. They have effectively "flipped" the property. This is getting scary. But occasionally this could actually happen. Suddenly the Agent has become a real estate investor AND an Agent all on the property you owned and has made more profit on it than you did.

Now some readers will claim that this is just a story and that it would never happen in real life. But it does happen in real life. Not every time because several factors need to line up. For example you need a desperate owner who wishes to sell, you need a rising market, you need a low asking price under the market, you need some friend or business associate of the Real Estate agent to be willing to make an investment and share the proceeds. And at this point you may scream at me "that surely this doesn't get any worse eh" Sorry but it might.

UnREAL-ESTATE CANADA

Where does the friend of the real estate agent get their money? Could they be "snow washing their money in Canada" In other words could this process be used to launder money from other countries or from crime? The answer is maybe and maybe not! And I don't know if it gets any worse past that –likely it does- big bucks are now involved not just the commission but the actual property itself.

So as a property owner you should be at least aware of the importance of listing your property at the correct price and what could happen if you don't.

Now lets go to listing your property at a higher price than the market would likely pay. You talk to the listing agent and tell them you want $650,000 for your house which the agent is aware should be in the $500,000 asking price level. But here is the problem. If the listing agent refuses to accept your listing then they will not get any commission. So they try and talk the owner into reducing the price. The owner refuses. So you have a choice. You can walk away and lose any commission from the sale OR you can offer to list the property at that price for so many days and then drop it by a certain amount. You reach an agreement and the property goes onto the market at $650,000. This raises some questions.

Is the Real Estate agent placing the property onto the market merely to ensure that they will get a commission if it sells later at a lower price? I guess the answer to this is "yes". But here is where the problems develop. At this point you really are not harming anyone. But what happened if in edition to being the listing agent you also bring a customer over who wishes to make an offer. Do you tell the prospective buyer that the property is over priced? That is higher than is should be? If you do that they might make a low offer but if they do that the owner may not accept it. And remember you are collecting the commission from the owner of the property. Are you breaking any laws here? I think that you are. But here is the problem.

How would you prove this? What if after the sale occurred you obtained an independent evaluation of the market value of the property and were able to show that the property was sold at a price significantly under that evaluation. By significantly I mean $50,000 or more dollars than the actual sale price. Could you then have a lawyer do a claim for the return of the commission you paid? I don't know. You made the mistake by setting and agreeing to the price but your realtor should have warned you that your asking price was too low. If they did warn you and you still went ahead then personally I think the blame is on your head. But if they didn't tell you what they should have known as professional real estate agents that your asking price was too low then surely a court would find some degree of blame and responsibility for the loss on the agent. And if you brought the case up to CREA (the Canadian Real Estate Associate) which sets laws and regulations for real estate agents then surely they would act against the Agent although exactly what they would do is a question I cannot answer.

Now if after the sale it was discovered that the same agent sold the property again a short time later lets say a year later for a substantial amount over the original purchase price by the new owner then I suggest that something pretty serious is going on here. But there is an even deeper potential problem.

UnREAL-ESTATE CANADA

What if there was in fact money laundering going on here and the new owner was laundering money obtained from criminal sources and you as the original owner of the property complained to CREA the real estate office and the police. Here is the problem. In a case like this you would be going up against organized crime.

In Canada every year billions of dollars of organized crime money is laundered and the "snow washed" money is re invested into real estate. Well dress me up and call me a chicken but in my opinion it would not be a good idea for an individual to take on organized crime! The best option and the safest option would be to learn from the mistake of placing the property on for significantly less than the market value and remember for next time to first determine an accurate asking price that represents the true value of the property. I suspect that you wanted a better answer but I just don't have one for you. Sorry. Just think that there must be a reason billions of dollars of criminal funds are being laundered in Canada. If our governments and legal system and police and sellers of property to criminals wanted the process stopped it would have been stopped years ago but today there is more criminal activity going on in real estate in the form of money laundering than ever before in Canadian history. Why? Because in 2017 there are markets in Canada where real estate prices are rising at an huge rate even higher than one could make in other investments so of course it is attracting criminals to launder their cash obtained from crime.

YOUR NEIGHBORS

If you are considering purchasing a property one factor that you should consider are the people in properties close to your house which we will call your prospective **neighbors**. You should do some research. Look up their addresses on your computer. Look up their names. Ask your Agent if they know anything about the neighborhood. What sort of cars do they have as that is an indicator of their wealth. What do their houses look like as that is an indicator of their financial situation. Are there any rentals in the area? If there are rentals then perhaps your area is an area for investors and land prices may be going up but if there are a lot of people living in the homes perhaps the owners are using the property to generate revenue. The odd person will use their home for weekly garage sales or to sell lots of stuff on kijjii. Are there any halfway houses in the area were convicts with federal offenses are being reintroduced into local communities? There are over 130 of them in Canada. Is there any construction going on in your neighborhood? Are some properties all owned by the same owner? If that is the case perhaps they are getting ready to knock down houses and build a higher density building. What races do you see in the neighbors around the property? Are there any religious buildings close to the home? What is the parking like? Check this out in the afternoon, mornings and evenings as the traffic often changes significantly during the day. Go for a walk around the neighborhood as you can get a much better feeling that driving around on the streets.

If you see something that you like that is good. But if you see something that you don't like that is bad and much better to see it now rather than after you invested your money in the property. Now some people will note that I mentioned race and they will be upset and suspect that I am a racist. In fact I know people from several races and I have no problems with them. In fact I like them! But the reason I mentioned race is that for some strange reason in Canada although races seem to get along well often they tend to congregate in the same neighborhoods and then gradually you have entire neighborhoods with a majority of people from the race that is congregating there. As an example in Toronto we have areas where there are lot of Chinese, Greeks, Italian, middle eastern and Jewish and others with similar racial or religious backgrounds. My point is that if your prospective house is in one of those areas where there are noticeable racial components that is not a problem you just should be aware of it prior to the property purchase. And if you prefer to live in an area with a mix if races or in an area with races the same as yours then this is your opportunity to do that.

And if you still feel uncomfortable about race consider this. In Canada we have two official languages English and French. And in Canadian communities we also have mostly French communities in the Province of Quebec where French is the official language and also pockets of English in the Montreal area. In Northern Ontario despite the fact that there are two official languages there are areas where French is the main language although usually everyone can speak English too. In Quebec the majority of the communities there are French speaking and many residents may not be able to speak English. A similar thing happens with other languages and races where often English or French is not the main language and the people there speak in their language in the community they live in.

So what happens if you are an English speaking Canadian and you move into an area where there are mostly people from one race or language that does not speak English? They may have a different religion, go to local restaurants that serve their favorite foods and they may also elect representatives from their race to represent them in local, provincial and federal governments. The term "**politically correct**" comes to mind where one should never say anything about people from other races, religions or languages but I am not trying to be mean or racist here I am just trying to help you get a property that you will be happy living in and checking out your neighbors is a good first step before you make the decision to purchase the property.

There is a Latin phrase that is often heard when discussing a business deal and that is *caveat emptor*—**buyer beware.** You are making a big decision perhaps one of the largest purchases in your life and you need to try your very best to understand what you are getting into. And doing that will help to identify the risks you face. Are we approaching the top of the real estate cycle? Will the prices level off or start to plunge soon? Or will they keep on going up? And now that I have told you about the billions of dollars of criminal money laundering that occurs in Canada every year what do you think will happen to that if the real estate prices suddenly start to dip. Will the criminals remove their investments and will as a result the values really dip down?

You have the option of placing complete trust in your Real Estate agent and not worrying about anything regarding the property you are considering bidding on. In other words yes it is entirely possible to not use your brain for anything. And I wonder why you are even reading this book then? Anyway that is one option and often people do it and sometimes they are happy and there are no problems.

Let's use an example. Lets say that you owned a home in Victoria BC and the prices were rising each year by between 5 and 9 percent. Then let's say your job required that you move to Ontario. You had owned the home in Victoria for over 12 years and you had a mortgage on it for $50,000 but it was now worth $400,000 and you wanted to purchase a home in Southern Ontario for $400,000. You could simply sell the home in Victoria and use the money to purchase the home in Ontario. Or you could mortgage your home in Victoria place most of the money into a new property in Ontario and rent out the Victoria home. You would then have an excellent investment in Victoria real estate that would continue to increase in value and the rent would cover any expenses there and would generate some income too. My point here is that it is something to think about. There is nothing worse than selling a home in an area where the real estate is rising in value only to see your home there ten years later being values at three times what you sold it for!

And for a moment consider what a Real Estate Agent might suggest to you the best thing to do. If you rented out your home in Victoria they would make how much on it's sale? Nothing. Not a cent. So what do you think they would tell you?

BUYING REAL ESTATE HOW MUCH DO YOU WISH TO PAY?

Now here is a classic problem. You go to a real estate agent and you tell them that you wish to buy a property at no more than $400,000.00. You describe to them what you want.

Remember that the agent makes a commission on the actual selling price of the property. In Ontario the commission rate is 5% so for every $100,000 there is a $5000.00 commission. So while you want a property at $400,000 maximum they want you to spend as much as possible on the property because that will boost their commission.

The term for this is **upselling** and it is a common activity in the real estate business, Your Agent will likely show you properties at and below $400,000 but then will also likely show you properties at $450,000 and $500,000 with the hope that you will buy then instead and they can make a larger commission.

There are two clever ways of reacting to upselling. You can say **no thanks** and not even look at the property. Or you can look at the property and if you like it make an offer at your maximum offer of $400,000.00 And I suggest that you make it a short term offer of no more than say one day. There is a term for a short term offer and it is called a "**pressure cooker**" and it could be as short as 2 or 4 hours. I like the idea of a one day offer because it gives the seller an opportunity to sleep on it and reconsider it. It is possible that you will receive a counter offer from the selling agent but my suggestion would be to stay with your maximum $400,000.00 offer. This does two interesting things. First it opens up the possibility of obtaining a property worth more than you want to pay for the price you want to pay and it also lets your agent know that you are serious about the maximum price. They may be furious with you but they tried to upsell you and failed so you aren't at fault they are. Nevertheless they will view you differently from that point because you beat them they didn't pressure you into a higher commission product.

It would not be fair to leave this topic at this point because to be fair sometimes upselling is not such a bad idea! Why do I say that? It's simple. Often the buyer will request a certain type of house in a good area and set an unreasonably low price for that house in that area.   In this case I am not sure the term "upselling" really applies. It would be more realistically called actual value buying or something like that. You can't really expect to purchase a home for $500,000 that is regularly selling for $600,000 in the area you are looking in. So in that case you can't jump up and scream at your agent not to try and upsell you. You really should be meek and realize that your agent is telling you the truth about prices in the area for they type of house you want. Or to use more descriptive language they are not trying to screw you and rip you off on commissions they are trying to explain what the reality of prices is for the type of house you want.   And if you do decide to look at the house in this case I am not suggesting that you also put in a low ball offer for your previous maximum amount. If that in fact is the price range for the type of home you want then you need to reconsider your budget and see if you can come up with more money and if you can't do that you need to reconsider the type of house you can afford. And if you do that let your broker know that you have changed the type of house you are looking for.

Broker Pressure to Buy or Sell

We need to remember that the broker has a tough job. At times if they do nothing and just allow the buyer and the seller to think and not act then there is no sale and no commission. So they often need to apply pressure. They could suggest to a prospective buyer to place an offer on a property they have viewed but weren't completely happy with. The Broker could suggest to them to place a low ball offer on the property so that if they did get an approval from the seller they could used the saved money to make necessary changes. For an example the buyer could remark that the concrete floor in the garage was all cracked. The broker could say reduce your offer by $6000 and you can place a new floor in and that would look a lot better. So the broker has offered a solution and also placed some pressure on the buyer to make an offer.

Another way of placing some pressure on the buyer especially after they have viewed a few properties and not placed an offer is to tell them that prices are going up and the longer you wait the more expensive the properties will get. Or they could say that offers are building up on the property and unless they make an offer somebody else could buy it. The broker will always have an offer form and a pen ready and this ads to the pressure. They might also list several advantages to the property and again this will add to the pressure. Remember you wish to purchase a property and your broker wishes to help you buy a property because if you don't buy a property they don't get paid.

Now if you are selling a property how does a broker place pressure on you to sell it?

One way to apply pressure to the seller is to give them an offer only good for four, six or 12 hours. The shortest one puts the most pressure on them. They may resent the pressure but they will also see it as an opportunity to sell the property quickly. A broker can also use psychology. Let's say that the owner is a senior and will be going to a retirement home and has lived in the home for several decades. The buyer's Agent could deliver the offer to the owner and mention that the prospective buyer is a young family with two young kids and they are looking for a home to bring them up and since this home is close to a school they are quite interested in it. The owner may possibly then reconsider the offer which although it is lower than they want it to be the people seem nice and they like the idea of helping them. This does place some pressure on the seller to accept or negotiate an offer they can accept.

Brokers sometimes use a trick to place pressure on prospective buyers who have been looking at several properties but so far have not made an offer. They ask a buddy to come over at the same time as the viewing to make it appear that more than one person is interested in the property and that therefore the prospective buyer will need to make up their mind quick to make an offer or lose it to the other person. The technique is called **double booking** and in my mind I see it two ways. One view is that the broker is getting anxious as they have shown properties several times to the prospective buyer but they have not made a single offer. I do understand this because each time a broker shows a property to a buyer there is time and energy involved and a cost too. You can't keep on doing this and somehow the buyer needs to decide to make an offer. So in a sense the double booking is understandable. But from another viewpoint the double booking is misleading and it is sending false information to the prospective buy from their broker and that makes me uneasy. Because once the flow of false information starts one tends to stop trusting the person sending it.

Sometimes when a buying agent has a customer who is willing to place a low ball offer they use the following technique called low bid strategy to make the seller consider the offer. The first offer is a very low bid so low that the seller would immediately say no to it. For example if the asking price was $300.000.00 and the low bidder was thinking of offering 250,000.00 the agent for the low bidder will phone the agent for the seller and say that they have a low bid for $200,000.00 and of course the selling agent would contact the owner and they would say no. Then two or three days later the buyer's agent would say he had a bid for $225,000 and again the sellers would say no. Then a couple of days later the buyers agent would give them the first real offer of $250,000 and the sellers would likely carefully consider this and might offer a counter offer. It is possible the **low baller** was expecting some sort of counter offer and who knows perhaps an agreement could be reached. Now the problem here is that there were no offers for the two lower amounts. What makes the problem more complicated is that the broker could say that the low ball offer was at that level to start. It would be difficult to prove that this was not the case especially if the low ball bidder worked with the Agent. But is this honest? Clearly the Agent is trying to obtain a sale but just as clearly they are attempting to do it by lying about fake offers. So again I can see why they are doing it but should you catch them doing it you no longer trust them.

A Realtor Dirty Trick??

First you need to understand that a realtor makes money only ONE way and that is when there is a sale. They earn a commission on the amount of the sale. Now also remember that there are a lot of Realtors out there competing trying to get customers and trying to sell houses. Ok the next key fact is that in Canada and in many other countries too the commission is split between the agent who obtains the original listing and the agent who presents the winning offer. And then the commission is split again from the agents to their real estate companies who they work for. So what first appears to be a big commission is actually just a fraction of that commission for each agent.

It does not take a genius to understand that an obvious objective for an agent or real estate office is to perform both functions which is called in the trade **double dipping**. So your listing agent also presents you with an offer from a prospective home buyer that they know. Or another agent in the same office as the listing agent does the same thing. Consider the impact on the commissions. In one case the agent would receive both the buyers and sellers commission and although they would still need to share between 30 and 50% of it with their office the amount they get on the sale is exactly double the amount that they would have got if another agent from another real estate company made the offer that was accepted for the purchase. And not only does the Agent double their income but the agent's real estate office also doubles their income. So both the agent and the agent's office would be very supportive to the plan of controlling the sale by double dipping. And the real estate term for this is called **"dual agency"** where a specific real estate office represents both the buying and selling broker. Now there are rules and the Agent must inform you that they are also representing the buyer.

In the case of properties with small values say a property selling for $200,000 compared to a property selling for $1,000,000 the total value of the commission say in Ontario where the commission rate is 5% would be $10,000 or $50,000 so the agents portion would be significantly smaller with a selling price that is much less than say an average property in Toronto. So in the case of smaller deals one can see the advantage to the realtor to double dip and try their best to obtain both commissions. And when you consider it even in the Toronto areas where the commissions would be very large they would be twice as large. Now consider what is happening here. As the seller YOU are the one paying the commission!

Ask yourself a simple question. Do you wish to pay your broker TWICE the commission on the sale just because they also found a buyer? There are two ways of looking at this. One could argue that they are performing both functions so the commission paid for each function listing and selling is earned by your broker and their office. But there is another way of looking at it that will really piss off your broker and their office but what could save you several thousand dollars! The brokers will hate me for this. I understand that. The sellers will love me for this! I understand that too. Here is my suggestion.

When your broker tells you that they have a buyer that they would like to represents tell them that is great news! But then say the commission needs to be reduced by 25%. So on a $200,000.00 sale you would save $2500.00 and on a $1,000,000.00 sale you would saver yourself $12,500.00. I think that is fair. I don't think it is fair to your broker to take ALL of the extra commission they would make. But I do regret that your broker would love to punch me for telling you about this.

And there is another problems associated with double dipping. Your broker may make almost no effort to sell your property by advertising it if they really want to double dip. They will instead look for a prospective buyer themselves. So you may wonder why there are no open houses or open houses of very short durations during slow times or poor quality photos or an apparent lack of effort to use media to sell your property. In my opinion double dipping is a reflection of the desperation facing some real estate companies and their brokers in a very competitive market and or in a stagnant or falling market. Yes they need to do things to survive but as long as sellers allow double dipping to take place and continue to pay full commission rates the process will continue.

And speaking of commissions one factor about commissions that always bothered me was that in a six month contract if your broker sells your property on the first day they get exactly the same commission that they would get if they sell it on the last week of the contract. I do understand that there are issues. I just don't think that this sort of commission structure is fair. Nor do I think that a commission should be a constant percentage of the actual sale price because that means when the sale prices increase as in Toronto and Vancouver the commission increase for doing exactly the same work.

And when commissions on falling prices decrease even if the home owner suffers a loss on their investment they still must pay a commission to their broker which only ads to the loss. Is there an answer to this? BC charges 7% commissions on the first $100,000.00 and then 3% on the remainder. That is an improvement over Ontario where a constant 5% is charged no matter what the selling price is. But one could argue that the owner of a very inexpensive property of $100,000 or less is actually charged 4% more commission than richer folks with more expensive properties. I don't think is fair either but for more expensive properties I think the two part fee structure is better than the one part fee structure.

There are problems with real estate sales in Canada. Our three levels of government –municipal, provincial and federal all see real estate as a source of revenue in the form of taxes and fees for services, our lawyers and all people associated with real estate sales all see real estate sales as a source of income. As a result the cost to own real estate in Canada is growing past the point where the average Canadian can afford to purchase it and maintain it and so instead more and more Canadians are now renting real estate and also selling the real estate they have to richer folks and more of them have higher mortgages too.. Somebody in our Governments needs to sit down with those involved and come up with a better plan or at some point in the future there will be a major market crash and many people will lose their investments and go broke! Even criminals in both Canada and in foreign countries are using Canadian real estate to launder their money and establish investments which are taking advantage of rising property values.

YOUR REAL ESTATE DEAL

Let's consider this fact for a moment. In real estate you are either the buyer or the seller. You normally have a real estate broker to manage your sale or purchase but YOU are the one making the final decisions and you are the one signing the contracts. So in some cases you can enjoy what we would call a good deal or an excellent deal or perhaps a bad deal or a terrible deal or whatever. Remember that you are not a real estate expert. As a buyer or seller you may only engage in a limited number of transactions in your entire life time. So you tend to depend on the experts who work in the field every day. But remember folks it is still YOUR real estate deal and one way of obtaining a better deal is **negotiation**.

I suggest that agreeing with everyone is NOT the way to go. Negotiate. Your lawyer may give you a very large bill. Negotiate. Your broker may be able to double dip and provide both a listing and selling service. Negotiate the commission you will be paying to them. Your offer on a property may not be accepted but you still want it. Negotiate on the details. My point here is that real estate is a complex subject and although it first may appear simple with only buying and selling involved the actual process to arrive at a price and the resulting costs could get quite complex and a bit of negotiation on your part could help you get a better deal and could save you thousands of dollars.

Try to eliminate emotions and just concentrate on the business deals. Be polite and be friendly but also be a business person. You are negotiating to achieve the best deal for yourself and your family. Don't just stand there and agree with everything and sign whatever they give you to sign. Do they want a six month contract? Think about that. Think about the time of year and where you will be in six months. If that is OK with you fine if not try two months or four months. See what they say. Negotiate. They think you are asking too much? Negotiate to keep that amount for the first month or for the first 15 days then consider lowering it. You might have a sale you might not. But my point is that even as a non expert the bottom line is that YOU are involved in this deal and YOU need to negotiate to help find the best deal. Listen to your Agent and some agents are excellent. But some are desperate and may do things to increase your costs in the deal or to reduce the amount you get paid for the sale. Just try your best and negotiations are a way of doing that.

For a moment look at life from the point of view of your agent. Let's say they have 50 properties for sale at their office. Your property is included in that number but your property is on the lower quarter of the list as far as asking price goes. Other properties have doubled the asking price your property has. So an agent obtains a client who is looking for a property and they have a good sized budget. If the Agent sells your property to them they may get half the commission that they would if they sell a higher end property to them. It is that simple folks. If the prospective buyer had a very limited budget your property might be on the list you broker promotes to their buying client. You can't really blame the agent for this. In fact if they have your property and don't promote it they are effectively removing your property as competition to the higher priced properties they are trying to sell. If another firm only had a few properties including yours and they were desperate to make some money then they might actively promote the sale of your property! Complicated isn't it?

But let me tell you something very positive that should make you happy! If you read this book carefully and think about the facts and ideas I am telling you then you will find yourself with a much better understanding of how real estate really works. You will notice subtle changes when you read a listing or visit an open house or talk with an Agent or owner. You will find yourself looking at the business from a different and an improved perspective and consequently your chances of making a good decision which will either save you money or make you more money will improve. Significantly. That is my objective and even as your Author after doing a lot of research for this book I now understand real estate much better than I ever did and I understand that when a subject is complex you really need to study the topic more so that when a decision point is reached that you make the best one! .

HOW THREE LEVELS OF CANADIAN GOVERNMENT TOTALLY SCREWED UP THE CANADIAN REAL ESTATE MARKET

In Canada we have three levels of government: municipal, provincial and federal. At first that seems fairly simple but the deeper you look into it the more complex it gets. In fact the subject is so complicated that I would need to do a full book on each level of government in order to describe how it relates to real estate in Canada. And that would provide you only with a basic introduction. And I have no interest in doing that anyway! As an alternative I will try and give you an overview and with that feel free to do some more research if you wish. But if you have an overview you will have a much better understanding of the topic than over 95% of Canadians.

Now let's start off with the three basic levels of government in Canada –**Municipal, Provincial and Federal**. All three levels have elected government representatives and government employees. I suggest that you check out reports from Stats Canada to review voter turnout for each of the three types of elections. They show very interesting results from each age range. Surprisingly municipal elections result in the lowest turnouts and those voters in the 18 to 24 year old age range are the group with the lowest voter turnout in all elections. Sadly between 21 and 46% of the voters don't bother to vote in Canadian elections.

Finances in each level of government are different. In the Federal and Provincial governments most of the income for government expenses comes from taxes and fees for services and they are allowed to run a deficit if the income is less than the expenses. But in the municipal government deficits are not allowed and they raise most of their money from property taxes and fees for services. They charge something called a **mill rate** on the assessed value of the real estate they do not charge taxes like the Provincial and Federal governments charge on the actual income. To make it a bit more complicated if your property value goes up at the same average rate of other properties then you do not pay any more municipal taxes and if your property value actually goes down compared to the average value of other properties you pay less income taxes. But if your property value goes up at a greater percentage than other properties then you pay more municipal taxes. Every four years your municipality assesses the value of your property and that is the value that the mill rate is applied to. Simple?

No, not simple. There are several different types of property including residential, commercial, industrial and multiple dwellings where there are over say 7 properties per location as in an apartment building. In the case of an apartment your municipal taxes are included in your rent and in other properties you receive a separate tax bill. And to make it more complex the mill rate on apartment buildings is actually higher than single family residences. There is no standard mill rate for all properties. The mill rate makes up the largest single source of income for municipalities approximately 40% of their annual budget.

Let's consider what happens when say you are retired and your income is not going up each year but the value of property is increasing at a greater rate than the average rate of increase in your city. So your municipal property taxes go up! You are screwed! Every year in a rising market it is possible that your property tax amount will increase. Note that your income has not increased simply the asset value of your property and it gets worse folks much much worse. Your municipal taxes are not applied to the amount of the property that you actually own they are applied instead to the assessed value of the property! Think about that. Let's say that you purchased the property a year ago and you placed $100,000 down on a property which was worth one million dollars. So you actually had a debt of $900,000. Your taxes are the mill rate applied against the million dollars not the $100,000 that you actually own. One might argue that the property value is going up so if you sold the property you would still make lots of money even after the taxes. But what happens if the property value drops? Let's say it drops by the value you invested in it and now it is only worth $900,000 or the value of your mortgage. Now you are paying property tax on a property that you have no net asset value in.

Now let's step back and consider this. Since we have three levels of government each level is concerned about its own operation and expenses and revenues. They do not consider the total costs to the property owner they simply wish to maximize the income they can get from the property. I once worked as a civil servant and I understand what happens in government. The people are honest and hard working BUT they concentrate on their departments. It would be impossible for them to consider all three levels of government and so in real estate transactions each level of government is out to maximize their revenue from these transactions. And none of our "experts" in real estate consider all three levels of government when they attempt to explain how real estate works to their clients. A really good Accountant who specializes in government taxes would be your best bet. Do you really think that your hard working real estate Agent is going to warn you that your taxes will be increasing in a rising market? They won't say anything about that because they desperately need to ensure a sale of the property or they don't get paid. Will your Lawyer or Home Inspector tell you? Nope. Will the media tell you? Probably not as the subject is too complicated to explain in a few words or paragraphs.

Now let's consider real estate in Canada's largest market. Let's use Toronto as an example. Toronto is the biggest city in Canada and in fact the GTA (Greater Toronto Authority) is actually bigger than most Canadian provinces in population and the amount of wealth located there is also bigger than most Canadian provinces. And each level of government collects taxes and fees for services. Now just try and relax because what I am going to tell you next may upset you.

At one time Canada had three main sources of wealth and employment; natural resources, manufacturing and agriculture. Canada has trillions of dollars of natural resources in the form of oil and minerals and just about anything you needed. We have huge forest, huge stocks of fish, huge numbers of farms. But we had a very small population. In WW1 we had only about 9 million people and in WW2 we had about 11 million and today in 2017 we have about 36 million people. But we also have the second largest land and water mass in the world! And the distribution of our population may really surprise you. Almost 90% of the Canadian population is located in a few communities located in a 100 mile band clinging wimp like to the US border. The rest of the country only contains a few million people perhaps 4 million or so and they are spread out in small communities with vast amounts of empty spaces between them. You might wonder at this point what am I getting at?   Well here it is...So despite having vast amounts of space in Canada the desirable places to live are mainly in that tiny 100 mile band AND not the entire band just a few communities in that band. Vancouver, Toronto and Montreal are three of the most desirable places to live in Canada and just these three city areas have a total population of about 11 million or about 32% of the entire Canadian population. So in that 100 mile band just these three city areas take up a large proportion of that population. And people are flowing into these three cities as the years go by not into the other areas of Canada. Ok we are getting close to the monster problem. Here goes...

The world economy started to change with the growth of the economy of China starting in the mid 1980's In 2009 China became the largest producer of cars. They are the largest producer of renewable energy and they are growing at a fantastic pace of approximately 10% per year when the rest of the world is down to approximately 3% and as a result the amount of wealth in China has also grown. To some degree a similar growth has occurred in India. And what do people do when they have large amounts of wealth? They invest it into safe investments that make more wealth. These are intelligent, hard working people who continually make good decisions.

In Canada our economy is in serious trouble. Our Canadian owned manufacturing industry in Canada is almost dead. Our resources industries are now owned by foreign countries. Most of our large retail stores and restaurants are owned by foreign countries. A lot of wealth flows out of Canada each year to foreign countries and now a lot of foreign people are purchasing property in the most desirable areas of Canada in Vancouver and Toronto and they are driving the prices in these areas up to levels where average earning Canadians cannot purchase properties because they don't have the wealth required to do that. This problem has also happened in other Countries like Switzerland, Australia, Hong Kong, Mexico and these countries have implemented rules to limit foreign ownership of their property. But Canada has done absolutely nothing and so the foreign purchases are flowing in by the billions. But it isn't just the foreign purchases that are ruining real estate for average Canadians.

With over a decade of rising real estate prices a home owner who is going to purchase a bigger and better home now has two basic choices. They can sell their existing property and use the money on the new one or they can re-mortgage their existing property to take out the increased asset value and place those funds in their new property. And they can rent their old property out which should cover the costs and mortgage payments and so they then can take advantage of the rising asset values on not one but two properties.

And since the Canadian economy is in such horrible shape in the other sectors real estate is now providing the best return on investments and will continue to do so as long as the real estate prices continue to climb. So this has caused people with enough money to invest in real estate instead of stocks and other commercial venture and as a result thousands of Canadians own multiple properties which they are renting out. And because average Canadians can no longer afford the high cost of purchasing properties in cities like Toronto and Vancouver they are entering the rental market so there is more demand for that and the people who own several properties are continuing to purchase more and rent them out. It all sounds good in a way but in another way we all know that real estate values go up and down they cycle and they always have and at some point the real estate values will hit a peak and then start to fall. And then what will happen?

Asset values of properties will fall and people will not be able to afford high rents. Instead of making money every year in the form of increasing asset values the people who own several properties will see their asset value drop and the main advantage of owning property will disappear so they will wish to sell. But when they sell they will need to pay off outstanding mortgages and what happens if the sale price of the house is not enough to pay off the existing mortgage? What do they do?

If they have available cash they could use that to pay off the mortgages but what happens if they decide to sell all their rental property and they don't have enough money to pay off the balance of the mortgages? This is not good. If they have ten one million dollar homes in Toronto and the asset value of the homes nose dives by 20% they are out $2,000,000.00 in asset value and that is a huge loss. If the market dropped by 40% which is certainly a possibility they would be out $4,000,000.00. Are you thinking what I am thinking? **Bankruptcy**? Yes it is possible that if an owner had to sell multiple properties when the price nosedives down then bankruptcy is a possibility. With a big price drop there would be billions of dollars of net asset value disappearing in Canada. There is a huge pending disaster lurking here!

UnREAL-ESTATE CANADA

Why isn't Canada doing anything you say? Our governments are aware of the fact that foreign ownership is propping up the Canadian economy and if they limit it the real estate values will fall and the economy will collapse so they are very reluctant to do anything about limiting foreign ownership. So what we are seeing in real estate in 2017 and what we will very likely see for the next few years is the movement of billions of dollars of foreign investment into Canada and the ownership of hundreds of thousands of Canadian real estate properties by foreign investors from China, India, Saudi Arabia, the Middle East, the Far East and other areas in the world where wealth has accumulated. In addition we have billions of dollars of money obtained from criminal activity that the owners want to "snow wash" in Canada and invest that wealth in Canadian property that is going up in value. So does Canada have a problem? Yes it certainly does? Is there anything that can be done to solve the problem?

Absolutely but our three levels of government need to sit down and identify the problem and discuss solutions and them implement them. If they don't do this the problem will only get worse. Canadians will be forced out of our most desirable areas and into the less populated areas in Canada. And even now if you check out the prices of real estate in areas surrounding Vancouver and Toronto you will see that happening. So that is the bottom line.

As a potential buyer or seller of real estate in Canada you now know what is happening here and you can use that knowledge to decide which area you would like to invest in and which area is affordable and which areas may likely go up in value over time at a rate faster than other areas of Canada where our population is so spread out in rural areas.

226

My suggestion would be that the Federal Government should establish a Ministry of Real Estate and each Province should do the same. Each Canadian municipally should have a Councilor of Real Estate on their city councils. And all three levels of government should then start to work together to better manage Canada's real estate resources. I also think that the Mexican approach to limiting foreign investment in certain areas should be applied to Canada and NO foreign ownership of property in the 100mile band containing 90% of the Canadian population should be allowed. And all foreign ownership of land north of the 100 mile band should be limited to 40% of the ownership of all properties and the 60% ownership of the remainder of these properties should be available only to Canadian citizens. Obviously this suggestion would make foreign investors and sellers in Canada to these investors furious with me. Because what I am suggesting here is that ownership of Canadian property remain Canadian. If we continue to allow foreign ownership we will be effectively selling Canada to foreign interests and we will no longer have a Canada. Imagine for a moment what those tens of thousands of Canadian troops who fought and died in WW1, WW2 and Korea and Afghanistan would say if the Canada they died for was sold to foreign interests.

HOW A NON CANADIAN CAN BUY CANADA

The world population in 2017 is over 7.5 billion but the population living in Canada is less than one percent of the world's total so over 99% of the world's population live in countries outside of Canada.

When you review the size of each country in the world the numbers are very interesting. If you only look at land area then Canada is number five after Russia, Antarctica, China and the USA. If you look at land and water area then Canada is number 2 or three after Russia and after Antarctica which although is not a country is owned by several countries.

When you look at population Canada is 38 with only 4 people per square km. And the numbers get very interesting when you look at world Gross Domestic Product because Canada is the 10th highest country for GDP

Now let us look at murder rates per country. Brazil is the worst country in the world, India is next followed by Mexico, Russia is 9th, Pakistan in 10th and China is 12th the USA is 14th and Canada is an amazing 80th in the world in murder rates. Remember that depending on how you count them there are between 195 and 206 countries in the world.

So those are the numbers and now we need to figure out what they all mean. Obviously Canada is one of the safest, largest, richest places to live in the world. So one might think that people with some money and even people with no money would like to move to Canada. And here is where we should take a closer look at both groups. There are billions of people on

Earth with very little money. And there are millions of people on the earth with millions of dollars and lets review those numbers:

Rank Country Number of US$ millionaire households

- United States 8,008,000
- China 2,070,000
- Japan 1,081,0004
- United Kingdom 961,000
- Switzerland 519,000
- Germany 446,0007
- France 445,0008
- **Canada 440,000**
- Italy 354,00010
- Taiwan 324,0001
- Australia 230,000
- Hong Kong 223,000
- Netherlands 222,000
- Saudi Arabia 214,000
- Belgium 202,000

Now let's look at which countries have the most billionaires:

	United	5	Bill Gates

States	36		
China	2 51	Wang Jianlin	
United Kingdom	1 20[3]	David and Simon Reuben	
Germany	1 20	Georg Schaeffler	
India	8 4	Mukesh Ambani	
Russia	7 7	Vladimir Potanin	
Hong Kong	5 5	Li Ka-shing	
France	4 7	Liliane Bettencourt and family	
Italy	4 3	Giovanni Ferrero and family	

0	🇨🇦 Canada	3 3	David Thomson and family
0	Taiwan	3 3	Tsai Eng-Meng
2	Turkey	3 2	Murat Ülker
3	Brazil	3 1	Jorge Paulo Lemann

At this point you have a better idea where the money is on the planet Earth. The numbers change every hour and it is entirely possible that some wealth is hidden and let me give you an example of that.

I will tell you a little bit about crime. I say a little bit because if I tell you exactly what is going on that would place me into a very dangerous position. And you might share that position. First of all world crime is not a million or billion dollar activity. It is a multi trillion dollar activity and we will never know the precise amount of criminal money out there because there is now way that it can be reported accurately. However there is an activity that goes on in a regular basis that world police forces are aware that exists and that is called **money laundering**. There are four phases to money laundering. First of all the money is acquired by criminal activity such as the illicit drug trade, theft, prostitution, tax evasion or whatever. Then the money laundering process starts with something called layering and here funds are deposited to banks then transferred to other banks often in other countries via electronic transfers or cheques. This process could involve several countries and several banks and then the final phase is called the **integration phase** where funds now in legal forms are returned to the ownership of the criminals who acquired them.

And at this point I will warn you that we are entering a zone which will surprise and possibly horrify millions of Canadians and which will make many non Canadians and criminals both in Canada and in other lands very interested. So my suggestion would be to take a rest. Have a coffee or a beer or a rum in coke if you are ex-Navy like me. Because I need to inform you about what is really going on in order for you to understand real estate in Canada. Yes there are some good opportunities and yes some of them are criminal in nature and yes there is an element of danger and yes our three levels of government have fucked up big time and yes they need to make some big changes!

In 2016 10% of the world's millionaires migrated to other countries. 11,600 of them moved to Australia, 10,000 moved to the USA and 8,000 moved to Canada. When you look at the 8,000 millionaires migrating to Canada you will see that the largest migration came from France and China. The millionaires from Europe tended to move to Montreal and Toronto and the millionaires from China tended to move to Vancouver. Why did they move you ask? Three reasons. They wanted to ensure that their kids went to good schools and universities and they wanted to enjoy the much safer living standards in Canada and also they wanted to invest in real estate that was going up in value. Not surprisingly the three levels of Canadian government were unable to identify how many people from foreign countries purchased property in Canada to either launder money from criminal acts or to transfer money from successful investments abroad to a safer area. And there is one more fact about foreign investment that will surprise you.

Canada has something called a Canadian Limited Partnership or LP and Canada is now one of the most opaque countries in the world disclosing the actual owner ship of limited companies and just to make it even more ridiculous Ontario is the most secretive province in Canada for maintaining the secrecy of the actual owners. What one can do if you wish to form a Canadian LP is simply to pay somebody else to act as a company Secretary and CEO and as an example one Lady in Quebec did this with over 200 companies and had absolutely no idea of what the companies really did. I could do an entire book on this topic but I just wanted to alert you to what was going on. And if you wish you can research it more online to find out more information. Because the actual owners of the Limited Partnerships were not living in Canada they did not need to pay taxes in Canada. They could use the money that they transferred into these companies to purchase real estate in Canada to transfer the funds back into other companies they might own elsewhere.

So what is really happening here? To use a non politically correct term the Canadian Governments have fucked up when it comes to the areas of foreign investment in Canada in the forms of Limited companies and foreign investment in real estate and as a result Canadians are being forced to pay more and more to live in certain cities and are being pushed out of these cities and the resources in them so that rich foreign owners can come in and take over.

And there is one more point I better mention about foreign ownership and money laundering in Canada. The media and our government are beginning to focus in on two major communities Toronto and Vancouver with some additional focus on Montreal. But the story does not end there. The foreign investors are not stupid. They understand that Canadians are being pushed out from these cities to outlying areas and guess what they are doing? Yes you got it right! The foreign investors are investing in real estate property in outlying communities and they are also investing in areas in areas outside that 100 mile population band clinging to the US boarder. They are taking over Canadian resources and land and any area where they see possibilities for future investments and profits. And entire neighborhoods are becoming empty because investors are not renting out the properties. That means that Canadian businesses in those neighborhoods that once supplied services are seeing their business plummet. What we are seeing is a horrible mess and a pending disaster.

Because what happens when more and more of your available income goes to your residence costs? That money is taken away from other activities and gradually you realize that you can no longer maintain your residence and must move to a less costly residence. In Toronto condo monthly costs and apartment rents are going berserk. How many residential properties do you think are owned by foreigners who do not pay ANY Canadian income tax because they have moved their kids into their new Canadian homes to attend University in Canada while they stay in their home country? The Government has no idea of how many people are doing this today. Yes they do pay municipal taxes but no they don't pay any Provincial or Federal taxes. So guess what happens with the tax rate for tax paying Canadians? It slowly goes up. At this point you are likely pissed off so I will end it with a happy event.

 The birth of a child. We all love children. We were kids ourselves once. A birth is a happy time! So if you are not a Canadian but you are pregnant why not visit Canada during the last few months or weeks or even days of your pregnancy and have your child here? Guess what happens? When a child is born in Canada they are officially Canadian citizens according to the Canadian Citizenship Act and they have ALL the rights associated with a Canadian citizen. They have access to free education and health care and many other services and rights. You might think that our three levels of government are not screwing this one up eh? Wrong. They have absolutely no idea of how many foreign women are giving birth in Canada despite the fact that there is a well known term called **birth tourism** that describes what is going on.

It comes in two forms poor folks and rich folks. The rich folks are willing to pay between $10,000 and $20,000 to help deliver their kids so that they will have two passports one from Europe and one from Canada. The poor folks may not even be able to pay for the expenses associate with the birth. In 2016 there was one hospital in Richmond BC that delivered babies to 299 foreign mothers out of a total of 1938 births. That is a staggering 15%. And that is also only ONE hospital in Canada. What the hell is going on here? Our governments don't even know what the numbers are and we have companies in Canada selling Birth Tourism services and we have people providing temporary quarters in **birth houses** prior to the birth. We are not talking about a million dollar problem here folks. We are talking about a problem that is rapidly increasing and that is resulting in potential future expenses of billions of dollars that will need to be covered by Canadian tax payers. I love kids and I think it would be pretty accurate to say that we all do but surely there is a better way to manage this.

I think that I better end this chapter here. I have shared the issues with you and I have given you areas to do some more research on if you wish more information on what is really going on. The bottom line is that Canadians are being taken advantage of and if we don't smarten up and admit that we have goofed and that we must and will make some changes then the problems will continue and Canada as we once knew it will no longer exist. Canada is dependent on immigrants for growth and to maintain our country.

There is absolutely nothing wrong with an immigrant that wants to be a fellow Canadian citizen and who has applied to do so and been allowed in. But money laundering or snow washing money or birth tourism or foreign ownership of Canadian real estate that drives up prices beyond the ability of Canadians to pay are problems which must be solved. Somehow our three levels of government and our politicians and citizens must get together on this and fix the problems. Now let's go on to other topics!

CROOKS

As we all know there are crooks out there. These are dishonest people out to do no good. How does one identify them and protect oneself against them? Occasionally you will read about a real estate agent who was showing a client a property when he attacked her sometimes even killing her. So it is possible even for a trained individual who deals with people all the time to be fooled. The crook may be out to physically hurt you, rob you or steal items from the property. If you use a Realtor they take on this risk and if you are showing the property it is your risk. The crook may also attempt to steal your identity and or commit a mortgage related fraud. Now we are getting into a particularly dangerous area where organized crime may be involved. These boys are serious crooks.

There is a big difference between a small time crook trying to rob some goodies from your home by stuffing them into his pockets as you show him around and people in organized crime attempting to commit fraud against you. The organized crime people would think nothing of killing you and dumping your body into the lake. Remember with real estate you are dealing with involves large amounts of money. This is why organized crime gets involved in real estate fraud.

You may find that organized crime has several professionals involved in the scam and each is taking a share. You may have a lawyer, a real estate appraiser, a realtor, a police man, and a banker all involved. The incentive here is to make a quick buck- a lot of them- without getting caught. And when they do it once and succeed they will do it again and again.

Your identity and good credit rating may be used to purchase property which is then resold and the equity removed. This is one good reason for checking your credit rating on a regular basis.

A crook could gain control of your property while you are away and rent it out to several innocent people while taking deposits from each of them. Then on the first of the month you might see ten moving trucks in your driveway with lots of angry people trying to move in. And they all have a receipt for their deposits with your signature on them and you never signed any of them. Think about it. They all paid a month's rent say for $1,500 and a damage deposit of say $1000 and that could be $25,000 for the crook. They have cashed the cheques in an account they set up with your name on it and they have withdrawn the money leaving you with huge problems.

There are several types of mortgage frauds and we would need another book to go into the details of how they were constructed. A basic idea is that the valuation of the property is inaccurate (too high) and the consequent mortgage obtained from the bank or wherever is much more than the property is worth. This is one reason why banks now send their own appraiser to verify the actual market value of the property before approving the mortgage. Another idea is to use somebody else's identity without them knowing about it to conduct a real estate transaction.

And imagine how much money could be involved if the crooks sold your house! They would receive the full purchase price on the day of sale and simply take the money and the new owners could move in while you are off on your annual vacation and after the crooks had moved everything out of your home. So you get back to your home only to find out that somebody else is in it and now they have your title. Just think of the problems that would develop here not only for you but also for the new owners! And we could be talking of hundreds and hundreds of thousands of dollars. And when you get into that much money the dangers increase. Nobody wants to tell you about crimes like this. Not the real estate company, not the legal community, not the banks and not even the media.

I will give you one example of how criminal money was used to pay for houses in Canada and the example I will use is a very attractive home once used as a grow op in Manitoba. It was confiscated by the government under the Criminal Property Forfeiture Act after in 2008 the police discovered an amazing 850 marijuana plants in it and in two other attractive homes in the same area they found over $3.4 million dollars in marijuana plants. The crooks were even stealing power. The home was placed and purchased by honest people and repairs were done to bring it back to excellent condition. If you were in the neighborhood you would never think that something like this criminal act was going on but in fact there are thousands of grow ops in Canada and this is just one example.

And when you begin to think about it ask yourself why if there are thousands of grow ops in Canada why are only a very few being confiscated by the Government? The reason is simple and that is they are not placing enough resources on fighting crime and what is the reason for that I wonder? Could it be the money? When you have a multi billion dollar drug trade occurring the obvious suggestion is that some of that money is being used to bribe government officials so that they won't be caught. For many years the largest cash crop in BC was marijuana and over 9 billion dollars was generated each year. When you have that much money being generated by crime in just one province and over 70 billion being generated nationally in criminal acts then it starts to sink in that billions of dollars of real estate in Canada are related to criminal activity of some sort. So my point here is that when you consider investing in Real Estate in Canada be aware of real estate that is related to criminal activities If you are intending to invest in an area with high rates of crime then don't expect the three levels of government in Canada to do much about it. And what does one do when a Real Estate Agent knocks on your door and asks you if you wish to sell your property to an individual who you are not aware is laundering money or establishing a location to commit criminal acts?

A very nice residential area in Manitoba where three grow op properties were discovered, confiscated and sold to honest owners. One would never think that the three homes had 3.4 million dollars of pot plants in them. How many other homes in Canada are being paid for and used by criminals?

CROOKS IN CANADA AND REAL ESTATE AGENTS

I am going to start this by telling you something that you may or likely may not know. There are a lot of Canadians who break the law or bend the law or operate in an unethical way! By a lot I don't mean a few dozen or a few hundred or even a few thousand. I mean a few million! How many million? Nobody knows because many of the crooks are never caught by Police. Our police tend to concentrate on violent crimes because these are the most dangerous and they usually require immediate help. But non violent crimes including business crimes, unethical behavior and bending the law happen all the time and relatively few of them are identified and charges laid. And what am I getting at? Let me explain.

Yes there is crime and unethical behavior happening in Real Estate buy also yes there is crime and unethical behavior happening in health care, education, retail, food, transportation, and just about any activity you wish to name. The problem is similar in all fields -it is the money. People need money to pay the bills and support themselves and their families. As their standard of living goes up the need for money goes up too. And so they look to ways of maximizing their revenue. At times they are desperate. And during those times the need for money goes even higher. And things start to get complicated. Why? Because there are levels of criminal activity.

UnREAL-ESTATE CANADA

Each occupation appears to have their own level of criminal or perhaps we should call it unethical activity. This level is usually reflected in how the public reacts to that occupation based on the concept of trust. As an example a person working as a used car salesperson does not have the same level of trust as a Doctor or Fireman. But at the same time there are completely honest used car sales people and criminal Doctors or Firemen. But as a general rule you can expect to place more trust in certain professions and occupations than others while at the same time remembering that there will always be exceptions to the rule.

So my point is that while you should treat a real estate deal as a business deal and you should be careful dealing with Real Estate Agents you should realize that while there are problems with unethical behavior and even criminal behavior there are also Agents who are completely honest and behave in a ethical way. There are over 110,000 real estate agents working in Canada and thousand and thousands of them are honest, ethical and hardworking for you! And a few are crooks! Just like every other profession ion Canada.

As an example have you ever purchased coffee at a restaurant and have the cashier make a "mistake" in giving you your change? Some of them actually do that to cheat you! And often it works! I remember going to a restaurant in Europe where we were presented with a bill that was over $30 over the actual total because of a "mistake in the addition". We pointed that out and the server was furious. They were making a good income from doing this to tourists. If you realize that not everyone is as honest as you are or might be then that places you in a much better position during a business deal.

One way of protecting your position in a business deal is to focus on the numbers. Be objective not subjective. When an Agent suggests an asking price for your property find out how it was obtained. Which sale properties did they compare your house to? What factors made your property worth more or less than the properties that sold. When did the sales take place? Is the market steady, falling or rising? When an offer is presented what is the percentage below the asking price or in some cases in a rising market –above the asking price.

For example if your property is valued at $425,000 and the prospective buyer offers you $25,000 less what is the percentage reduction? Actually that is 5.8% less than your asking price. On one hand $25,000 is "a lot of money" to use a subjective term. You could buy a new car with $25,000. But 5.8% means that they are offering you 94.2% of your asking price. That's "not bad!" To use another subjective term.

Normally when an offer is made they offer you the price they are willing to pay not the amount of the reduction. They don't say "I will offer you 5.8% under your asking price" they just say I offer you $400,000 as in the above example. You need to do the math. Be sure that you have a calculator.

BRIBES a.k.a. "gifts"

When somebody gifts you a wad of money that usually causes a positive reaction because there are no taxes no records and suddenly you have some money that you can use to do whatever you want to do. It is usually done in secret with nobody watching and you can stuff it into your pocket or purse immediately. But usually this is done for a reason.

If you are selling or even purchasing a house is there a way of paying extra money to achieve your goals? In other words can you bribe somebody outside of the regular commissions charged to obtain the property at the price you want or to sell it at the price you want? And let's be frank about the term "bribe". You could use a much more positive sounding word like "gift" and it would be much less offensive both to you and the person receiving the gift but essentially it is still a bribe. If we look at the U.K. there was a recent survey taken about how many people bribed people in the Public Service and 1 in 20 said that they did. Apparently globally the ratio is 1 in 4 which is horrifying but probably very accurate. And if this type of bribery exists in the Public Service of a very well respected country how much of it exists in the private sector of countries like Canada?

Here is the problem. Commissions are taxable. There is a record of the commission paid and who it goes to. And so the government takes a share of it. In the case of Ontario they take 13% of the commission for sales tax! So in the case of the $400,000 house with the $17,500 commission the government collects $2275 in taxes! Talk about a rip off. But this is what happens.

What if you were to give a Real Estate Agent a gift of say $5000. A gift is not taxable. What if you gave the Agent the gift IF the house that you are selling was sold for an amount that you stipulated? If it was less than that amount there would be no gift just the agreed upon commission. There would be no written agreement only a verbal offer and the stipulation on the price would be made very clear.

The question is would this "bribe" work? The other question is "how many times is this done in reality?" Clearly most Agents would be very reluctant to participate because of the risk of being found out and the effect that would have on their employment with the company they work for. Some agents would find the offer insulting. But in very tough conditions were annual sales and commission income were down and the Agent had lots of expenses the bribe or "gift" might be an option. And what if you received say $15,000 more for your property than you asked the agent to sell it for? If you gave them $5000 you would still have $10,000 more than you expected on the sale.

And let's look a little deeper into this. What if in a given market there were say 100 people who were buyers and 500 properties for sale and your property was priced in the lower quarter of the prices. In a normal situation the Agent would prefer to sell a higher priced home to one of their potential customers because the more the home sells for the higher their commissions. But if you said they would get a $5000 gift that changes the situation entirely. In the case of a $100,000 sale an Agent in Ontario would earn a 5% commission which would be split between the sellers agent and the buyers agent and then would be split again between the agent and the company they work for and lets say that is a 50:50 split although it could be less. So if the Agent was say only the selling agent that $5000 commission would be split into two $2500 payments and then down to $1250 for the Agent and $1250 for the Agent's company. Now sit down and relax because that means that if you gave the agent $5000 if they sold the property for $115,000 that would mean that the agent would receive $1437.50 in a taxable commission AND your $5000 non taxable gift or in other words they would receive the equivalent of the income they would have gotten by selling 4.5 properties of the same value. That would be a huge incentive. One could also argue that a "gift" is perfectly legal. One could even offer a gift in a non cash form like giving the agent a vacation or a used vehicle or a boat motor and trailer or a skidoo. And another point here is that perhaps you really don't need to make the gift that big! After all it is 4.5 times the normal commission they would receive. What if you offered them $2000 instead? Possibly that would work too. My suggestion is that you consider the option and as we all know the larger the gift the more incentive it carries. And in this case a gift of $5000 is several times larger than the taxable commission they receive. Do you really think that a lot of sellers would consider doing something like this? I doubt it. Would it work? It could. If you took some care on how you introduced the idea to the Agent it could either work or not.

I understand that some readers will be upset by this suggestion that bribes or gifts could be used and however what I am doing here is describing how business deals really work. Trust me. I have worked in business for decades and have worked in both the private sector, the military and the governments and in my own businesses. Imagine for a moment that it is winter and a truck pulls into your driveway and unloads a large box and the driver comes to your door and asks you to sign the delivery slip. You look out and see a crate with "Ski Doo" marked on it. Somebody has just given you a $10,000 snow machine. That somebody is a business that you deal with on a regular basis. In fact your company does over a million dollars of business with them every year. Do you think that this never happens in business? Think again. It is not something that people will talk about and you will never read about in the media but it does happen.

In some cases the gift will be a bottle of wine and in some cases the gift will be a case of scotch. Do you know what a case of scotch would cost? In some cases it is a new car or a new snow machine or a bunch of tickets for your family to attend a baseball or hockey game that would cost hundreds if you bought them yourself. These are gifts not payments and so many treat them as non taxable. And there is a relationship between the value of the gift and the amount of money that the individual receiving the gift generates for you. If they helped make you $1000 in extra revenue you might give them a bottle of wine and a box of Christmas chocolates. If they helped make you $100,000 in profits you might give them a much more substantial gift. And as you know real estate deals generate very large commissions and very large fees for services and so one might expect that "gifts" would be distributed.

In fact there are companies which specialize in supplying business gifts. You can purchase bottles of cases of wine with your company logo on it, e-readers, gift cars, gifts designed to make the recipients happy and help them and their families and subsequently make them want to do more business with you.

And yes folks there is a good story here too! Often what an agent will do is provide their customers with a gift when they move into their new home. Depending on the size of the commission it could be relatively inexpensive yet thoughtful or it could be even something like a snow blower! Usually the gifts are unexpected and the customer is quite happy to get them and essentially it is a marketing technique where the customer will tell their friends what a great agent you were so if they were looking for on you would be the person they would recommend. And that gift could go both ways. If you were happy with your Agent and the pre sale "gift" I mentioned wasn't involved but the sale went very well and you got more for the property than the asking price then what would be wrong with giving your agent an appropriate gift. This is how business works!

GOOD AND BAD DECISIONS IN REAL ESTATE AND THE CONSEQUENCES

Most of us would agree that we live by the consequences of our decisions. Yes it is an oversimplification and yes there are exceptions but it is a good general rule and a place to start. Let's consider some cases.

You are in your twenties and own a mortgaged home in Victoria. You get a job promotion to Toronto and are faced with the decision of either selling the Victoria home and buying one in Toronto or renting out the Victoria home and attempting to buy one in Victoria based on the equity you have in your Victoria home. So you decide to sell. Is that a good decision or a bad decision and what are the consequences?

Here is what happened. You sold your home for $200,000 and over the next five years real estate in Victoria doubled. The home is now worth $400,000. You purchased a property in Toronto at the top of the market for $400,000 and after five years it has fallen to $350,000. Had you kept your Victoria home your equity would have increased significantly. But it was reduced significantly instead.

If you make a bad decision like purchasing a property prone to flooding or at the base of a hill prone to wear or on a beach prone to wave damage or a property near an industrial zone or on a dangerous corner for traffic or whatever you very likely will suffer the consequences.

Real estate decisions are critical events where a wrong decision can ruin you or a correct decision could make you a millionaire! There is a song by one of my favorite Canadian singers that I think you should listen to while considering real estate. Sarah MacDougall from Whitehorse, Yukon sings **Sometimes you Win Sometimes you Lose**. The song, the version with the dancing bears in it is on Youtube and well worth a listen. Sarah was not singing about real estate but she was making the point that some times things go well and sometimes they don't. A beautiful song! And the song places you in the right mood to decide which is your best deal! Thanks Sarah.

THINK AHEAD AND PLAN AHEAD!

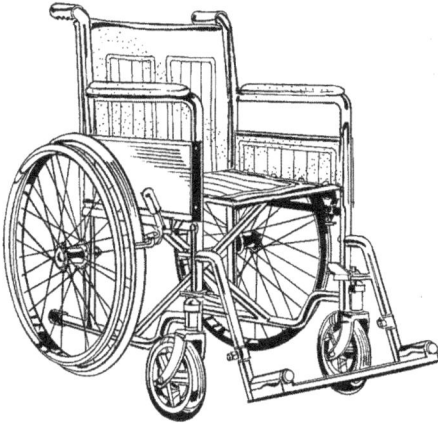

Over the years I have noticed a very odd tendency regarding how people think. Every day something happens in our lives some of it is expected and some of it is unexpected. Sometimes you grow old and enjoy very good health and other times you end up in a wheel chair!

Another example would be going to school. You go and take a course in some subject and as the days pass you realize that you are understanding it well or not. You know that a test is coming up and you realize that you need to study for it. But here is what happens. If some people are asked by their friends to go to the pub a couple of days before the test some will say sure and some will say sorry I need to study. So what is happening here?

Some people react to what happens and enjoy the moment but other people think of what will happen and decide to prepare for it rather than enjoying the moment. So some people will go to the pub and drink all night and others will stay home and study all night. And guess who does better in the test?   Now let's consider real estate.

Let's say that you have a mortgage and a three bedroom home in town and you are told by your employer that you will be transferred to another province in six months.   Some people will wait until the transfer occurs and others will think about the best plan for their home. Will they place it on the market or rent it out? Is the market going up or down or is it steady? Are the homes in the new locations more or less expensive?   In other words some people plan ahead and when the transfer does occur they are ready for it and have made the best decision. But other people don't plan ahead and so when the time comes in panic they phone up a real estate agent and place their home on the market. That could be a good plan but if the market is steadily going up they may be making a bad decision. Perhaps what they should do is re-mortgage their home and use the funds to purchase a second home in their new location.

So the main point here is that when you are investing in real estate you really must plan ahead. What will happen in the next couple of years, the next five and ten year periods and the next 20 years. Sit down and write up a plan. There are so many variables you need to consider.   And the danger is that if you wait to make a decision the moment the events occur you will likely make some bad moves. .

WATER AND REAL ESTATE??

I took this picture at Cowichan Bay on Vancouver Island. Thousands of Canadians live on boats and Canada has the largest coastline in the world. We lived on our sailboat for three years and it was fantastic! An alternate life style to consider!

Your first reaction to this chapter might be – what the heck has water got to do with real estate –unless he is talking about waterfront? And I am not talking about waterfront. In fact having served in the Royal Canadian Navy and having lived on a sail boat for several years I love water. But lets consider what happens when you mix water and real estate.

Humans are approximately 57% water by weight and the average human will have the equivalent of about 70 litres of water in them. Humans start to die off after three days without water. We use water for so many things from cooking to cleaning to swimming to putting out fires. Because water is so important to human life you might be surprised when I tell you that water and real estate sometimes don't mix. In fact water can sometimes completely ruin your real estate investment. Here is the problem.

Water is what a chemist would call a **universal solvent**. More material dissolves in water than in any other liquid. If you get a flood in your home the water will ruin thousands of dollars of material. If water gets into your basement it could result in rot and insect infestations and warped wood and destroyed machinery and electrical problems. Water can make one heck of a mess.

I once watched a house built in our neighborhood where they dug the basement quite deep into a blue clay soil. Then they hit the water table and the basement started to fill with water. So they pumped it all out and then installed some sort of double foundation with huge sump pumps all at great cost and proceeded to complete the construction of the house. That foundation probably cost at least four times what a foundation would cost if they had not run into the water table. When you are buying a property be sure that you know where the water table is. As an example if the water table is only a couple of feet down then it would be very unlikely that any homes in the area would have a basement and if they did flooding would likely be an issue. And the water table depth is usually seasonal too and may rise with melting snow and rain and in fact it can rise several feet so you may think you are safe during the dry times but during other times that basement of yours may flood! And if there is a problem here with the water table who do you think is going to tell you about it? You will need to ask. And it would be better to ask someone who is not directly involved in the sale. Sometimes a city worker in the planning department would be a good source of info.

SPACE VIEWS

Traditionally, a prospective buyer will drive by your property to see if they are interested in viewing it. They obtain what is called a **street view**. They may also review photographs of your property again from the street view perspective. Modern technology has given us another view option which is not generally appreciated yet in the industry. That view is from outer space! Try looking at the property with a program called **Google Earth**. Not only is this program very effective and very efficient it is very FREE!

But the problem is that despite the fact that Google Earth has been around for several years prospective buyers are not using it. Some do but most don't. So as a reader of this book if I have managed to talk you into using Google Earth and if you found it useful then we will both be happy! And if you are a millennial I trust that you already know about communication and technology and will already be using services like Google Earth so in your case I am only reminding you!

Google Earth gives you a view from a satellite. You can zoom right down to your house. **The huge advantage of this aerial view is that you see your house and it's relationship to other homes, roads, rivers, forests, developments, etc etc etc.** There is a lot of information to process. And remember normally with traditional real estate advertising you are not made aware of these facts. You can get a feeling for development in your area and what might develop in the future. You can see potential problems where roads exist. You can even see potential flooding areas. I strongly recommend that you spend an hour or two looking at the Google Earth views and then noting any information you can glean from them and then investigate those facts. And remember you have several options for viewing property in Google Earth. As an example you can view development over several years, distances, elevation, the direction that the sun travels and an amazing amount of information at no cost to you. My point is that it would be a mistake to simply look at Google Earth images and stop there. Check out the menu at the top of the screen and you will be amazed at how much additional information you can obtain. It will take a few minutes of experimenting to see what else it does. And remember the amount and quality of the information goes up each year.

In the case of higher end housing an aerial view gives you a better idea of where your home fits within your area. Is it on the margins next to a higher density area? Is there much room for expansion? If not and if your area is a desirable area then limited room for expansion could help with the appreciation of the value of your property.

I used this technique to view a home in a very desirable neighborhood of Toronto. From the air one could clearly see that the northern side was a river at the bottom of a ravine. There would be no growth there. The southern side was a major highway so no growth there. Both East and west sides were effectively forming a parcel of land with parkland on one side and a major street on the other. All the housing in this area was high end with properties in the one million to five million dollar range. This area is a good example of an area that is only going to get better over time. All homes were single family dwellings. And consider that because if you were living I a million dollar plus home would you really want to live next door to a 15 story apartment building? And so in this example this is another sign that values will only go up over time because there are no apartment buildings here. You could look at the homes in this area from a drive by view but a quick review of the satellite view gave you information that you would not get by driving by or walking in the neighborhood.

And a final point. You don't even need your computer and the big screen on it to see a Google Earth view. You can view it on your cell phone or tablet. You can view it during an open house. It only takes a few seconds to open the program and see the property from space and see what is around it. You can also use Google Street View to look around the property from a street perspective and that will show you even more about the property in a very short period of time. This raises a privacy issue because most people are not aware of what people can see about their house online. They even can identify the type of car that you have and what sort of condition your home was in the day the photo was taken. We have all this new technology and some people know how to use it and others don't. So join the nerd club when it comes to real estate and modern technology and end up with a better deal.

And one more interesting point about google street views of a property. It is shocking how much personal information about your property is shown on Google Street Views They obtain these images by driving a camera equipped car down your road. So out of curiosity I checked out a few friends homes and discovered something that is not obvious at all but very significant. If you want everyone in the world to view your front yard then don't plant any trees there but if you want a decent level of privacy simply put a few trees near your property line at the front of your yard. And what happens? Google Street View can't see much at all. But without the trees everyone can look at the front of your home and determine information about it that you want to keep private. Check it out to see what I mean.

Google Earth is a key information source for real estate property and be sure to take advantage of this free resource. Technology is something that changes daily and as I write this book in 2017 this program has been around for a decade or so and every year there are improvements. It is another example of how complex real estate is and how nobody can possibly understand all factors associated with it. All we can do is try our best ask experts in each field for their advice and information and then make decisions. And the better the advice and the more accurate it is the better chances that your decisions will result in success.

THE WORST or the BEST HOUSE ON THE STREET?

We once purchased a house in the James Bay neighborhood of Victoria, BC. It was a nice little modest home built about a century ago. It was also probably the most modest house on the block. And we purchased it at the bottom of the market more as a result of blind luck than anything else as it was our first house. As the market went up so did the little house and we did well when we sold it. There is a lot to be said for purchasing a modest house on a desirable street when your house is less expensive than most of the others.

Strangely this relationship seems to work in reverse when you purchase the best house on the block. When you reach the time when you decide to sell you will find that prospective buyers are looking at the selling prices of other sales on that block and then discounting the value of your home. Also the type of person who would like to buy a higher end house often will want that house to be grouped with like houses in a like neighborhood. In other words they don't want to live with the common folk in the lesser houses. I know that sounds terrible but I think it is accurate because that's what people do!

Another problem with the best home on the block is that it becomes a target for crooks. Bad guys will look at your home and think that because it looks much better than others on the block that it will also have many more good things to steal.

BATHROOMS

There are basically two questions about bathrooms and your home. How big and how many? And let's start in a home without a bathroom something you might find very odd.

My Grandparents had a beautiful cottage on Lake Superior that we visited as kids. They had a dock a small boat, gardens and a beautiful yard. But there was no bathroom in the house! Instead they had an outhouse about 30 feet from the home on the edge of their property. *(The image here is similar to the size they had.)* The reason for this was that the street they were on was not connected to the sewer system. And I should tell you also that the outhouse was spotless. So I can tell your from experience that it is possible to have a home in the country without a washroom in it and instead with an outdoor outhouse.

UnREAL-ESTATE CANADA

But in the city all properties are connected to the municipal sewer systems and they don't have outhouses so the question there is how large should your bathroom be and how many should you have? We are going to talk about pee and poop which I hope does no offend you.

Here is a large bathroom that looks quite nice!

Every day on average a person will pee about 8 times. Possibly on some days they will pee less and other days they will pee more but let's use the average pee rate as an indicator. So if only one person lives in the home then the bathroom is used for that purpose up to 8 times a day. A couple will see 16 times a day. A family of five will see 80 pees a day. And add poop to that. Then add brushing teeth and shaving and washing and you can see what is happening here. While it is possible to have just one bathroom and it is possible to have just a small bathroom of say 30 square feet including a sink, toilet and shower there are many people in the real estate market who demand having more than one bathroom and demand that the spaces available are larger than the minimum size. .

So you have a decision here. How many people will be living in your home? Will you have guests? Do you have visitors regularly? It is possible to have small room with only a toilet and sink in it. If you have lots of room in your home and a basement and or second story then the number of bathrooms is an issue you need to consider.

A small bathroom in surface area but it does have a shower, sink, toilet and cabinet and so you can do all your normal human functions here in a small space!

One consideration would be the cost of installing an additional bathroom. The main problem is usually the plumbing. A workable rule of thumb might be to have one bathroom in a home up to 1000 square feet without a basement and two bathrooms in a home of up to 2000 square feet and 3 bathrooms or more with larger homes. If you are having guests or wish to establish a space that can be rented out then you need a separate bathroom for that space. I know that thinking about bathroom requirements seems kind of silly but peeing and pooping is a normal human activity and the more people doing it the more resources you should have to enjoy a comfortable life style.

REPITITION OF SIMILAR EVENTS AND HUMAN NATURE

For some strange reason humans enjoy an event if it is similar to an even that has previously occurred. For example if they purchase or sell a piece of real estate from one broker they love to go back to the same broker the next time they want to purchase or sell more real estate.

People enjoy going to a favorite restaurant and having basically the same meal they had previously there. They often prefer to live in a neighborhood where all houses look similar and where other homeowners are in a similar demographic.

In any area you will find people who are not normal.

UnREAL-ESTATE CANADA

So you take a chance when you deviate from the herd and go for a strange design for your home or paint it an outrageous color or decorate it in a strange and different way. I remember one house that was a beautify log home and it looked beautiful inside and outside. It was a work of art. However it was the only log home in the neighborhood and when it was sold it was difficult to sell for that reason and it did not get the price it should have gotten. Not only was it one of the best houses on the street but it was also the house that looked different from the other homes. What I find unpleasant is when a neighborhood has all the same sorts of houses all with similar designs and colors. I guess that some people like that but I don't.

Let's say that your house has vinyl siding on it but every other house on the street is brick. It is very likely that a prospective buyer will discount the value of your house because it does not conform to others on the street. So when you are considering a home consider where it stands with the other homes in the area. Is it at the top or bottom of the list? Something to consider!

Some neighborhoods in Canada are almost identical and after viewing and photographing thousands of homes I personally do not like areas where all the colors and designs are similar. Some people love that approach. But people are not all the same. Sometimes it is refreshing to see something different and something attractive or entertaining. Over many years of history this has attracted millions of people to view the unique structures and examples like the Statue of Liberty, The Eiffel Tower the Wawa Goose and let me give you an example from North Bay, Ontario.

At 1135 Cassells St. in North Bay Ontario Canada we have the home of Daniel and Roberta Seguin. Daniel is an Artist and he was constructed a unique home that is a source of joy for thousands of fellow citizens. This home is not only unique to North Bay, Ontario it is unique to Ontario, Canada and the world! There is no other home like it anywhere.

When you drive by in your car you see a glimpse of the home but you really need to park your car and take a closer look! What you will see will amaze you and as you realize that you are looking at a work of art the items in it become more and more interesting and you will appreciate the talent and work required. If you have ever visited an art gallery you will realize that this home IS an Art Gallery. One of the things I like are the positive feelings that this home has shared with thousands of people over the years.

There is a combination of color, balance, variety, collectables, and several other factors that generate a positive feeling and a smile An Artist can take almost any material and combine it into an art form which viewers will love.

When you walk down the side of the house you see a wonderful structure and so many interesting items to look at. It is almost like a magnet. The work required to collect these items and display them with such an artistic flare is amazing. And remember this photo is in black and white but in reality there are colors here which are wonderful.

I had the opportunity to speak with Daniel Seguin and I was amazed by his energy, love of Art and his abilities. When you complete a work of Art some people will love it and others will not. Since the beginning of time any Artist learns this very quickly. I took a couple of Fine Art courses at my University, I do some Art myself and I have been lucky enough to visit the Louvre in Paris and other Art galleries in Canada. So I can tell you that I do have an appreciation of what Art is and how to recognize those with great artistic talent. Here is proof that not all real estate in Canada is the same and that variations from the normal can be a great source of joy.

CATS

Your first impression might by what on earth have cats to do with real estate? In fact Cats can represent a total disaster for the seller and buyer. Cats have three issues with real estate. They pee, they have fleas and they have very fine hair. Cat urine is very concentrated and very smelly and some owners may have several cats who are allowed to pee inside the building. The urine soaks into rugs and floors and even concrete to the extent that the only solution is to remove the soiled material. That means ripping out the carpets and the flooring and even the concrete pads in some cases. If you don't do this the odor of cat urine will persist in the home. So you could be looking at tens of thousands of dollars to solve this problem.

Another problem with cats is that they attract fleas. Once the fleas nest in the home you need to get rid of them. This can be done and the cost is not excessive but it is a health issue until it is done.

The last problem with cats is that they have very fine fur. The fur becomes airborne and will be carried into the heating system. In a forced air system the ducts will become contaminated with it and require cleaning. In the worst case the furnace may require replacement. This is a significant expense.

I love cats and millions of people love cats!. But my recommendation is that if the home owner has multiple cats in the home that you should pass on it. I once visited a home where several cats (over a dozen!) had lived and the owners were having a home and yard sale. The smell of cat urine was so strong in the basement of the home and on the first floor that you found yourself choking on it. It was horrible and I remember that cat house to this day. Yuk.

Now some will argue that the cat pee will reduce the asking price of the home and that therefore it will be a better deal. There is no logic in this statement. The reduced price is because the cat pee damage makes the home worth less. Others will say it is cheap fix simply replace the carpets clean the walls and repaint. Again this is a lie. If the cat pee has gotten into wooden floors in large volumes they will need to be replaced. If the cat has been using the basement as his toilet the concrete slab floor may be soaked in cat pee and it won't be possible to get that smell out.

Another problem here is that it places the real estate agents in a difficult position. Remember they only get paid when there is a sale. The selling agent will tend to minimize any problems with the cat pee. The buying agent who works on the buyer's side would be tempted to also minimize the issues or suggest that there are relatively easy fixes available.

The question becomes do you really wish to live in what is now a giant cat box? The ammonia smell will linger for years. Do yourself a huge favor and avoid a house like this. If you are an owner consider the downsides of cat ownership before filling your home up with them. If you are a renter consider the damage cats may do to your property before renting it out to cat owners.

Again I like cats. I like dogs more but Cats are ok too. We once had a neighbor's cats visit us or years for snacks and he was wonderful until one day he suddenly disappeared and to this day we still feel sorry for him. But cats and real estate do not mix. Do you really wish to buy a cat pee house? So to speak. If you are going to buy the house anyway and you know it had several cats and you can smell cat pee at least talk to a professional cleaner and see if they have a solution and how much will it cost. Perhaps you could discount that amount from your offer.

HOARDERS

There are people out there who collect things. This is usually a normal behavior. A normal person will collect something and then when they no longer need it they will sell or give it away or toss it into the garbage. This allows them to make best use of their property. And yes some of us tend to collect more than we need but usually after a few years or so we start to get rid of it. So far so good.

There are also people with problems out there. They collect everything and throw away or recycle nothing. As a result their residences become packed with stuff so that after a few years there are narrow pathways through their homes and garages where they can walk and stuff is packed from floor to ceiling. These people are called **hoarders**. Some of the stuff will begin to rot or decompose and the home becomes a health risk with possible vermin contamination.

My experience is that Hoarders exist in a range. Let's call it three stages. The first group will collect a bit too much stuff but their residences are still livable except they may be a bit messy. The second group which I will call **mid-horders** are people who simply have too much stuff and more stuff than they need. Instead of having one bike they have three possibly none of them in good working condition. They have multiple copies of equipment and other items when they only need one. They are a little over the edge but not wacko.

Then there is the **full horder** who is basically nuts and who collects everything in piles sometimes neat piles sometimes not. These people have a mental disorder but they do exist. And when their properties go up for sale the prospective buyer needs to carefully consider what to do. Sometimes there is significant value in the collection of stuff the Horder has and sometimes it is all or mostly garbage. Here is an example. A Hoarder loves cars so they collect dozens of them in a field or large barn and much to your surprise the cars have considerable collectors value or parts value. Some old cars are so collectable that they are worth thousands of dollars each. So buying the property and calling the junk man to haul them all away is not the smartest thing to do. I am not suggesting that you should keep them all but possibly you could have a big sale or hire an auctioneer or put the cars on kijjii or contact local collectors or do something to clean up the property and make a few thousand dollars more than your costs to do the clean up.

Even scrap metal has a certain value these days and so my suggestion here is take a close look at what the horder has left and consider your best options. Often a property can be acquired at a relatively low cost because of all the collected items on it and sometimes it is all junk and needs to be picked up and taken to a local dump and that could cost hundreds or even thousands of dollars.

On the good side a house full of junk collected by the neighborhood packrat will significantly lower the price of the property. Unfortunately, if you purchase the property in this condition you really don't know what sort of damage had been done to the home. Again on the good side there are people who will cheerfully load up their truck and take the stuff to the local dump for a reasonable price. What is more likely to happen is that a hoarder's home will be cleaned out prior to placing it on the market and you may not be aware of the fact that a hoarder lived there.

If you can obtain the home prior to it being placed on the market there is a good chance that you could get it for a significantly reduced price and that spending just a few thousand dollars to clean it out will result in obtaining the home at thousands of dollars under the market price. Your biggest risk is that the hoarding has caused structural or other damage to the home that may be more expensive to repair. And remember there is the possibility that the hoarder may have some good stuff there with an actual dollar value. In fact there could be significant value there in which case you may end up with an inventory of value that you can resell.

So should you run into a situation where hoarding is involved take a second look at the situation and determine if there is any opportunity there or should you just stay away?

SMOKING

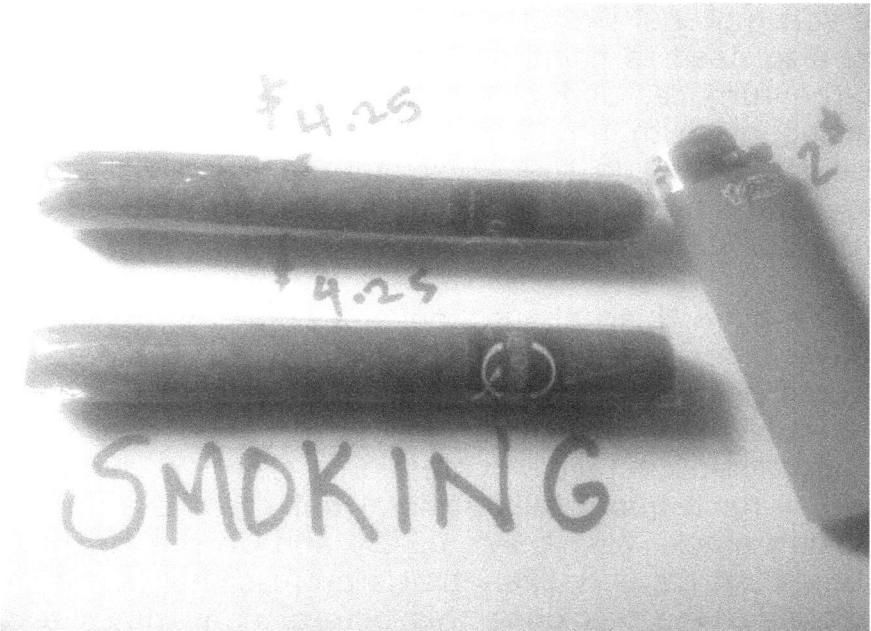

Here are two small cigars that really stink and cost $4.25 each. With the lighter your cost is just over $10.00 plus tax.

Every year I have a couple of cigars. I also love the smell of pipes and the different styles of pipes and being a collector by nature I can see myself with several of them and all types of expensive pipe tobacco. Instead I have decided not to smoke. I think I learned that from my Dad who gave up smoking when be became a senior citizen and because he did that he lived on for many more years. When people smoke inside their homes the smoke filters through the home and collects on surfaces. The smoke gets into fabrics and any porous surfaces. The result is that the home stinks like an ashtray. This is very unpleasant to both smokers and non smokers and in most cases is a show stopper when trying to sell the home.

Ridding the home of smoke smells involves a huge cleaning job. Even then you may need to take out all the soft material like drapes and carpets and furniture. You also need to change all the light bulbs, the filters on the furnace, and give the home a deep cleaning starting off with products like TSP. Yes you can get products that hide the smell but the smell will come back unless all the smoking compounds are cleaned out of the home.

The good thing about smoker's homes is that from a buyer's perspective it lowers the price. If the price is lowered below the cost to clean out the smoke then it is possible that the buyer will get a good deal. The buyer should contact a professional cleaning company and ask for a quote telling them that there is a strong smoking smell. Yes you could try and do the cleaning yourself but it's very likely that a professional cleaner – somebody who has done this before many times and has the right equipment –could do it better and for quite a reasonable cost. Cleaners work hard but are not paid high wages and so you get a good deal.

Many years ago we had a fire in an apartment building we were staying at. There was smoke damage to nearly all the apartments including ours. What really surprised me was the excellent job that the cleaning company did. We were covered by our insurance so there was no cost. From this episode I learned that smoke damage can be reversed if you know what you are doing and have the right equipment.

Ok a final thought on smoking. If you smoke your chances of dying of lung cancer are much higher than if you don't smoke. You could also get throat cancer so why bother? There are so many other things to do in life that surely you could come up with an alternative for more fun than smoking. And from a real estate perspective by not smoking you would only add value to your home and the fact that you were able to live longer would give you more enjoyment in your home. Something to consider eh! .

INTERIOR GARDENS

We all like plants. The problem begins when we start to grow a lot of plants indoors. Some people have a veritable garden inside their homes. The plants generate a higher level of humidity. This humidity settles on windows and runs down into the sills. If the sills are wood they begin to rot. Once the rot starts you have a big problem to solve.

There are two messages here. If you are living in the house or have a renter in the house then limit the number of plants you have in the home. If you are buying the house and somehow find out that the people living there had a lot of indoor plants then start checking out the condition of interior walls and window sills.

As mentioned, most of us like plants. They look great help with establishing a pleasant appearance in a home. But when there are too many plants in a home we start to see the damaging effects. A classic example of this is when a renter decides that they will start a grow op in your rental property. This generates huge amounts of moisture which will ruin just about everything and require an interior rebuild to repair. I should end this topic by saying again that most of us love plants. But while you can have a few plants in your home it is not a greenhouse and most or nearly all people have reasonable limits on the number of plants they will have. I say most because I have been in homes, very nice homes, where there were dozens of plants growing in the same room. And yes they did look great but remember all that moisture may result in some structural problems and when you encounter a home with lots of plants in it that is one thing to check.

And I do recall moisture running down the inside of windows and moisture on the walls despite the fact that the plants looked gorgeous. I feel a bit uncomfortable suggesting that you limit your plant collection because that is one of the things people do to enjoy their lives a bit more. I am just looking at it from an objective and mathematical perspective. If you can figure out a way of increasing your air flow and decreasing humidity then perhaps more plants would work. Possibly a dehumidifier would help! Just remember that if you visit a home for sale that has lots of plants to check out for rot and any damage associated with them.

FIRST NATIONS

In the United States they had Indian Wars and they took over Indian Lands. But in Canada we never had any Indian wars and instead signed 11 Treaties with our First Nations. Most Canadians do not have a very accurate knowledge of First Nations but the reality is that although Canada is 150 years old in 2017 our First Nations were here for thousands of years before Canada was founded. I think that it is useful to have a better understand of our First Nations as we consider different aspects associated with real estate in Canada.

There are over 600 First Nations Bands in Canada with over 3100 Reserves spread across the country. The largest reserve is the Six Nations 40 Reserve in Ontario with a population of over 20,000 band members. Yes there are issues with real estate and First Nations and in 2017 there are improvements being implemented. This may involve the transfer of land ownership back to First Nations bands and this will certainly affect land values. It is not really clear at this time exactly what will happen.

The First Nations fought for Canada in both world wars. They insured that Canada won the war of 1812 with the United States. Our First Nations are mainly located in regions north of the 100 mile band on the US boarder where most of the Canadian population lives. Over 5000 First Nations serve in a Canadian Army reserve service called the Canadian Rangers and they are the eyes and ears of our Northern regions. Over the years I have met and worked with many First Nations people. Yes there are problems in First Nations not that unlike the problems we have all over Canada. Too many Canadians are now aware of issues that our First Nations must face including the problems associated with our country not abiding by the terms of the 11 agreements in the form of Treaties that were signed by both parties. But it does appear that improvements are being made.

From a real estate perspective it would be helpful to both buyers and sellers to be aware of any First Nations issues that may apply to their land. So that is something to consider and investigate. And when doing that my suggestion is not to get caught up in the comments that our Trolls and Haters make against First Nations. If you understand what is really going on then it will be to everyone's advantage.

POOLS

We all know what a pool looks like. Then come in all sizes and shapes. On the lower end one can have an inflatable pool with room for one person or a hot tube with room for up to four or even possibly more. The bigger pools again come in several sizes from small to large to huge. When you visit a home with the purpose of reviewing it for possible purchase the pool causes an almost immediate emotional impact on you. On a hot day you might want to go for a swim or sit down beside the pool and have a drink or just look at the people swimming in the pool. The water in the pool looks beautiful and there is nothing better than floating around or swimming in it during a hot summer day.

The last thing you will think about is what we are going to tell you now. But before I tell you this information I would like to share my experience with pools. We once looked at a house for sale in Victoria, BC that looked like a normal home not too big nor fancy not too expensive but it also had a large pool with a roof and walls. It was not an outside pool it was actually attached to the house. It was fantastic to look at and I still remember looking at it and thinking that it would be an excellent home to buy. Not because of the home itself but because of the pool. I think the home and the pool were about 40 years old when we looked at them. We ended up buying another house but I still remember this one with fond memories. The example here is how a pool can generate a positive emotion and a desire to acquire it.

I have also visited friends with pools and have used pools while staying at hotels in the summer months. I love pools! But here we are talking about pools and real estate.

The question is – Is a pool a good addition to a real estate property? This is an important question because if it is a good investment it should make the property worth more money and if if is a bad addition to the property it will likely make the property worth less. Now the question gets complicated because as I pointed out there are several types of pools and in addition to the different types of pools they all tend to age some at different rates. That is some pools like inflatable ones might only be good for a season or two. Other above ground pools could be ok for several years and certain types of in ground pools could last decades. A hot tube is actually portable so if you don't like it you could remove it fairly easily or even move it to a better location in your yard. Many above ground pools could be taken down fairly easily and possibly even sold. An in ground pool once established is much more difficult to remove or move. Yes you could have some heavy excavation equipment come in and dig it up and yes you could then have some big trucks with fill come in and fill up the hole but you are talking about several thousands of dollars to do this. My guess would be at least $10,000 to remove a small and mid sized in ground pool and more to remove a large in ground pool.

And yes it does get complicated. I have seen pools that add to the value of a yard and not only look beautiful there were incorporated correctly into the back yard so that the back yard remains a very useful place to visit and enjoy. But I have also seen pools which dominated the back yard to the point where there really was no useful backyard except for the pool. And in those cases I suggest that the pool detracted and lowered the value of the property. Fewer people would wish to purchase it and people would want to spend less money for it. So from an investment perspective there are two possibilities. A pool will either add or reduce the asset value of the property.

From a buyer's perspective if the property had an in ground pool that was old and needed work there is an opportunity here to make a reduced offer on the home that the seller may accept. And if you obtain the home at the reduced offer it may be possible to fix or remove the pool and still be ahead financially.

However what if the pool looks great and is in good condition and you like pools and the back yard is large enough to allow other uses? Is a pool a good idea? That depends.

If you can afford to maintain the pool and if you enjoy the pool then yes the pool may add to the value of the property and may be a good idea to purchase. But if you have limited funds and the new property will take most of your available funds then likely obtaining a property with a pool is a bad idea even if it would be a good idea if you had the funds and it was in good well maintained condition.

There are several potential good points to having a pool. First you can get some good exercise. Second you can appreciate being in your back yard more. Third you can entertain your friends with a pool. They might even bring over some free beer for you! Imagine the fun you could have in your back yard with a BBQ, a pool party, a few beer some outdoor music and those drinks with the colorful umbrellas and ice cubes in them.

And I should mention one more fact about pools that often people might not consider. If you are located in a densely populated area like Toronto or Vancouver there is a tendency for those with enough money to also own a cottage near a lake and an example for Toronto would be the Muskoka area north of Toronto. While thousands of people do this there are a few problems. Yes it is wonderful to relax on a beach in front of a lake in the summer time it is also very expensive to purchase and maintain the cottage and drive back and forth on the weekends where traffic is sometimes bumper to bumper. So what some homeowners are doing is installing pools in their back yards and not purchasing or renting additional homes in cottage country. And while you might point out that the pool could cost a lot of money it is unlikely that it will cost as much as a cabin in cottage country and there will be zero time spent on driving back and forth in crowded conditions. You can literally step out the back door and jump into your pool in about a minute or two. If you are selling your home with a pool this would be a good sales point to make to any prospective buyers!

I do have suggestions for you regarding pools. Be objective. Be analytical. Forget your emotions. Follow the money and identify the value of the pool in it's present condition, the cost of maintaining it, the number of months that it can be used each year, the potential cost to remove it and does it fit the back yard well. Is any additional work required to make it fit better? Obtain an accurate description of it with the dimensions and the water capacity. I am referring to an in ground pool.

If the pool is an above ground pool find the same information and be careful of the actual condition of the pool as above ground pools are often built with liners with a limited life span. In the case of hot tubs the condition of the tub is also important. The good thing about both hot tubes and above ground tubs is that they both can be removed relatively inexpensively compared to in ground pools. In the case of hot tubes I suggest that you have a rail of some sort to help you enter and exit the tub as it is quite easy to slip when your are climbing in and out without something to grab onto. As you get older and heavier the risk goes up. I say this because I was once invited into a friend's hot tube but when I tried to get in my bad right knee prevented that and there was nothing to grab onto. . It is one of those things you don't think about until it happens and you try to enter or exit a hot tub!

There is a potential privacy issue with hot tubs that usually can be solved relatively easily but if the owner has already done something about that there is one thing you won't need to do. Resting in a hot tub with a drink is actually quite pleasant. With a good view or a TV screen close by it could even be more fun! It would be wise to review the electrical safety of the hot tube as they usually are powered by electricity and as you know water and electricity are not known to match well especially when you are in the water! And remember one alternative in a hot tube is just to relax. No music. No computers or cell phones or TV screens just you and the warm water . Nothing wrong with that! After a few minutes you can do something else but in a much more relaxed and better mood!

An inflatable hot tub is an option where you can still have lots of fun but at a much reduced cost for example this one is approx $350 and actually holds 4 to 6 people!

So to review the points made here –pools of all sizes and prices do have advantages and disadvantages. Condition is important. Monthly costs are a consideration. You can really enjoy them or really resent the costs and appearance. So there is no simple factor that describes all situations regarding pools. It depends on several factors and you need to sit down and consider them all before making a decision.

There may also be other issues that you wish to consider possibly related to health and age and physical condition including recovering from injuries. I hope the ideas have helped. I still remember that first pool that I saw in Victoria and I know I would be happy having it in our home today! And I know of two absolutely fabulous back yard pools one above ground and one in ground both of which were incorporated into backyards in a wonderful way that made them even more attractive and useful. I am sure that if you had either one of those pools in your backyard you would be very happy! So good luck with the pools if your real estate search uncovers the potential for one!

EXPERTS

Now for a deceptively simple topic that becomes worrisome almost immediately!

An expert is somebody who understands a given topic and who can be depended on to give good and accurate advice about that topic. Seems simple enough? But what if a person claimed to be an expert or believed they were an expert in a given topic and the reality is that they do not understand the topic and are in fact giving bad or inaccurate advice about that topic? Or what if the information they were giving was designed to help them and not you?

When I began researching this book I naturally looked for experts in the field. It took a while to realize that people claiming to be experts did not seem to fully understand real estate and that in many cases the information they were giving was faulty or designed to help them and not you! Sometimes they just wanted your business and there is nothing wrong with that but you should try and realize what their objective is.

Family members and friends will wish to help you with your real estate decisions. In some cases they may have purchased or sold real estate in the past and because of that they may feel that they have a better understanding of the topic than you do and that therefore they can give you advice. In fact they may have a better understanding of real estate than you do but my point here is that they are not experts in the field.

Man is a social animal and there are constant interactions between friends and acquaintances. There is nothing wrong with listing to or talking about real estate with a friend or acquaintance. At the same time if you wish to make the best decisions regarding real estate then you should have access to expert opinions from people who understand the topic and the situation that you find yourself in.

My suggestion is that nobody is an expert in all aspects of real estate. It is such a large and complex topic that you really need to consult with people who have expertise in sections of this topic.

Even a genius has a sense of humor so how do you really know when they are kidding?

Let me give you an example. When I went to University I took a course in computer programming and this was when programming was done with paper cards. You would wrap an elastic around the cards and then take them down to the computer centre where the main frame was located. There you would enter the cards into a card reader which would transfer information to the mainframe and cause it to perform certain functions.

This was also the time that desktop computers called PC's were beginning to be introduced. It was possible during these times to have a expert level of knowledge about the entire computing industry. As an expert you could answer just about any question about computers and the programs that were available. But things quickly changed and then we had geometric growth in the number and types of computers and programs and suddenly it was impossible to be an expert in the entire field anymore. You could become an expert in a certain type of hardware or software but that was about the best you could do. The same sort of situation applies with real estate or medicine or stocks or teaching or just about any human activity.

People with levels of expertise in real estate include Realtors, Lawyers, Economists, Bankers, Accountants, Contractors, Designers, Tradesmen, Home Inspectors, Town Planers, and I am sure that there are others! You simply cannot expect one person to have a level of expertise in all aspects of real estate.

And yet members of the public do have what I will call "**unreasonable expectations**" when it comes to assigning expert status in real estate. Many expect that

Realtors are experts in all aspects of the field and can be depended on to give them the best advice. Others depend on friends and acquaintances and family members who have purchased real estate in the past to provide them with accurate expert level advice.

And this is where things become troubling. Have we accepted advice from others in the past expecting that they were giving us good advice when in fact it was wrong? Just who do we go to for expert advice?

I have identified areas of expertise. My suggestion would be to match these areas to the area of knowledge that you require advice on and start taking notes and doing your research.

Here is an example. Many years ago we purchased a house in Victoria BC. I was a little concerned about the traffic so contacted the local planning department. I received excellent advice advising me that the street was something called a "secondary arterial" and that traffic would gradually increase over time. We owned the home for over ten years and that is precisely what the traffic did. Every year there was more traffic and less parking and more people but it wasn't a surprise because an expert in town planning warned me it would happen. That also meant that the real estate prices were on the way up and yes they were!

Remember people are sensitive beings. If they feel that they are experts in a field when in fact they are not you should not challenge them on it. That will only make them angry with you. Be polite, listen to what they have to say and be sure to obtain advice from experts in the particular segment of real estate that you are enquiring about. And one approach that can help is when asking a question phrase it in a specific way so that the person you are asking the question to can focus on that particular aspect of the subject.

For example if you were considering buying a truck you could say "what truck would you recommend?" And you could get the wrong response. But if you asked "what would be the best truck for hauling a 26 foot trailer" you would likely get a much better answer. The same idea applies to real estate. When asking questions try to be specific. Don't say "what is the best neighborhood to purchase a house in Toronto? Say something like "Where would you recommend to purchase a house for no more than $800.000 that is within 15 mins driving time of downtown?" My point is that often your can obtain better advice if your question is specific to your information needs rather than a general questions that applies to a much bigger field.

Some people will understandably claim expert status when they encounter a bit of luck in real estate for example when they happen to buy at the bottom of the market just prior to it rising substantially. Were they experts or just lucky? If you do as they suggest will you be lucky too? Or is the market moving in the opposite direction?

People that like you will want to help you. They will have the best of intentions. You need to be sensitive to this while still keeping your radar up to identify information which may not be true. Real estate is complex, the stakes are high in that the financial transactions will be some of the biggest in your lifetime and making a mistake could result in a financial disaster that will affect the rest of your life.

And one more point here. I have stated that Real Estate is an extremely complex subject that because it involves so many things that one person is incapable of knowing it all. Imagine one person trying to build a cruise ship. How could they do it? You would need several expert trades to do the work and several designers and accounting experts and there would be no way that just one person would be an expert in the entire process. However your real estate agent will be an expert in certain aspects of the process, your Lawyer will be an expert in others your home inspector and banker will have their areas of expertise and you as the buyer or seller need to have access to all the experts. Show them respect and ask the right questions and beware of those who seem to believe that they understand everything. Good luck!

COMPLEXITY

Study this there will be a test in 30 minutes!

In our world some things are simple and some things are complex. The simple things are usually easier to understand. Let's consider some examples. Water freezes at 0 degrees Centigrade or 32 degrees Fahrenheit. If you have a thermometer you can tell what the temperature is. So when your thermometer falls to the freezing temperature of water you can watch it as it freezes. Simple right? Yes.

But let's increase the complexity. You ask your friend how cold is it and she says "really cold". Suddenly you have a problem. The thermometer gave you an **objective** measurement in the form of a number. But the phrase "really cold" is a **subjective** term and there is a wide range of possible temperatures attached to it. And it might be a variable depending on what the person was wearing not the actual temperature. Another person asks you a question. Will water freeze now? They say. You need to decide if "really cold" means that the temperature will be at freezing temperature or not. But how can you do that? You have a complex problem! Life is not simple anymore!

And now back to real estate. There is a tremendous amount of complexity in real estate. And there are all sorts of reasons why a buyer will decide to buy or not buy your property. There is no single factor in most situations. And where there is a single factor often it is difficult to identify it. They may like the color of your house, the curb appeal, the size, the design, the condition, the location within a neighborhood, the distance to a mall or hospital or school or whatever. They even might like that very attractive blond neighbor that you have who was in shorts and a T-shirt and smiled at them! Factors may combine some of them causing a drop in interest and others causing a rise in interest. There are dozens of factors involved in a real estate deal and as a result some properties sell almost immediately and others take months or even years to sell. Some sell for more than the asking price and others sell for less or much less.

And there are more problems in trying to understand real estate. Some experts will tell you that it all depends on one factor. **Location location location**. They will say. And in fact location IS important but it is not the only factor that determines if a real estate sale will occur. Most property owners only have a couple of real estate sales in their lifetimes and some have a few. But in Canada there are thousands of real estate sales every day and on average the number of home sales per month varies from 30,000 to 45,000 homes.

So what am I getting at here? My point is that real estate is so complex that there are no simple rules to understand it. But if we recognize that there is great complexity suddenly the subject becomes easier to understand! For example if somebody who thinks they are an expert talks to you and tries to tell you all about real estate relax because what they are telling you is not really all about real estate! It is only about some factors in real estate that they encountered. Don't be rude. Listen to them. But remember they really don't know what they are talking about! They may know about specific facts and those facts could be very useful to know. For example they might know if a local market is rising or falling if there are a lot of properties for sale or not enough –if there is a great demand for one specific area. All this is very useful information.

And there is one more point I would like to make about expertise and friends and real estate. A friend or family member may not be what I would call an expert in real estate. However they can still give you excellent information on the topic and you really should listen to them. I have often received excellent information from these sources and that information has helped a lot when making decisions on real estate.

Now the big question is how do we manage the complexities of real estate? Is there a way we can gain an advantage? Are there ways to avoid getting screwed by those in real estate – people like the seller and the agents and the lawyers and the bankers? I think that there is. I suggest to you that there are ways to simplify real estate transactions. And you will discover those methods in this book.

DRESS

If you are engaged in a million dollar business idea and look like a slob that sends a message to the people you are dealing with. Not a good message.

When you are engaged in a business deal think of the perceptions that are occurring. You will be dealing with a Real Estate Agent who will either be attempting to get an offer to purchase from you or will be attempting to make you accept an offer from a buyer. The Agent will have a paper document that requires your signature. They will also have a pen. They will be looking at you and you will be looking at them. They will be listening to what you say and you will be listening to what they say.

UnREAL-ESTATE CANADA

What if you were wearing a pair of shorts with paint on them and a T shirt with holes and dirt on it and you hadn't shaved that day or had a shower or haircut. And your breath smells from those three beer you had after supper. What sort of impression would you make? The Agent will be well dressed, clean, shaved with a recent hair cut. What I am getting at here is that the Agent will be able to exert power over you by the fact that you look like a bum and they look like a professional. Do you really want that to happen?

Over the years I have participated in many senior business meetings. There you are at a board room table with several people each one responsible for a certain section of the organization. Normally the CEO or Chair person will run the meeting and there are several subjects to discuss. Often board members have the opportunity to express opinions or provide reports. You don't go to a meeting like that dressed in shorts and a T-shirt without shaving and with dirt on your hands. I mean you could do that but the reality is that you would normally do that only once and you would be fired –unless you were the boss in which case you could do whatever you wanted to.. And it is unlikely that dressed like that you would be able to convince anyone at the meeting that your approach is the correct way to proceed. So what is my point here? A real estate deal IS a business meeting. Dress for it. You are not dressing to work on your car or the back yard or to go fishing you are going to a business meeting.

So my suggestion is that you don business attire. Clean matching clothes, recent haircut even consider a tie and sports jacket. If you have a tie and jacket on there is a good chance that the Agent will not and you will be exerting the subtle power that business dress exerts. And if the deal proceeds to a sale or purchase continue on in your Lawyer's office in the shirt, tie and sports jacket mode.

I know that some of you will not believe me that dress is that important. My suggestion to you is to do a bit of research. Take a look at photos of business meetings. Visit a large office building and look around. You will begin to see a trend in the way people dress. The higher up in the organization a person is the better they seem to dress. Appearance is important and so during a business session appearance is one factor that you must manage correctly.

As silly as it sounds a **brief case** can set a standard often unexpected. When you go to a meeting with a brief case the other side has no clue why you have it or what is in the case. At one time brief cases were often carried to business meetings but now in the digital world they are not used as much as you can have a lot of information on your tablet or cell phone. You can often pick up a brief case that would sell for $75 or more at a thrift shop for under ten bucks. I am telling you this because I collect them myself and keep one for each website that I manage. It works for me! At last count I had 26 of them and my family worries about me. But they work! Usually they have locks on them too and that gives you one additional level of security for your laptop, phone and anything else you might wish to place there. Try it you might be surprised!

.

TALK

When a business deal is made it is surprising how much depends on dress, facial expressions and movements.

There will likely be a lot of talking in a real estate deal. And again I am going to draw your attention to the fact that you are engaged in a **business deal**. This is not a social occasion where you are trying to make friends. This is a time when you are trying to negotiate the best business deal you can obtain. If you do a good job you will obtain thousands of dollars of benefits either in a higher selling price if you are a seller or a lower purchase price if you are a buyer.

There is no need to be rude. But focus on the deal and the numbers associated with the deal. When the agent attempts to use a subjective term like "large bedroom" try your best to convert it into objective terms. Ask them what the square footage is. Ask what the measurements are and make a note in your note book. If you continually do this the Agent will be under pressure because the traditional subjective terms that they use in a real estate deal just aren't working! Keep focused on the deal. Don't start talking about your kids or hobbies or cars or whatever the Agent is trying to get you to talk about so that a type of friendship is established. Remember the Agent does not get paid a penny until the sale occurs so what they are tying to do to you is to have you complete the sale. And being your friend is one way they do this. They are not being evil or sneaky they are just trying to obtain a sale.

Brevity is a good approach. When you get into prices and changing offers and counter offers a brief statement is very powerful. For example you could say...." $390,000 is my top offer. He can take it or leave it. ..... That sends a very strong message to the Agent –to both Agents. But if you said "let's try $390,000 I think that might work. We are pretty close and he might accept that..." What you just told the Agent is that he may be able to get a higher offer from you. He might pass that message on to the other agent! And the other agent might come back with a higher counter offer. But with a brief to the point distinct offer everyone knows where the line is. And you can move that line if you wish later.

So the message here is to be brief. Focus on the deal and nothing else. Dress and act business like. No need to be rude but no need to be overly friendly either.

NEGOTIATIONS

Let's introduce this chapter by drawing your attention to two possible sales. In one case you ask for $400,000 for your property. To your surprise and happiness the buyer sits down and writes you a cheque for exactly $400,000 and shakes your hand. Wow! There was no negotiation required. Now let's consider a second case.

You ask $400,000 for your property. The buyer comes back with an offer of $380,000 and includes the following conditions:
1. That all the furniture be included
2. That the 1967 mustang presently in the garage be included
3. That the offer is subject to financing
4. That the offer is subject to a house inspection
5. That the offer would have a closing date of six months from this date.

You come back with a counter offer at $390,000 but insist that the closing date be three months from this date, the 1967 mustang be kept by the seller and that the brown leather chair in the living room be kept by the seller.

The buyer counters with an offer of $385,000 and you keep the chair and car and that the financing be finalized in one month and the deal closed in two months.

At this point you counter with $390,000 and they keep the car and chair and a two month closing date.

And so on. The negotiations become complicated. They become frustrating for both parties. The buyer tells you to go screw yourself and he walks. Oh Oh.

What I am suggesting here is that the negotiation phase can become complicated and can result in failure. People's emotions can control their actions. This is a situation where a Realtor can help by working with both parties to arrive at a sale. Remember the Realtor doesn't make a penny until there is a sale. So they will want to do all they can to make that sale happen. This is a good thing and a bad thing because they may not be acting in the best interests of the seller. On the other hand by obtaining a sale even at terms that the seller may not completely be happy with they are providing a service to the seller.

If you have the type of mind that only sees in black and white you may have a hard time understanding this process. If you accept that there are also shades of grey then you will see the light here. It is just that the negotiation process can be complex and arriving at a sale may involve some give and take from both parties.

LET YOUR MONEY DO THE TALKING

A stack of $100 bills is worth $10,000 and that could purchase a lot of whatever you wanted. It is amazing how well money talks!

When tendering an offer for real estate or for anything for that matter the buyer often feels a need to explain why the offer is lower than the asking price. In fact they may be quite nervous offering the lower amount especially if it is a **low ball offer**. The problem with this approach is that it potentially sets up arguing points with the seller. For example if you don't like the floor coverings and wish to change them it could cost you several thousand dollars despite the fact they are in good shape. The owner could take this as an insult of his design sense and he may not focus in on the dollar amount. My suggestion is to simply let your money do the talking. Present the offer without any negotiating banter about why it is lower than the asking price. Let the owner focus in on the amount not the reasons why you are offering it.

When a property is first put on the market the seller may have what turns out to be unreasonable expectations about the selling price. After a few months or even years they may be open to other offers.

If you are one of the first offers on the property your offer may be immediately rejected but remember it is possible that the same offer will be accepted later. When an offer is tendered it should also include a time expiration.

The time expiration is a bit tricky. If it is a long period the seller could use your offer as an incentive to other potential buyers to offer a little more in a mini bidding war. If your offer has an unreasonably short period like "take it or leave it" or you have three hours then the seller might be insulted. I would suggest 48 hours as being reasonable. Possibly 24 hours would work too. But it is something to consider because there are variables here. And there are emotions from the buyer and seller. But remember everyone the buyer, seller and agent all have one thing in common and that is they want a sale. But there needs to be agreement on the terms of the sale.

PRESENT ALL OFFERS

My suggestion is that if you are using a Realtor that you include in the contract that he or she is to present all offers to you. At first this seems a bit confusing. After all isn't the job of the Realtor to filter the unlikely prospects out? And won't it cause you stress if a unqualified buyer submits a silly low ball offer? There is another reason.

When a Realtor lists your property they also get half the commission when your property is sold by another realtor. But they get the full commission if they sell your property themselves. So let's consider what happens if they get a quick offer from another realtor shortly after your property is listed on MLS. Let's also consider that your listing realtor has a few potential clients that wish to view your property. If the other realtor's customer buys your property your listing Realtor will earn half the commission which will be around 2.5%. And they could double that commission if your listing realtor sold the property to one of his or her customers. This is a messy little fact surrounding how the commission splitting goes in the real estate industry. By stipulating that all offers must be submitted to you the problem is solved. And to be sure it is solved you should ask your Realtor in front of witnesses if there are any other offers.

It is possible that your Realtor could delay the presentation of the other Realtor's offer so that he could get his in and hope that the negotiation process could be finalized before presenting the other offer to you.

I am not suggesting that Realtors are dishonest. I am simply attempting to introduce the reality that your Realtor must work in. In a tough market when sales are scarce and prices are falling and sellers are upset and the bill collector is pounding on the door and threatening to take back the car –what does one do while still trying their best to keep honest and provide a good service to their customers?

And remember there are what I will call "levels" of legality. There may be another term for it but this one gets the idea across. On one level there is total honesty. Step down from that a bit and you bend the laws of ethics for your profession. Drop down a bit more and you start breaking laws listed in the Criminal Code of Canada or Provincial or Municipal laws. And within those laws there are additional levels from minor infractions to serious criminal charges.

And laws vary quite a bit from country to country. You can be placed before a firing squad in some countries for behavior that wouldn't even generate a charge against you in Canada. My point here is that when you are involved in a Real Estate deal you need to be aware of anyone breaking the laws or the ethical standards because if you notice them doing that you really need to be alert as to what is really happening.

DECISIONS

In a real estate sale or purchase there are several decisions that you must make. And if you make a mistake you usually pay for it later. Lets for a moment consider just what a decision is. You find yourself in a situation where you realize that more than one option is available for a certain need. So which option do you choose? The right one or the wrong one?

Let's consider vehicles. There are thousands of options there. You need to be aware of what you need the car for, how much money you have to invest, what style and color you want, and dozens more decisions. And this is where it gets interesting. If you deal with a car salesman they will attempt to make some of the decisions for you based in part on the vehicles that they have available to offer to you. But you may find later that they were wrong. And you may be wrong. You may not have read the reviews on the car you buy and find out later that other owners recognized problems that you didn't notice. And the gas mileage might not be as good as you wanted to be. Or if you purchased a truck perhaps the truck can't tow weight well like you boat and trailer. What am I getting at here? When you are placed in the position of making a decision sometimes you lose and sometimes you win.

So let's get back to real estate and decisions. Here are some examples:

1. Do you want to buy or sell?
2. Do you want to move out of the city to another area?
3. How much do you want to sell for?
4. How much do you want to buy for?
5. Do you wish to use a Real Estate Agent or try and sell the house yourself?
6. What commission are you willing to pay?
7. If you are buying do you want a house, a condo, a trailer, a boat, a foreign property?
8. If you are selling where are you going to move to? And what are you going to do with the money from the sale?
9. If you are buying which area do you wish to settle in?
10. What sort of offers would you accept from a buyer or offer a seller?

And there are many many more decisions but this short list gives you an idea of what you are up against. Now let's consider how to make a decision.

I would like to introduce to you the idea of being objective and subjective. At University I took a lot of science courses and I graduated with a degree in the area of human behavior –Psychology. So I have a good understanding of how decisions are made. I also know that many people without a good background in math and science tend to lean towards the subjective point of view rather than a number orientated objective viewpoint. I spent many years on boats including sail boats. If you ask a person on a boat what the wind is like they may answer subjectively or objectively. They may say the wind is "strong" but what does that tell you? What does "strong" mean? Or they might say the wind is 15 knots steady from the North East. Now you know precisely what the wind is doing. Let's consider another example.

You are a doctor seeing a patient. You ask the patient how they feel. They say "a bit hot". So you take their temperature and you notice that it is 104'F. This is not a "bit hot" it is a "high fever" The patient has a real problem! My point here is that unless you are objective when considering a decision you may make the wrong decision.

So how does one be objective when making a decision about real estate?

First of all get a note book and a pen and a calculator handy. When you come to a decision point list the options that face you. Then try to convert the options into numbers. For example if you see a house that you like and it is selling for $423,500 what sort of bid would you place on it? If you offered them 10% less than they were asking for it would be $381,150. That is 42,350 less than they asked. Their Real Estate broker would lose about 3% of that or $1270.50 and would make a commission of about 3% or 11,434.50. So as you can see here that your offer of 10% less than the asking price results in significant changes to the amount of money the seller and seller's agent will collect. However they have already factored into the pricing the probability that they would receive an offer rather than the asking price.

Now if you were the seller in the above situation you have a decision to make. Should you accept the offer or should you counter with a reduction in the asking price? If you counter with a higher amount the buyer might walk away? They may also counter your offer. So should you take a risk or should you just accept the offer? A lot depends on the state of the real estate market and the amount of time you have available and several other factors. You could go to your agent and request that he drops his commission. They would hate you for this suggestion but it is possible that they might agree.

Now let's go back to the buyer! The seller does not take your offer but counters at $402325 which would be 5% less than the asking price not the 10% less you offered. What do you do? Another decision point. Lets consider your options:

1. accept the counter offer and buy the house for $402,325
2. refuse the offer and walk away
3. new offer
   a. say $390,000 or
   b. a surprise offer of less than your original offer say $375,000

3(b) would certainly generate anger with the seller and the seller's agent. You would have done something completely unexpected. You have just placed the seller into a stressful position. Do they accept your offer or not?

3(a) would be a tough but reasonable offer. You are close within $12.350 of the seller's counter offer. This is only a 3% reduction over the seller's counter offer.

The point here is that you need to make a decision and your objective is to make the **correct** decision. If you make that decision you will acquire the property for the minimum price. If you make the wrong decision you may not acquire the property at the minimum price or you may not acquire the property at all.

Canadians are by their nature polite and friendly. But this is a business deal. If you make the wrong decisions here you may not acquire the property. But and pay attention –if you make the right decisions here you may acquire the property but you may also acquire a life long enemy. The Agent will hate you because you cost them a reduction in their commission. If you don't buy the property the agent will hate you because they don't make any commission. The owner will hate you if you buy the property at the minimum costs and they will also hate you if you don't buy the property. But again please remember that this is a business deal. The idea is not to be polite and make friends and help people in the normal Canadian way.

Now I have given you an example of how to apply objective reasoning techniques instead of subjective approaches. I have also given you an example of how to make decisions in a business deal. Each deal will be slightly different. You may have different options and the prices may be different and the market may be different. Yours may have been the only offer in four months. Or it could have been one of ten offers that week! Try and remove the emotions and think in numbers. Forget about being sad or happy or mad or frustrated. Forget about trying to be friends with the Agent or the Owner. Be business like.

WHY REAL ESTATE AGENTS ARE NOT YOUR FRIENDS

Now I need to be careful here. Because when a lot or most Realtors read this they will hate me! They will tell you that NOTHING in this book is true and that it is ALL bullshit. And that you shouldn't believe ANYTHING that I am telling you. But I will tell you anyway. Real Estate Agents are NOT your friends.

Yes they can act like friends and smile a lot and say friendly things. But they are NOT your friends. There are two main things that they are trying to do with you. They want you to commit to a sale or a purchase and they want you to tell your friends that they have done a good job. So you are being used as a source of **income** and for **future advertising**. They will actually hate you if you do not go through with the sale or if you reduce their commissions during the sale by either paying less for the property or taking less for the sale of a property.

Just to be clear I am NOT saying that Real Estate Agents are your enemies. I am just saying that they are not your friends. After the sale is over they might make good friends!

Friends help each other. But a Real Estate Agent is NOT trying to help you. They are trying to make money off of providing you with a service. And they will do just about anything to earn that commission and many of the things they do are on the line or even crossing the line of legality or their code of ethics. As an example what if the Agent was aware of the fact that four properties beside the house you wish to purchase have been purchased by a developer who might want to put in an apartment building beside you! They know that if they tell you that you will not want to purchase the house. So they don't tell you and four years after you purchase the house bull dozers come in and take out the houses next to you and for the next few months a 10 story apartment building is constructed just beside you. The municipality approved it because they had pressure from people wanting to rent and a ten story building would generate much more taxation revenue than four houses. If the Agent had been working for YOU they would have told you about this potential development. But when they work for THEMSELVES and their main objective is to collect a commission they won't tell you. But to be fair I will also say or admit that some Real Estate Agents *will* tell you. My main point here is that some won't. And from a legal perspective they have not broken any laws. But from an ethical perspective they have acted like rats. And there is the problem.

You need to understand that most Real Estate Agents do not make very much money. Some do! But most don't. The last time I checked their average wages were approximately $60,000 a year. And it depends on the market and often the time of year. Imagine how desperate an Agent would get if they are trying to support their family and pay for food and expenses and they haven't had a sale in a couple of months. And then you appear on the scene. Let's be fair here. I am not saying that all Real Estate Agents are evil. But I am saying that many Real Estate Agents are understandably desperate. And when you are desperate you often allow your ethics to slide a bit or a lot. Something to consider.

Let's consider for a moment how a Real Estate Agent can obtain a commission by ensuring that you either buy or sell a property. In order to convince you they need to do the following:

1. Maximize any benefits of the property
2. Minimize any problems with the property
3. Apply psychological force on you to sign the agreement
4. Try to maximize their commission
5. Convince the people you are dealing with to go ahead with the deal
6. Convince both sides that the price is right.

When you review what the Real Estate Agent is doing you will see right away that some of the things they do are the same things you want done too! If you are purchasing a property you might agree with points 5 and 6. IF you are selling the property you might agree with points 1, 5 and 6. But if you are a buyer or seller you can also see that the Agent is doing things that are not to your advantage in order to get a purchase or sale completed. So they do help you but they also help themselves too.

There is an obvious danger here dealing with Real Estate Agents. You may purchase or sell a property once or twice in your life time. Possibly more times. But the Agent works in this field every day! So you are dealing with an expert. And you are NOT an expert. So there is an opportunity here to learn a few things from the Agent. And don't let them see this book or mention to them that you have read it. Because it gives you an insight and a better understanding of just what they are doing and it is best that they don't know that you know this! That way they will just think that you are an average customer not a person familiar with how real estate really works.

Now I have said that the Agent is NOT your friend. I have warned you that they will attempt to act like your friends. I have warned you that they may or will act unethically and possibly outside the law in order to get a sale and earn a commission. I have explained to you how many Real Estate Agents don't make a lot of money and can be quite desperate at times for a sale. My point here is not to suggest to you that the Agent is your enemy. The Agent is doing business with you. The Agent wants to do business with you. Because this is the only way that the Agent makes any money! I think that your best bet is to consider a real estate deal to be a business deal and to treat it like a business deal. And that means lose the subjective attitude of "that's nice" "big yard" "nice trees" "I love that house" to more objective terms like 65X130 foot yard, asking price $450,000 but I think it is only worth $375,000. Lose the emotional terms and take up the objective terms. At least until the deal is completed!

BUYERS MARKET VS SELLERS MARKET

How can you tell if it is a buyer's market or a sellers market? This is a fact that is good to know because it affects what your offer should be and what the final purchase price might be.

If homes are selling in the first 30 days on the market that is considered to be a **sellers market** and prices are normally rising. If homes are taking more than 30 days to sell that is a **buyers market** and selling prices are normally steady of falling.

In both cases remember the difference between listing price and selling price. In a rising market a **bidding war** can develop and the selling price can exceed the listing price. In the case of a falling or buyers market the selling price can be lower than the asking price.

There is a common problem with both types of markets and that is you don't really know how long the process will last. Sometimes the markets rise over a period of years and at the end of a cycle you might be in the last few days. You also don't know how far the market will go. Will the prices go up or down 40% and then stop?

A major change in prices is due to a correction in the market and smaller changes are due to normal market cycles. A correction could be due to the loss of a major employer in a small city or a recession or depression or other very significant factor. Prices in a correction are difficult to predict. In the worst case entire neighborhoods could be subject to foreclosure and the value of real estate investments could plummet. In contrast it is very difficult not to make money in a rising market. It is easy to lose money in a falling market. Remember what happened when the American housing market collapsed. It hit a high point in early 2006 then started to drop due to the sub prime housing crisis and prices fell in 2006 and 2007 and nose dived in 2008. The situation got so bad that there were thousands of empty homes and crooks entered them and took away furniture and wiring and left the homes is very poor condition. Billions of dollars were lost in the real estate market in a matter of months. When a market rises like the one in Toronto has been doing for years there comes a point when a correction occurs.

A housing crisis in Detroit resulted in thousands of abandoned houses. Criminals broke into them and took copper wires and

plumbing supplies and pretty much destroyed houses which were once good places to live. Many of the houses were knocked down and the land sold. A disaster!

TYPES OF MARKETS

There are several types of markets and here are the main ones:

1. **Rising** Market
2. **Falling** Market
3. **Steady** Market

Let's consider them. Starting with a Rising Market.

In a **rising market** nearly everyone is happy. The sellers are happy because they are getting prices higher than they likely paid and profits are being made. Real Estate Agents are happy because volumes go up and commissions go up and even buyers are happy because as soon as they own the property its value goes up! This process can go on for years. Billions of dollars of financial gains are made and everyone is **happy.** Even the government is happy because now they collect more taxes on the increased value of the property and the taxes collected during sales.

There are several interesting aspects to a rising market and lets consider one of them. Let's say that you list your home with an agent in a rising market when a large volume of people wish to purchase homes, There are two unexpected sub problems here. One of them is that given a large number of prospective buyers why would a seller's agent look to the buyer's agent to participate in the sale process. Why not **double dip** and perform both functions either by themselves or within their office so that the commission is not split. So perhaps the buyer's agents have prospective buyers who want to bid more than the person the sellers agent has offering a bid but the sellers agent does not wish to present that offer to the seller. What a filthy rotten thing to do! You as the seller could possibly be losing out on a much better deal. So that is one problem. Another is that your selling agent may be very busy and may have lots of customers and despite the fact that they have several offers on your property they wish to set a time when the bidding process will end. Why? Because they want to collect the commission on the sale and have enough time to sell other properties. So what happens? What could happen is that if they hadn't set a deadline you would have been offered a bigger offer and made more money on the deal. I realize that the bidding period can't go on for too long but it does worry me that in a market like this where the prices are zooming up and everyone wants to buy that you might be losing some money. Something to think about in a rising market.

However keep in mind that like any business cycle there are ups and downs and the prices won't keep on going up forever. At some point they will reach the top and then start falling. The challenge is knowing when this will happen. And yes it is possible that the prices will reach their top then fall a bit then start rising again! But it is also possible that there will be an abrupt drop in prices also called a **real estate correction** and suddenly billions of dollars will be lost in a large real estate market. If you are in the market at that time you actually might not need to sell but still the value of your property would have decreased. If you do sell you actually take the loss in dollars rather than just in asset value. If you keep in the market the prices as I already noted might go back up and you may recover your losses in the value of your assets.

So the bottom line is that a Rising market is very interesting! It is also a very happy time for everyone. You love your Real Estate Agent for getting more money for your property than you asked for! They love you for the big commissions they earned!

Recently Vancouver, Calgary and Toronto were examples of a rising market and Calgary was an example of what can happen when the process is reversed.

And there is one more very interesting aspect to a rising market that is not obvious at first to most people. When big money sees an area where the real estate market is rising they often start investing in that market. They will purchase property and not be too interested in ensuring that the property is populated. In the case of Vancouver many very rich people from China purchased high end residential real estate over $3 million dollars in value simply as investments and not as places to live. In Toronto developers are buying properties with the same objective. They aren't that interested in generating rents they are more interested in the increasing prices of the property. Some home owners are doing the same and purchasing more than one home with the assets they have in their main residence because they know they can make better money on the rising assets than they could make in investments on the stock market or by keeping their money in the bank.

So if you consider this situation as it develops you will see the danger. Too many people are treating real estate as an investment to take advantage of the increasing values of the property instead of as a place to live or work. And this activity tends to force the prices up even further and faster and you know what will eventually happen! The prices will top off and start to correct. And suddenly the prices will fall and people will want to dump their properties and the prices will fall even faster! You may be surprised to learn that during a **falling market** Real Estate Agents still make a lot of commission income! Lots of properties are selling and often quite quickly and each one sold or bought creates a commission for the Agents.

STEADY PRICES

When prices are steady there is a problem. No growth. No increases in the value of real estate. Investors do not invest in real estate because there is no investment income available. If nothing else is available that is generating income at the time they may keep real estate that they own but it is unlikely that they will purchase more. This type of market is a problem for Real Estate Agents. Not a lot of sales so average income tends to fall because if there are no sales no commission income is generated. And there seems to be another problem for sellers.

If you are selling your real estate in a steady market there needs to be an incentive for the purchaser to buy it. They won't buy it for more than the present value because they know that prices will not increase. The only incentive is if you sell it to them at less than the appraised value in today's market. In other words as a seller you may need to take a loss in order to sell your property. This places your Agent in a difficult position. In order for them to get a commission they must somehow place pressure on you to accept an offer lower than the present value of the property. And so they delve into their bag of tricks some of them unethical and others possibly even not legal or in accordance with their code of conduct. But from their perspective this is the only way they can earn a commission and pay the rent and buy food for their families. And so in a steady market as a seller you need to be very aware of what is happening. I can assure you that you will not be aware of all the tricks your Agent can use to obtain a sale. But remember you have the final say. And things could get ugly.

FALLING PRICES

Oh dear. Where to start? Falling prices are the worst time in Real Estate. Almost nobody is happy and everyone who sells takes a loss over what they might have made if the market had continued to rise. If you sell during this time you will almost certainly sell for less than you wanted sometimes significantly less. You could call this a "loss" But the Real Estate Agents could still be happy if the volumes are up. Because they will make a commission on each sale. The amounts of the commission will be lower but the number of commissions will be higher with a net increase in total income. So they will be smiling while the buyer and seller are crying so to speak.

Usually real estate is an individual's main asset. So when they sell that asset as a loss their net worth decreases. The equity they had in the property is reduced and sometimes it is reduced to the point where they still owe money on the property even after the sale. This is a financial disaster for some owners. Even the buyers may not be happy as the value of their investment may continue to fall after their purchase and they will start to lose money on the value of their investment.

Now at this point you may be wondering what I am trying to get to. Yes you can understand that the market can be rising, steady or falling but so what? Here is my point. The market is different in each case and you absolutely need to know what is happening before you enter it. I guess I should have told you that at first! So how does one know what the market is doing?

1. Ask your Real Estate Agent. But beware they may have an answer for you that is different than what is really happening! It is still interesting to know what they will say. And yes they could tell you exactly what is happening.
2. Check out the number of sales in your area over the last three years and see if there is a trend
3. Check out the average price of properties in your area over the last three years and see if there is a trend.
4. Remember that every year in Canada there is something called **inflation**. Go to **the Bank of Canada inflation calculator** online and determine what the property would have been worth one two and three years ago in constant dollars.

After you do this you should have a good idea of what type of market you are entering. For example in a falling market if you are attempting to purchase a property you may wish to increase the discount on the asking price. So in the case of a rising market for a property that is asking $400,000 you may find that the only way you can purchase it is to offer more say $425,000. In a steady market you may be able to purchase it for $375,000 and in a falling market you may be able to purchase it at $325,000. SO if you were the seller in the first case you would make an extra $25,000 (less commission) or in a steady market you might lose $25,000 or in a falling market you might lose $75,000. So there would be a $100,000 difference in this example between the sale prices in a rising and falling market. That is a lot of money!

UnREAL-ESTATE CANADA

Having lived on our sailboat for several years I can tell you that for $100,000 you could invest in a used liveaboard sailboat in the 40 foot range that you could use to travel to the South Pacific. Or you could purchase a very nice motor home or cottage or both so $100,000 is a lot of money!

Here is an example of a "fixer upper" on Ebay that needs work but will likely sell for about $5000. You could purchase a new one for $75.000 but possibly one could fix this one up. Making a few thousand dollars more than you expected on a real estate deal could open some doors here. We once owned a 26 foot Winnebago and can tell you that they are lots of fun!

WHEN TO BUY IN A FALLING MARKET

In some ways there is an advantage to buying real estate in a falling market. You can often offer a lower bid and the owner desperate to sell his property might accept it. All is well if then the market hits bottom and starts to increase again. But if the market continues to fall you lose your shirt. Is there a time to buy in a falling marker? Yes!

All you need to do is figure out when the market will hit bottom and buy the property just before it does. Then the property will begin to rise again and every time it does you make money. So place some thought into it. Look at the numbers. Look at the trends. What changes are happening? Come to a decision. You might be right and you might be wrong. You might be close or the market could keep dropping for a year or two or more. But the potential is there to purchase your real estate at the right time and make a good return.

PROPERTIES WITH PROBLEMS

Not much on the planet is perfect. People are not perfect. It should be no surprise that properties are not perfect either. The question is what sort of problems does a property have and how serious are they?

A house could have an infestation of various bugs or critters. Termites or carpenter ants come to mind. Mice, rats and coach roaches follow. Then there is rot and mold and radon and asbestos and problems in the soils like old leaky oil tanks and such. And speaking of oil determine if the property was ever heated by oil. If it was then check to be sure there are no underground tanks and no oil spills from a rusted out tank that was replaced.

It could be that there are design problems with the house and that it is about to collapse. There could be electrical or plumbing problems or both.

A professional home inspector will be a help here. For a few hundred dollars they will inspect your home and identify all the faults. Unfortunately, like all other humans on the planet, home inspectors are not perfect either. Some are better than others. The same inspector will do a better job on some houses than others. The bottom line is that they may miss a few faults. And yes if the home inspector knows the real estate agent there is a possibility that the inspector will miss a point or two in order to help with the sale and possibly a gift in the form of cash or other clients will go to them from the Agent. I am not saying that they all do this. All I am saying is that we have two people who both work in the same business of selling properties and if they were to work together even in a small way it may be possible to generate a sale and a commission. I am sure that some ok a lot of agents would like to punch me for saying this but there would be a few who might say "oh oh!."

In an attempt to protect the buyer many provinces have a **disclosure statement** that the seller signs off. If the seller signs off on the form indicating that they are not aware of any faults and later it is found out that they were the buyer could pursue the matter in the courts and possibly reverse a sale or obtain a reduction in the price. I would suggest that you Google for more information on disclosure statements for your province or state as there is a lot of information out there much more than I can place in this chapter but it would be well worth reviewing it.

DESCRIBING YOUR HOME

Now for a topic that is much more complicated than you first might think. When you write an ad for your home you need to take considerable care in writing up the description. Why?

If you say something that is not true and the buyer purchases your home based on what you wrote then the buyer may have certain legal rights should it prove that what you wrote was false.

As an example, if you say that your home is structurally sound or perfect and only requires fresh paint what happens when after the sale the buyer finds that the house has a termite infestation and that several load bearing timbers have been compromised? Who pays the several thousand dollars required to fix the problem and get rid of the termites?

A good realtor should be able to write up a good description of your home that is both accurate and legally safe. If you are doing it be careful that what you are writing is accurate.

A description should provide accurate information about the home and it should highlight the advantages the home has. For example if your home is on a waterfront lot you might refer to the pleasant lifestyle with the ever changing water and skies, the large ships in the distance and the sailboats out in the bay.

This may surprise you but if you help your buyer or seller think it can be to your advantage. Let's consider some examples so that you understand what I am trying to say.

Let's use the example of a man attempting to sell a rowboat to another man who has a young son or daughter. He might mention all the fun they would have with it and all the good memories that would be made. He might also mention that a rowboat is a good starting point for teaching your children about boating safety before they are trusted with a motorboat. In other words you help the buyer think thru the advantages of having the boat. And then you mention that at this price you will always get your money out of the boat when you upgrade to a larger vessel. TV ads do this sort of thing all the time. One men's cologne suggests that all you need do is apply and a bevy of beautiful women will come running to you. The beer advertisers do much the same thing.

So if you are close to the lake or the shopping centre or school mention that fact and its advantages. If your home has a swimming pool mention how they can get healthy exercises from it and relief on a hot day and how your friends will want to come over and visit. It's probably not a good idea to mention the additional maintenance that is required and the extra insurance and the cost of heating the water etc.

Some of you will not believe me and suggest that people are perfectly capable of thinking themselves. All I can say is that in my experience I have found that helping a person by mentioning the advantages and the use of the item will often generate a sale. Try it and be surprised! I will give you one more example. In one of my businesses I sold vintage British outboard motors on our website to customers all over North America. At the time I had a very intelligent young student working for me part time and I asked her to stand by our front fence holding the motor. She said sure but said just a minute and then she let her hair down. She put her hand on top of the motor and then smiled. I took a picture placed it on the website and the motor sold the very next day! She sold the motor! It was her attractive smile and long hair that placed a positive image on the high quality motor. This is done in marketing all the time. The idea is to generate a positive thought with the prospective customer and they then make the decision to purchase the product.

I have been lucky over the years and have worked with many exceptional people. Real estate is an area where you also meet exceptional people. I am certainly not trying to pick on them. I am just saying that you are entering into a competition and various people may have different objectives. Your objective is to obtain the best real estate that you can for the best price if your are a buyer and to obtain the best price and terms if you can if you are a seller. And you need to be aware of the dangers and trends and business cycles and expenses and so many other things. So try your best and with a good understanding of how real estate works your chances of success are better the more you try! And working with exceptional people also helps!

HORROR STORIES

You just moved into your new home when you notice your neighbor for the first time.

In the worst case scenario you purchase a property at the top of the real estate cycle and shortly thereafter there is a correction in the market and prices rapidly fall. In this case it is possible and likely that your **mortgage is upside down** a term that is used when the mortgage is more than the value of the property. What this means is that if you decide to sell at this point you will lose the down payment that you placed on the property and you may still be left with a debt even after your property is sold. This could happen to thousands of people when there is a sudden correction in the market.

UnREAL-ESTATE CANADA

Another example of a real estate horror show is when you purchase a property and there are basic structural problems found. In British Columbia this occurred when the **leaky condo crisis** occurred. In Toronto recent information indicates that glass walled condos may only have a short lifespan before major repairs will be required to the glass. The frustrating problem that I see with these types of situations is that in all cases the plans had to be approved by a government regulatory agency and the government inspectors approved the construction but when problems develop the government steps back and claims it is not their fault leaving the property owner to hold the bag and pay the bills. The owners must pay sales taxes on the materials and services required to do the repairs and surely there is a better way to manage problems like this.

Water is another problem that can cause horror shows. I have seen homes built on lots where the ground water was close to the surface and where sump pumps had to run almost continuously and basement flooding still occurred during the wet season. As stupid as it sounds houses with basements are sometimes built in areas where the water table is just next to the surface. And if you check out the nature of water tables you will see that they vary in depth with the season. Naturally the basement floods or is filled with condensation and mold. If you have ever had a house with a crawl space that has flooded because the sump pump stopped you will understand what I mean.

Sometimes a neighborhood changes later in the day. I can think of one where if you drive thru it looks normal during the day but absolutely packed with cars if you drive through after five. Parking is often a problem in neighborhoods. I can think of one area in

Victoria where stately older larger homes were converted into rental suites and as a result there was no place to park resident's cars. Again surely the municipal government could have managed this problem better than they did. I have worked with government workers before and they are great people but they must follow rules and regulations and the elected representatives in a municipality or the Province are the ones that establish those rules. And there are also Federal Government rules. And yes there are reasons why they wish to be politically correct. Developers promise them more rentals and rental properties usually generate more taxes than single family dwellings and so they are reluctant to establish parking requirements for a property that suddenly has more people living in it.

In Canada we have a good tolerance for other races. One way that this is done is by the races congregating in specific geographical areas or neighborhoods. This is no problem if you happen to be a member of that race but if not you may find yourself to be the only ones of your race in the neighborhood. It will be like you are living in another country! As an example several races with a very small percentage of the total Canadian population have a much larger percentage of the population in cities like Toronto or Vancouver. For example the average percentage of the population could be 1% in Canada but could also be 3% or even higher in Toronto. You can check that out with records from Stats Canada. And the higher percentage in Toronto could be concentrated in a certain ward in Toronto with the result that although they are only 3% of Toronto's population they may be 10 or 20% of a particular wards population.

The race thing is not normally mentioned in government or the media because they feel that it is politically incorrect to do so. Instead of the word "race" or "religion" they use a term like "demographics". So what happens when you go to an open house, place an offer on it get it accepted and find out when you move in that all your neighbors are members of a particular race or religion that is different from yours? I am certainly not a racist and have friends from many races. However I do understand why people with certain demographics characteristics often like to congregate in specific neighborhoods. It is something that you should be aware of.

PRICE

Have you ever considered how the **price** of real estate is determined? It is a very complex process although you can make it quite simple if you wish by simply grabbing a number out the air and going with it! The real estate agent will look at properties that sold in your geographical area and compare the homes of similar size and build and their assessed value and selling prices to determine what your home's price should be listed at.

Let's consider the objectives of the players here:

Agent – wishes to get a listing and a sale knowing that a sale is easier at a lower price

Owner- wishes to get the maximum price in the minimum sales time

Buyer – wishes to get the property at the minimum price

Banker –wishes to finance the property at an accurate evaluation

One obvious trick the Agent can use to obtain the listing is to over value the property to make the seller happy and then after a month or two go back to the owner and suggest that the market has changed and that the price should be reduced. The danger here is that the seller will refuse or that the market is in fact falling and even the suggested price is not low enough to sell the house with the result that the listing is not renewed and no sale occurs. This sort of approach would work well in a rising market where the inflated price would soon be reached.

Another problem with this method of setting prices is that one house may have many extras built in compared to a standard house of the same size. How does one set the price there? Another problem would be maintenance and condition. If a ten year old home was meticulously maintained how would that compare to a ten year old home that need several thousand dollars of maintenance and repairs?

The bottom line here is that the real estate agent is concentrating on the asking price. The asking price is almost never the price the property sells for. But it must be in the ball park of prices that would not put the buyer off and result in them not even considering the property.

So what does it all mean? It means that when an agent sets the asking price for your property that you agreed to -it is NOT the sales price and it is only an educated guess of the approximate price your home should be listed at. The actual sales price could be less or if a bidding war develops it could be more than the listing price.

The seller still owns the property and can decide NOT to accept an offer even if it is at the asking price. Although unusual this could happen in cases where there seems to be a large and unexpected demand for your property and a quick offer. As the seller you control the property.

There is a definite relationship between the asking price of a property and the amount of interest as shown by visits and offers. What would happen if the fair asking price for your property was $300,000 and you asked $325,000 for it? Everyone will have an opinion. In my opinion you would reduce your number of prospects by 50% and by 100% if you asked $350,000 for the property. And yes I could be wrong because you don't really know what a property will sell for until an offer has been placed and he owner accepts it.

As the asking price goes down the level of interest from prospective buyers goes up. The key question here is what is that relationship? And more importantly when does that increased interest translate into offers?

Recently, in Toronto when gasoline was selling for $1.35 a litre a special promotion offered gasoline at 50cents a litre. This generated a long line up of drivers who wished to purchase gasoline at this gas station. Now the interesting point here is that the same line ups could have been generated by a significantly smaller reduction in the price of gas. My guess is that a 20 cent per litre reduction would have produced similar effects.

To the 85 cent per litre reduction. Let's go back to real estate. Suppose that a home was fairly priced at $300,000 but there were no offers after several weeks. Let's look at the prices that would attract attention from buyers and why:

>**$299,500** For some strange reason dropping the price by only $500 gets it below that bigger sounding $300,000 number

>**$289,500** Now the price sounds significantly less than $300,000 but it is only $11,500 or approx. a 4% reduction

>**$279,500** Again the price sounds significantly lower than $300,000 in fact it is a 9.3% reduction

If you were a prospective buyer and you thought the house was in fact fairly priced at a $300,000 asking price then at what level would you be tempted to put in an offer?

I would be tempted at the $289,500 asking price and would likely place an offer of $260,500. And yes that would be a low ball offer but I would be trying my best to get the best deal. And I can always raise the offer if I wish.

WHY DO PEOPLE LOOK AT PROPERTIES FOR SALE?

- To help set the price for their property
- Neighborhood curiosity
- For design ideas
- To find out if they can obtain household items at a good price or for free
- They are in the market for a friend or relative
- To sell you services
- To entertain themselves
- To see if there is something they can steal and how to break in.

- To obtain a real estate listing from you
- They presently own property and are trying to decide if it is time to sell
- They are genuinely looking for a new home

Given that the seller's objective is to sell the home you can see right away that most of the reasons people have for viewing your home will NOT result in a sale. If the home is being sold via a real estate agent the agent can filter out some of the people who are not genuine buyers. If the home is being sold by the owner then they normally will need to deal with all types of people who wish to look at their property.

An area of frustration is that you are not sure if the buyer is genuine or not. Are they just wasting your time or are they seriously interested in buying your property? I think you only know for sure when they submit an offer to purchase.

THE PENDING CRASH IN CANADA

When you are looking at a home also be sure to look at how the traffic relates to it. Are you on a corner? Is the home too close to the highway? Every year hundreds of vehicles crash into homes! When a vehicle is in motion it has lots of energy and your house is just not that strong. And the accident could happen in a second leaving you little time to get out of the way.

We are publishing this book in May 2017. Most of the topics are going to be useful for decades in the future. They will be useful in both Canada and other countries. However there is one event that as I complete this edition I also realize is pending and could happen at any time. And that is the real estate crash we are going to have in Vancouver, Toronto and Montreal and smaller crashes in other parts of Canada. As we all now real estate is a business activity and business goes up and down in sales activity so prices go up and down. At the present time it is very obvious that real estate values in these three major activity areas are very close to their high points.

And the next step will be for the prices to peak and then fall likely will a rapid fall or as we say a real estate **crash**. Investors know that this will happen what they don't now for sure is exactly when it will happen and they also don't know if the prices will peak and then stay at that price for some time while annual inflation rates slowly decrease the value of real estate assets.

They also know that if real estate prices reached a peak and remained steady that their asset value could possibly keep up with inflation or may dip only slightly and they realize that they may not need to sell their properties. They could keep the properties for the next upturn.

But there are other risks. If they only have a minimum amount of their funds invested in the property a downturn could wipe out the net asset value that they had. They still may not need to sell but if they did need to sell they would lose their down payments and incur additional selling costs that would possibly place them into debt.

There are options. If they really thought that we were getting very close to a downturn in the market and if they owned more than one property one option would be to keep one property as their home and sell out the other properties to convert those asset values back into cash. If they managed to do that they would likely make a profit on their investments. And if they waited for the market to hit bottom before investing in real estate again they could possibly turn that profit they made in the sale into two or more properties at the bottom of the market which would then begin to appreciate again in value.

Another option would be to sell all their real estate at the top of the market before the crash and place the money in the bank and simply rent some property to live in or move to a much lower price area.

There could also be a financial disaster looming. If their investment crashed and they had what is called an upside down mortgage where their mortgage was larger than the new value of the home then even if they sold the home they would be in debt. Bankruptcy would be a possibility.

My advice if you are reading this book before the very likely crash occurs that you should really sit down and have a plan. Consider your options depending on what the market does then if and when the crash occurs apply what you consider to be the best option. There is a risk level associated with each option and not everything we do in life is successful or a failure either. Good luck!

LOCATON LOCATION LOCATION!!

I suggest that one of the most deceptively simple descriptions of real estate value can be attributed to the phrase "**location, location, location**" often given with a superior tone as if the speaker is explaining an essential building block of the universe to a young student. What does it mean?

When I first began studying real estate I thought the phrase meant the actual location of the house on a given street. Wrong.

First of all consider that the location of every single piece of real estate is different. You could have a condo in a building which had a desirable address. But your condo could be located on the least desirable side of the building or on the least desirable floor. Or you could have a neighbor who likes to play loud music. We once had one who played his bag pipes. We liked him but he sure generated a lot of noise!

It is also possible that your condo, while being a desirable address, was too far from your job. Or it could be that your building was attracting a large number of owners from a specific religious or cultural group that you felt uncomfortable living in.

Your house might be the best house on the street. The problem here is that if all the other houses are significantly priced less than your house then when you go to sell you might find it difficult to get your price. It is also possible that your house is of a different design or color than other houses in your area making it less desirable to buyers.

The location of your house in relation to the water table may be a concern. If your house is in a wet area where the sump pump is working nearly all the time or if it is in an area prone to flooding then this could make it less desirable to a buyer who discovers this.

What is the crime rate in your area? How close are you to a hospital? Where are the power lines and railway tracks? Are there any industrial zones close by? What is the air pollution like? Which direction does the sun rise and set from? Is your area declining or improving? Are you close to parks or a pub? Are there lots of kids in your area? Is it a retirement area? How is your house set on the lot? How close are your neighbors?

My point here is that the phrase "location location location" refers to not one but dozens of considerations. When somebody flips this phrase at you ask them which factors they are considering.

If you consider the phrase from a simplistic point of view it means that an identical house and lot will be worth more or less depending on its location. As an example if you took a home located in North Bay Ontario where property values are lower than many larger urban areas in Canada and you placed the same house in the Oak Bay area of Victoria or Toronto you will find that the value of the home is quite different. Now here is where the complexity of the phrase reveals itself. Just why is the value different? Let's look into that!

Not only is the physical location of the property important the proximity of certain other features to the property is important and here are some examples:

1. Proximity to water (ocean front, lake front, river front, pond front)
2. Proximity to the main business district and or place of employment.
3. Proximity to homes of similar value, construction and design
4. Proximity to residents of similar race, religion, interests and wealth
5. Proximity to roads and transportation networks such as buses and the subway.

In each of these five cases one could take an even closer look at the property to better understand how it stacks up against others. As an example in the case of ocean front property there can be a wide variety of situations ranging from a beach type property with a gradual incline to the ocean and shallow waters to a more abrupt hill or cliff type setting with deeper water that may not be as accessible. In some cases there is little protection from winds and waves and it others properties may exist in sheltered waters where boats could be moored. Depending on the type of water freezing could occur during the winter months or storms could occur. Normally the value of a property will be significantly higher if it is on waterfront. As an example we live on a one mile road adjacent to a large lake. On one side of the road there are waterfront properties and on the other much deeper properties which extend into the forest. On average the properties on the lake side of the road are twice or more the property value of homes on the forest side of the road.

One of the reasons that waterfront is desirable other than the obvious fact that people love water and the views is that one side of their property contains no people. In a normal lot you will have people on all four sides of you, while on waterfront you have then on only three sides.

Let's consider the proximity to roads and the transportation networks. When we lived in Victoria we were on a **secondary arterial road** close to downtown on the bus route. We had the option of walking to work or taking a bus or driving. We really did not need a full time car. In Toronto we have friends and relatives who live close to where they work. Again they do not need a car as they are within walking or subway distance to work. When a car is required they rent one and they may do that five or six times a year at a cost of perhaps $500 or a fraction of the cost of having to maintain a car and pay for gas, insurance, license plates, parking, maintenance, etc.

If you compare these sorts of properties with those that are far outside the city and many minutes away from work then you can better understand the additional costs involved. Transportation costs become significant and your most precious asset **time** is involved too. Some people can adapt some work to their travel time but others cannot.

Proximity to homes of similar value, construction and design

For some strange reason people like to group together with other folks of like interests. If you enjoy the look of a Victorian style home you may wish to have that home located in an area of like homes. In modern subdivisions you will note that most homes all have similar wall coverings design and colors. If you have a large prestigious looking home often you will wish that other homes in the same area are similar. From an investment perspective if your home is significantly different from others in the area you will likely have a problem when the time comes to sell it.

If as an example your home is say significantly larger than other homes in a desirable area then why should buyers pay more for your home to live in that area?

So when it comes to location location location how in earth would one arrive at a home value for a given style and size of home in good condition when different physical locations are considered. Just how much is ocean front worth? How much is a stable neighborhood or a neighborhood with a low crime rate worth? How much is it worth to be close to a very good school that you may wish to send your kids to? As you can see the exercise to value a property becomes very subjective. The tolerance becomes large.

There is good news here too. You can now understand what goes into determining a reasonable price for a home. As a buyer you can be analytical about the process. The claim that the property has water views could be changed to an argument that the property only has water glimpses. If you are a seller you can point out that the water views are in fact a complete vista on one side of your property and that therefore you have a million dollar view! But by gong into more detail about each of the aspects related to location location location you better understand the property and its value in the market.

CURB APPEAL

Curb appeal refers to the reaction a person will have when they approach your home. Some homes are impressive some are not. Some homes are more impressive on the inside than the outside while in others this could be reversed.

Here is an example of a home with really bad curb appeal. But it would be so easy to fix! And if you fixed it that would result in a higher sale price. If you purchased it without it being fixed you should be able to buy it at a lower cost.

When homes are originally designed often the new home owner is not given a view of what the house will actually look like. They may be shown a one dimensional drawing. Newer homes may be built using a three dimensional drawing with a computer aided program and it may be possible in that case to see an improved perspective of how the home will look from the curb. In the case of an existing or resale home the buyer only needs to visit the home to see what it actually looks like from the curb.

So what happens is that with some homes the interior of the home actually looks better than the exterior. With many older homes the garage was a separate building at the back of the house but with many newer homes the garage is either in the front of the home or on one side. In the case of homes with the garage in the front of the home that is the first thing that you see and the garage tends to dominate the rest of the house. Personally I don't like that. You can build a home with a garage at the front with a narrow lot and so you can place more houses on a city block. Modern homes seem to mostly have garages in the front. Over the years I have taken pictures of thousands of homes and I prefer having a separate garage in the back yard with the driveway on one side of the house. And if it was my house I would prefer a garage that could hold two cars AND a place to call a workshop so that would be equivalent to a four car garage. You will note that some of the modern so called garages can only hold one car and they don't even have enough room for your basic workshop tools so the term **garage** can refer to a real attractive man cave or a fake little structure to hold a small car in which case I would say "why bother?" I kind of doubt that you believe me so please take a look at tiny garages and good sized ones like I described and you make up your mind which one you like best. And the last point on this topic is that if you do have a large garage and workspace that opens some activities for producing some products on your property that could be sold. You actually could have a small factory running back there generating thousands of dollars of revenue every year and a huge amount of fun and enjoyment. Something to consider!

Also when a garage is incorporated into the house design often it takes up less floor space than a stand alone garage raising an issue over its actual use. You may find that what first appears to be a two car garage is actually not a two car garage because it won't fit two full sized cars in it.

Often landscaping will help with curb appeal. But there is a problem. One can put in rockwork and a driveway with pavers and some transplanted trees and spend tens of thousands of dollars. But when you go to sell the property you will likely not get your money back for all the extras you put into the house to make it look nice.

A house with excellent curb appeal which will boost it's asking price!

My main message here is that if you are buying a resale property or having a new home built for you that you must consider curb appeal. Curb appeal will factor back in when you try and sell the property at some point in the future and it will also impact your enjoyment of the property while you own it.

This is a very interesting topic! Each property will have a quality called "curb appeal" which is the visual attractiveness of the home as one approaches the property. The theory is that the higher the curb appeal the more likely a prospective buyer will be attracted to the property and will wish to view and possibly purchase it.

Curb appeal can be boosted by landscaping, paint, architectural treatments and the basic design of the home. Often the curb appeal of a property can be significantly improved with modest funding. An improved curb appeal normally means the value of the property will be improved too.

Here are a couple of examples. If you clean the grunge and grime off the outer walls of your house with soap and water you can do that for very little money but you can increase the value of your home by thousands of dollars. Not convinced? If you have an older roof you can hire a professional cleaning company to clean it off for a few hundred dollars and again you can increase the value of your property by several thousand dollars. A new roof on a 3000 square foot home could cost over $7500 but simply cleaning it off professionally could only cost you under $1000.

There can be certain problems which are more difficult or impossible to fix. If your property is located under power lines or near a railway track or beside a run down building or a commercial building there may be no way to improve your curb appeal. If the front of your home shows poor design in that it is not balanced or it looks odd or it does not fit into the neighborhood then fixing it may prove very difficult.

Curb appeal should be a key design factor when the home is originally built. You should study the drawings showing the front of the house, or study a model of the home placed on the lot in a smaller scale and you should make the architect aware of your needs for good curb appeal if you are having the home designed for you.

But the topic of curb appeal is not that simple. One might wish to keep a low profile in a neighborhood and not have the fanciest home on the block. When you drive a fancy car or live in a fancy home or wear a fancy watch you are screaming out to certain less desirable members in society that you want to be robbed! In other words there are ways to keep your curb appeal modest while enjoying a very attractive home interior.

In recent TV programs on the Home and Garden Network there are several home improvement programs where paint and landscaping are used to improve the curb appeal of a property. Simply by de cluttering a front yard, painting that entrance door a better color and doing a bit of touch up work one can often make some big improvements and now the average buyer is expecting that these improvements have been made prior to looking at the property.

UnREAL-ESTATE CANADA

As a buyer if you encounter homes with poor curb appeal that cannot be significantly improved then stay away from the home. You will have the same problem when you try and sell it. If it is just landscaping and paint – not a problem- that can be fixed!

There are homes that go over the top in an attempt to establish curb appeal and the results can be a house that nobody would wish to purchase. I have viewed homes where the owners have gotten carried away with concrete statues. They might get away with one but oh no they have several to the point of making the home look kind of funny. Filling your front lawn with painted gnomes will do it too. The good thing is that with a bit of decluttering some of these embellishments can be removed in short order and any problems solved. In certain situations you can actually make money doing this as the over the top embellishments usually lowers the price people will pay for the property.

I have one more suggestion on this. Consider hiring a Graphic Arts student or a Graphic Arts professional to visit your home and make some suggestions on how the curb appeal could be improved. Trust me. I know some Graphic Artists and they are fantastic in applying design ideas and artistic talents to almost anything. Tell them what you wish to achieve and pay them cash. Yes there is a bit of a risk but again there is so much talent there that there are excellent possibilities to increase the curb appeal of your property for little money compared to the better price you can obtain for it.

RACE AND REAL ESTATE

In Canada (and other countries) there is a tendency for people of like races to congregate. In Toronto for example we find areas where Greek, Italian, Jewish, Muslim, Chinese and Koreans and other races congregate. Now here is the problem.

When a race congregates in an area this effects the restaurants, signage, churches, schools and even the elected representatives for that area. We also see people of the same races working together. The social fabric of an area is reflected by the people who live there. In some areas neither of the two official Canadian languages are spoken. You can feel that you are actually in another country which could be a good thing or bad thing.

The question becomes do you want to live in an area that is dominated by another race? Most people don't and that's why areas of like races exist because other races move out. Does this make Canada racist? In a sense yes it does. But in another sense it seems reasonable to want to live in an area of shared interests.

When purchasing real estate it is a good idea to find out if you are moving to an area where one race dominates the landscape. Because of the sensitivity and political correctness associated with expressing concerns about race it is a topic that is not normally discussed.

UnREAL-ESTATE CANADA

Crime is sometimes associated with particular races and here too it is wise to be aware of that when moving to a new home. And don't forget the politically correct term for race and religion is **demographics**. So don't ask about the racial content of an area ask about the demographics!

PHOTOGRAPY

Photography has changed a lot over the years my film camera on the left is German and fantastic and over half a century old and still works perfectly, the digital one on the right is from China and takes excellent pictures and I purchased it at a thrift store for $4.50. People are dumping excellent cameras for cheap just to use their cell phones instead.

We have a problem with photography. I once worked as a professional photographer in Calgary taking pictures of homes for sale. This was in the pre digital days and I used two 35mm film cameras with several lenses. I took thousands of pictures. And as you might guess I learned a few things. Since then photography has moved from analogue film cameras to digital electronic cameras and there has been lots of development in those cameras. The images do not need to be processed the same way film was. Yes they could be modified with a program like Photoshop but all you need to do is send the image to the person doing the graphics or advertising and that could be done via an email. If you wanted to you could take the picture and send it in to the office and they could place it online in minutes. The old approach took at least a day with film cameras because you first had to develop the film then print pictures.

But as with most things there are problems. Often the person taking the pictures is the real estate agent and that could be done with a cell phone. Very fast work here. However the agent is not a professional photographer like I was. They are using a camera with just one lens and they are not aware of some of the methods a professional photographer might use. And sometimes there is no one using a program to improve the photographs with the result that a photograph is posted and it does not show a good image of the property. I will give you an example.

When I took real estate photographs I used three basic lenses a wide angle 25mm lens a normal 50mm lens and a telephoto lens, I also had a very wide angle lens which was occasionally used in small spaces. This selection of lenses allowed me to take pictures at various elevations, distances and angles and I was able to show a property in its best views. I also had a flash available for certain shots when the light in a room was too low. And as a photographer my main focus was simply taking the picture to show a property in the best views. A Realtor has many more jobs to focus on and they simply do not have access to the equipment that I had even though the new cell phones and cameras are very good in many ways.

So here is the problem. On one had we have digital cameras today which are very easy to use but on the other we usually do not have professional photographers taking the pictures. As a result often the pictures for the listing are not that good and that sends a negative message to the viewer. And yes there are exceptions. There are professional photographers with good quality equipment that take real estate pictures and when they are used the images look much better and have a much more positive reaction with potential buyers. And to be fair there are Realtors who also take very good pictures!

This brings to mind one change that I saw occur in offices in the 1980's. Prior to that time a Director would use a tape recorder to transcribe a message that their secretary would then use a typewriter to produce. They worked as a team and the secretary controlled access to the Director. But then we got desktop computers and even the Directors and Managers had to type their own letters and further on the file systems were changed from legal to letter sized and then to electronic systems. And like photography in real estate we had all these changes in management which reflected the change from analogue records to digital records. But the frustrating thing was that the expenses required to run the computer systems skyrocketed and the records now in digital format often had less security than the paper records. Sorry for going on about this but I see a parallel here where the old technology was actually less expensive and more effective than the new technology. In the case of photography yes there are some definite advantages to the new technology but there are also some disadvantages. And sometimes when people apply the new technology in photography the results are not very good.

And unfortunately there is a level of complexity here. I would lean towards a professional photographer myself but I do understand that in some cases a seller or Agent might like to try taking pictures themselves especially when funds are very limited and time is very short and the property is priced at the lower end of the market. I think it would take about three hours for a photographer to travel to a local real estate listing take the pictures and go back to their office to transfer the images. They should get at least $50 an hour because they need to use their own transportation and equipment. So I would allocate $200 including tax for a simple real estate photo shoot. I think that would be reasonable given that you would obtain professional grade images from it. Yes it might be possible to obtain the images for less money by a person just starting out or working part time or a photographer with several jobs each day to do. And you really need to be sure that you are getting a professional photographer not a person who has an inexpensive digital camera and wants to learn how to take real estate photos. So that explains some of the complexity regarding taking real estate photos. Remember that your main objective here is to obtain a sale and spending say $200 to obtain professional pictures to get a sale of say $370,000 which is an average price for a home in Ontario would be a good investment. Yes you can take pictures on a cell phone for almost free but if the pictures are not very good you may not obtain the sale.

Here are a list of suggestions regarding real estate photography

1. Have a camera with a wide angle lens

2. Use natural light where possible
3. When taking a picture of a property with a drive way take the picture at an angle so that the house is shown more than the drive way.
4. If taking a picture of a drive way be sure the cars are not shown as they tend to dominate the picture and you are selling the house not the car!
5. if you are taking interior photos give yourself a time frame of at least one full hour and usually day time is better with more natural light
6. for each room ensure that the room is ready for a photo and arrange items so that the don't detract from the picture
7. have a splash of color in some rooms for example some flowers in the kitchen or living room
8. have some shots at dusk sometimes the horizon light sets off the building
9. use a tripod for some shots
10.   drone shots are now possible at relatively low cost. I noticed a small drone with a camera on it for $50 and that would give you some unique views of the yard and house that would attract a lot of attention. More expensive drones in the $200 range would likely get you better photos and you can invest a lot more than that if you wish but in most cases with the exception of acreages that would not be necessary.
11.   take images at different angles not all at eye level. You will be surprised how different they sometimes look
12.   Use pictures from Google Earth to display the area around the property. They are free and fast to obtain

13.   Consider using a GoPro camera as you can walk around the property and give an eye view of what it really looks like. You could even use Youtube to display it if you wish or your website.

14.   There are also cameras that will give a 360 degree view of a home and the viewer can get an amazing view.

One thing that the list points out is that photography is in itself an activity where skill and artistic talent and technical knowledge at the expert level can produce an excellent series of images to display the property. It is possible that some very talented Agents may also be able to to do this but I think it would be wise to hire a professional photographer who has this level of expertise. When I compare my days as a photographer to the technical advances of today there is a huge difference and if I was to enter today's market I would need a lot of training to learn all those new skills.

And I should mention the "full frame" camera. Yes they are expensive and yes the best logical use for them is a professional photographer but here is the problem. A standard digital camera has a relative small sensor to collect the image. The old style film cameras had a full size 35 mm wide frame where the image was collected. So what does that mean? It means that the full sized cameras will show more of the view than a smaller sensor digital camera. Significantly more in fact and so the image will look much better. The problem and there always seems to be a problem eh is that the damn full frame cameras are very expensive. Some of them are in the $8,000 range and they start around $1000 tax in. So if you are a professional photographer they are the way to go. If you are selling the house yourself that would be too expensive and if you are an Agent selling the house you would need to sell several houses and study photography before the expensive full frame camera would make sense. Is there an answer here?

Actually yes there is and it is quite surprising. People are dumping perfectly good older 35mm film cameras with different lenses on kijjii for between $50 and $150 dollars. This is unreal because these camera sets once cost two or three thousand dollars or more but now nobody uses them. So pick up a 35 mm camera set with a wide angle lens and go and buy some film and take film pictures. Your cost to get excellent pictures will drop to around $200 and after you are finished you could put the cameras back on Kijjii and possibly get $100 back thus you can get professional level pictures of your real estate for about $100. I would only advise a person with some photographic skills to use this approach. And when the pictures are printed it would be relatively easy to take digital photographs of them and use Photoshop to manipulate them somewhat and you are laughing and thinking to yourself what a nice person I was for telling you this. I hope. And yes this approach would take some time and if that is not available use your cell phone or digital camera instead.

So the bottom line on this topic of photography is that first of all images are very important. A good or excellent image will attract buyers and a bad image may repel them. Even a cell phone is capable of taking good images and the odd excellent one but to rise to excellence you need a camera with a wide angle lens and a full image frame sensor equivalent to the size of an older 35 mm film image. Or in theory you could also use an older but relatively easy to find at a low price 35mm film camera. As you compete with other listings you need high quality images to win in that competition. And unfortunately even today in 2017 we have many poor quality cell phone images being taken by non professional photographers to display homes to prospective buyers. Yes there are exceptions and yes some Agents are also very good photographers but my point here is that we are still seeing low quality images in the market place that result in little interest for prospective buyers to take the next step and arrive to view your house.

A final point here is that once you finish taking or obtaining your images you have completed that step of the process to sell the property. You can now concentrate on other things. The job is done!

NEW TECHNOLOGY

Times change and technology changes so one could ask the question has technology changed how real estate transactions are conducted? Is it easier to sell a home today than 25 years ago? Are fewer hours being spent obtaining a sale? And if technology is changing real estate should commissions be lower?

Another question might be are Realtors embracing the new technology and applying it?

In order to operate a realtor needs a phone, computer, digital camera, paper forms, a fax machine an office and a car preferably capable of taking four people to view a home.

The Realtor must be capable of integrating their phone preferably a smart phone into the listing and sales process. They must be a very organized individual. They also need to be very efficient. And on top of that women realtors need to be careful showing clients their listings as there are demented criminals out there that see that as an opportunity to attack them and or rob the property.

And there is a good part to the chapter on New Technology and that is the group we call Millennials. They understand new technology. They grew up with it and as it developed so did they. Let me give you an example as I have a nephew who is a Millennial. We were talking about the amount of advertising on Google and other websites and I was whining about how much of it there was. He looked at me and asked " Ron do you have Adblocker?" I had never heard about it before. So I admitted that and and he told me how to download it which I did and that solved the problem. Then we were talking about movies and he told me that there were a lot of free ones out there with programs called free Streaming sites and he gave me a couple of examples and again they worked perfectly. I thought I was a pretty nerdy guy because I have been working with computers since the mid 1970s and even worked as a Systems Analyst for a financial programs managing billions of dollars. But guess what? My Millennial Nephew knew a lot more about modern technology than I did! And my Son is the same and he too is a Millennial. So the message here is that you shouldn't think that you know everything about new technology and be sure to ask those that know more than you do for some help.

THE OFFER

A Traditional offer to a real estate agent is written with a deposit to show good faith. The agent then presents the written offer to the seller or the seller's agent. The offer is normally in force for 24 hours then becomes null and void. In some cases you can cancel the offer within a certain number of days but in others you can't.

This is one of the most exciting times in a real estate transaction. The offer can take many shapes. It can include clauses requiring a successful home inspection, the sale of an existing home, a specific closing date, the inclusion of certain fixtures or furniture and will likely be in an amount less than the listing price of the property.

If the offer is significantly lower than the asking price it is referred to as a **low ball** offer. While there is no definition of a low ball offer my opinion is that a 25% reduction in the asking price is definitely a low ball offer. A 15% reduction is probably the largest reduction one could offer without being considered a low ball offer. Having said that a sensitive seller might refer to ANY offer lower than the asking price to be a low ball offer. Sellers get agitated with offers that are lower than their asking prices and low ball offers are particularly annoying to them. As a general rule the lower the offer the least likely the seller will accept it.

And remember that there are three basic types of real estate markets. There are rising markets, steady markets and falling markets. So the definition of a low ball offer may change a bit with the type of market. As an example in a rising market the owner may consider an offer at the asking price to be a low ball offer because the plan was to set the asking price at slightly less that the estimated value of the home so that more people would be interested in viewing the property and a bidding war would develop.

At first glance you might think that the offer process is quite simple and uncomplicated. Yes it could be if you are willing to pay the asking price or a price very close to it. If the asking price is a very fair price that should be considered when placing an offer.

In most cases the asking price is slightly or significantly more than what the buyer is willing to pay for the property. In this case it does make sense to offer less than the asking price. There may be situations where it is a buyer's market and where the seller is under pressure to sell and where a reduced offer might be accepted. The low ball offer should be considered.

There is a shock value to a low ball offer and it will usually make the seller angry. For this reason there are advantages in making the offer via a buyer's real estate agent. He or she will contact the seller's agent and advise them that you are interested in making an offer but you feel that given the current conditions it would need to be significantly lower than the asking price. Your agent can ask if there is any interest and if so the offer should be given with as few clauses as possible as quickly as possible.

The seller will either ignore the offer if they find it too offensive or they may counter. They could counter with an amount that is slightly less than the asking price. Or they could counter with a significantly reduced amount that is say half way between your offer and their asking price.

Here is where things get messy and tough. Since your objective is to obtain the property for a low ball price likely for purposes of investment you need to stick to you price however you also wish to show the seller that you are not completely unreasonable. My opinion is that you should raise your offer slightly say by approximately 1%. The seller may counter or may walk away. You should stay with your offer and wait. Let your money do the talking for you. If the seller really needs to sell they will get back to you. If not then the sale was never meant to happen. This will not be a happy sale and you may have made an enemy for life.

But let's say that the offer is not a low ball offer. Let's say it is a normal offer to a maximum of 15% off the asking price. What happens then? How does the negotiation work? From the sellers perspective you want to be sure that anyone else with an interest in the property is aware that there is an offer in process as that may start a bidding war.

In the case of a normal offer there is an old adage in real estate that **your first offer is your best offer**. For the longest time I could not understand this concept then it started to sink in. Your first offer usually comes early in the sale process where you have just listed your property and have not reduced the price. Suddenly you get an offer that is lower than you were expecting but still in the ball park. What do you do? If you wait for another offer it might be weeks or even months away and by then you may have reduced your asking price and that offer will be yet another reduction on that reduced price and may in fact be lower than your original first offer.

You could accept the offer or counter. Tough decision. Whenever a person counters an offer they run the risk of losing the first offer and the buyer walking away. If you counter for a significant amount more the buyer may not agree. If you counter for a small amount more you still run the risk of losing the offer and do you really want to lose a sale on say a $300,000 property for five or ten thousand dollars?

If the offer is subject to several conditions then it might be easier to send a counter offer to the buyer but if it is a clean offer with minimal conditions you need to decide what to do.

For example in a falling market (buyer's market) with reduced sales it might be very difficult for the buyer to sell their property as a condition of buying yours.

When should you make an offer? Occasionally you will encounter a home in very good condition at a fair asking price that is a newer listing. It is basically a **turn key** home that does not require any additional work to move into. If you are one of the first to view the home you must realize that other prospective buyers will be looking at it too and that the first person to make an offer that is accepted will own the home. This is a case where you really should place the offer and quickly or you will miss out on the deal. If it is a rising market even more pressure is there to make the offer and close the deal as soon as possible.

The OFFER from a Realtors' Perspective

In a real estate transaction there are two basic parts the introductory phase when the property is listed and advertised and viewed and the final phase when the buyer makes an offer and negotiations begin to obtain a sale. It is at this stage that the selling agent acts as a true salesman to obtain an offer on the property. Unless an offer is obtained the transaction is doomed and no sale will occur. The viewing might have gone well, the agent or the owner has used their time and energy to show the home. But if no offer is made the process stops at this point.

What I have noticed is that the term Salesman is not generally understood in real estate. Perhaps there is a negative opinion towards the term. If you say "used car salesman" a person will be suspicious and tend to be critical of a person's character. If you keep with the term Real Estate Professional or Agent or Realtor there tends to be a better reaction to the term. The ironic fact is that the process involving the purchase of a property is in fact a sale and you need the services of a salesman or saleswoman to complete the task.

The sale begins with an offer often usually followed by a counter offer from the seller followed often by more counter offers until negotiation results in a offer to purchase signed in agreement by buyer and seller. .

When you consider the offer process ask yourself the question –Why would a prospective buyer decide to make an offer?

Let's consider the situation. Most people understand that real estate agents only get paid when a transaction is completed. They receive nothing for the costs of advertising the property or showing it to prospective buyers. They receive nothing for open houses. The only reason that a real estate agent will show you a home is that he or she has some expectation that the effort will result in a sale of either than property or another one.

No sale will occur until such time as the first step occurs- an offer to purchase is presented to the seller. And so there is pressure on the agent to obtain an offer from the prospective buyer.

This is where things can get ugly. This is where the salesman makes his appearance and uses tried and true techniques to obtain that offer. Up until this point the Realtor is friendly and will listen to the buyer's jokes and chat him or her up. A type of friendship may develop as the Realtor learns the buyer's needs and gauges their level of interest in the property. Up until this point there is usually no effort on the part of the Realtor to manipulate the buyer. But then it starts. Here are some of the methods used:

1. The Realtor has a pen in one hand and an offer form is close by within reach.
2. The Realtor attempts to introduce some urgency to the process by remarking that the property is being viewed by others or that offers are being prepared or that the seller is highly motivated to sell.

3. The Realtor suggests the market is better than it actually is and that there is some urgency to making an offer.
4. The Realtor suggests an unreasonable low ball offer to entice the buyer knowing full well that the counter offer will bring the amount up closer to the asking price.
5. The Realtor suggests the home is a turnkey home requiring no repairs or changes to live in when in actuality it is not.
6. The Realtor suggests a home inspection where he has built a relationship with an inspector to minimize problems
7.The home is a reno home after a grow op or fire or extensive damage from renters and this is not passed on to the buyer.   ]

VIEWERS COMMENTS

Here we have an area of complexity. On one hand one might think that a viewer's comments after or during viewing of a property might be of great importance to the buyer. In fact they could be or they could be meaningless too. For example if the viewer is not actually a genuine buyer but has looked at the house for the several other reasons then do the comments mean anything? But if the viewer was a genuine buyer and had comments which prevented them from making an offer then it would be very interesting to be aware of those comments.

Comments fall into two general areas :

Comments which the seller can do something about and comments which are beyond the control of the seller

If the viewer is concerned that the price is too high this is an area where the seller can do something. The seller can point out that the price is negotiable, that certain fixtures in the home could be included or additional information can be provided which supports the price such as an appraisal or recent sales trends.

If the viewer is concerned about the paint colors in the home the seller could offer to repaint it to their specifications as a part of the negotiating process.

If the viewer is concerned about the home being further away from their work location than their present home the seller can provide other advantages such as commute times, improved neighborhoods, reduced density, lower taxes, larger size etc that would tend to balance the problem with a benefit.

If the viewer has comments that are beyond the control of the seller such as basic design, height of ceilings, neighborhood, heating system, lot size etc then the best approach is probably to say as little as possible. In fact there is no such thing as the perfect house as there are too many variables and each person has a slightly different need.

The seller should not fall into the trap of being too sensitive or defensive to viewer's comments. Listen to them and try and understand where the problems are. Don't take them as an insult. The viewer should be able to express an opinion about their experience viewing your home.

You and your Real Estate Agent

There are so many different ways of approaching this topic! But I think I will start by saying that your real estate agent needs to make money to eat. If he or she does not make any money they will starve. Basically they will be very friendly in order to obtain the listing for your property. At first it will appear to you that you have made a new friend. This would be a mistake. You have just met somebody who wants to make some money by doing business with you. And this is a two way street because if they sell your home you will make money too.

You must consider the Agent to be part of a business deal. That does not mean that you cannot be friendly. But it does mean that you absolutely must conduct business to your best advantage. You may need to be quite firm with your agent. You may need to negotiate a sales contract with them that will reduce your commission amount. Emotions will be generated here including "hate" or "dislike" If for example you negotiate the commission so that the listing agent receives 3% and the buyers agent receives 2.5% then the sales agent will resent you. Why? Because on a $300,000 property you have just screwed them out of $1500 in commission.

It gets kind of complicated. Let's say that you sign an agreement with the listing agent and you notice that your property is not being advertised. What is happening here? Well it could be that the listing agent is trying to also sell your property to contacts they have so that the commission won't need to be shared with a selling agent. If after a few days they are unable to locate a buyer that they know they will then list your property for sale and hope that a sales agent will find a buyer for it. You might ask yourself a very good question. What makes the listing agent qualified to collect both the listing and sales agent commissions? While it is true that they have listed and sold the property it seems fair that since a sales agent was not required that only one commission should be charged to you. But the main point here is that as you can now appreciate greed is part of any business deal and any listing agent would naturally consider keeping all of the commission themselves if they could come up with a customer for you. And of course it gets worse.

Let's just say that the Agent has managed to get you to sell your property at a price that is under the market or in the case of a rising market at a price that will soon be under the market price. If they had a friend with whom they could do business with they could arrange for that friend to purchase your property and then he could place it up for sale and collect a second commission on it and possibly even make some additional money on the selling price too. While you can understand right away that this is a rotten thing to do depending on how it was done it might be considered to be within the law. But as the seller you could possibly lose several thousand dollars as a result of this deal. Is that fair?

Real estate sales are usually the largest financial transactions that you will have in your life time. And when that much money flows from one person to another you can be sure that several other people will have their hands out to catch some of it. Taxes, commissions, legal fees, land transfer fees, home inspection fees, MLS fees, open house costs, survey fees, etc. all combine to take several thousand dollars from the selling price and redistribute it to several parties. And everyone with their hands out will want to maximize the income they make from you.

REAL ESTATE BROKERS

There is a love hate relationship between people who sell real estate and real estate brokers or agents. The seller loves it when a sale is obtained for a price they wanted for the property. The seller hates paying the realtor their commission which is quite significant especially when the home has not been on the market for much time.

It took me some time to better understand the role of the broker and the problems and challenges they face to sell a property. Let's investigate this topic.

First of all a broker or agent or realtor –whatever the term you use- is not the owner of the property. The selling broker represents the owner of the property. But at the same time the Broker is not an employee of the seller but is instead a type of independent agent. **The sole purpose of the broker is to obtain a sale of the property**. Brokers are used in many financial transactions from commodity sales to insurance sales to car sales and real estate sales. Without brokers our entire financial system would likely grind to a halt.

The broker makes a living by a straight commission on any sale. They do not get paid a regular wage. On each deal they take a percentage of the selling price as their fee. If there is no sale the broker makes no fee and in fact invests time and resources in the process which are not refunded to him. And that big commission sellers hate does not all go to the broker. It is used to pay for expenses at the broker's office, to pay the listing broker and to pay the selling broker. Yes one can make a fortune as a realtor but most of them on average make modest or low incomes.

The broker works in all types of market conditions ranging from a buyers market when sales are sometimes slow to a sellers market where sales are sometimes brisk and high prices can be obtained. In each type of market the public acts differently and the broker will need to deal with people who may become very frustrated and angry. If a seller loses money on a deal or if a buyer pays more than he wanted to the broker will often get blamed. If there are no sales in a falling or slow market the broker will often get blamed. It gets funny. If the property sells in a matter of days the broker often gets blamed for setting the listing price too low. If the property is scheduled for an open house and nobody comes then the broker gets blamed.

I suggest that a sensitive person will correctly sense desperation in a realtor. If they don't sell they don't eat. There are many people with their hands out - sitting on the realtor's doorstep waiting for them to get paid that commission cheque. In a rising market with lots of properties selling times are a bit easier but in real estate times can get very tough both for the seller and the realtor. And this fact gives you more insight into the real estate market place. In fact the Realtor shares the same objective with the seller in that both parties wish to sell the property. However there are some not so subtle differences.

A common question is would a realtor suggest a seller accept a sale at a lower price simply to get the reduced commission? Let's look at some numbers. Consider a property that is for sale at $200,000 and the realtor suggests the owner accept an offer at

$180,000. The background is that it is a slow market and the buyer has told the realtor he will give the seller one offer only. If the seller accepts the offer the realtor is paid a commission on $180,000 and loses the potential commission on the other $20,000. The seller must pay a commission on the $180,000 but loses an additional $20,000 on the sale. This becomes very interesting and I think it is unfair to the seller. Why should the realtor receive their full rate of commission on a reduced sale price when the seller must incur an additional loss on the sale price of $20,000? If you continue on with this sort of logic in the ridiculous case where the property is sold at half price and a huge loss occurs the realtor still collects a commission based on half the property value while the owner loses half their asking price and the sale is a disaster.

When the commission is originally negotiated I suggest that the seller insist on an acceptable level of protection against reduced selling prices. In other words the commission would be significantly reduced as the selling price is reduced from the listed price. There needs to be some room for negotiation between buyer and seller. In the case of the home listed for $200,000 if it sells for say $195,000 there should be no reduction in the realtor's commission rate which they should receive on the $195,000 sale price. However in my mind it simply is not fair to expect a full commission when a sale is a disaster and the actual selling price is less than say 60% of the asking price. Now how does one fix this?

I introduce this problem realizing that the realtor is understandably very sensitive to not receiving their full commissions. They depend on this income to live. I understand that. But on the other hand we have the owner who may or may not be desperate for a sale and if they are required to agree to a sale where the actual selling price is very significantly under the asking price this can be considered to be a financial disaster for them.

Let's consider what the motivators are here. Money is the main motivator. The seller wishes to convert an asset into money. The Realtor wishes to convert the sale into a money payment for the commission. In both cases each party wishes to maximize the money payment they receive.

I suggest that the listing price for the property be divided by ten. In the case of a property selling for $300,000 this means that we have ten units of $30,000 each. Let's also make an assumption that the owner will accept an offer where 90% or more of the asking price is met. So what this means is that if the owner receives $270,000 or more for his property he should be reasonably happy with the sale.

The way many commissions are set up now is similar to this which occurs in BC. Ontario is a fixed 5%:

First $100,000   =7%   = $7000
Over $100,000   =3%   = $3000 per each
additional $100.000

Note however that in Canada there are no set commissions and all commissions are in fact negotiable however many realtors start off with a standard commission in this approximate format and amount. With the rapid rise of real estate over the last few decades the old methods of commission calculations have been revised and I think they still require work.

REAL ESTATE AGENTS AND THEIR COMMISSIONS

Let's take a look into the life of a Real Estate Agent. Some make excellent incomes and many do not. You only get paid when a sale occurs. No sales – no pay! The commission system in real estate is set up to pay an equal amount to the listing agent the agent who obtains the listing and the selling agent the agent who obtains the sale. While it is possible for an agent to list and sell the same property it is more likely that two agents will be involved. Some agents specialize in obtaining listings and others in obtaining sales.

Most sellers deeply resent the amount of the real estate commission. In previous years when houses were selling for $25,000 and commissions were 5% real estate commissions were in the$1250 range but now with the same houses selling at $400,000 the commission will be in the $20,000 range. Yes it is true that the purchasing power of the dollar has gone down however when you do the math and convert that $1250 commission to a modern day amount you will find out that today's commissions are still significantly higher that they were years ago and it is due to the huge increases in the value of real estate.

What if you decided to sell your home and so contacted a Realtor to handle the sale. He comes over on Saturday gets your signature on a sales agreement and on Monday afternoon you get a phone call telling you that he has an offer. To your shock the offer is your asking price less five thousand dollars and you immediately agree to it. Later when you have your payment for the sale you start to consider the commission earned by your realtor. On your 300,000 property you paid him a 5% commission or $15,000 and since he was both the listing agent and the sales agent he only had to pay his brokerage a percentage keeping $10,000 for himself. So your agent earned $10,000 for just a few hours work. It turns out he had another client who was looking for a home in your area and the sale involved only a simple phone call. Is this fair?

Sellers are more sensitive to real estate commissions when the market is falling and they are losing their equity in the property. When markets are rising and a profit has been made even with the commission the seller is more agreeable with the commission. So you have a situation where a seller will either be very resentful or reasonably happy with a real estate commission.

It gets more complicated. Your realtor does not make a penny until your property is sold. Up until that time he or she incurs expenses in both money and time. They may show your home to dozens of prospective buyers. Your home may be very aggressively priced making a sale near impossible in this market. Your agent may have suggested that you drop the asking price to generate some interest and you may have said no. The fact is that your agent is a professional. They have expenses. They need to eat and support their families. Most of them make modest livings and only a few make the big bucks. Some just list properties hoping that another agent will sell them and they will receive the listing agent's commission.

The sale is crucial so part of the duty of the agent is to close the sale. This may result in some pressure being applied to both the seller and buyer. We get into a grey area where the agent is acting for themselves to obtain a sale while also acting for one or even both of the parties. There are rules, there are legal concerns, there are ethics involved. However a bottom line is that there must be a sale for the both the buyer and seller and agent. If there is no sale there is no commission there is no new home owner and there is no money going to the seller.

Honesty is the best policy. The sad fact is that not all people are honest and this refers to buyers, sellers and real estate agents. Consider used car sales. The owner will trade in his used car and gloss over any faults. The dealer will check it over and if suitable will resell it. But the dealer may also sell it with faults. The new owner may buy a car with problems. The same or similar thing happens in home sales. The seller may not mention that he saw a termite the last time he was working on his crawl space changing a filter. The owner may have slapped some paint over some cracks in the wall or may have done second rate repairs to hide rather than to solve problems. Who is responsible? Can you blame the realtor? That doesn't seem fair. Do you blame the person who did the home inspection for you?

Often you will notice that Realtors are physically attractive people who dress well and are articulate and polite. Some tend to smile a lot and are very attentive to buyer's comments. Remember that a Realtor is a sales person and they are trying their best to produce a sale. Again if they don't produce a sale they don't get paid. People sometimes get confused that a friendship is being established. This is not really a friendship situation. This is a sales technique. That is not to say that the Realtor is not a friendly individual. My message here is that this is a business deal. There is nothing wrong with being friendly during a business deal but the idea here is to conduct business not make a friend.

I wanted to make several points concerning Realtors. First they are humans just like us. Most of them are pretty sociable. They are trying to earn a living to feed their families. They have taken courses in their trade and passed exams and most of them are intelligent and knowledgeable people who are entirely capable of selling your home and presenting you with a cheque for it. For this service they charge you a fee. And the fee is pretty big. Many would say too big. I think it is critical that the seller understand how a realtor operates to obtain a sale. They obtain a listing from you, write up the property, work with you to set an asking price and post it on MLS and then screen prospective buyers and show the property. They or a selling agent will obtain an offer from a prospective buyer and then enter into negotiations with you to close the sale. The amount of actual work that the agent does will vary from just a few hours to months and remember they don't receive a penny until the sale is finalized and the money changes hands.

LISTING AND SALES A BASIC PROBLEM IN REAL ESTATE...

The Real Estate Agent has basically two functions. First they must list your property for sale. That means that they must talk you into signing a Sales Agreement where you allow the Agent to list the property for sale for a specific period of time. The Agent who you sign the sales contract with is called the Listing Agent.

The second basic function is actually selling your property to a buyer. This Agent is called the Buyers Agent. In some cases both jobs can be done by the same Agent. That is called double dipping and it raises issues specifically who is the Agent really working for.

At first this relationship seems quite simple. But is it? Actually it is quite messy!

There are variables. In some cases an Agent will concentrate on obtaining listings. They are great at talking a prospective seller to sign a sales contract. And when that is done they take it back to their Realty Office and let other agents and MLS listings attempt to actually sell the property. And here is where the problems start.

If your property is in excellent condition in a good neighborhood with no significant problems and priced reasonably that will also allow a good commission then the selling agents will show a lot of interest in it. But if this is not the case then they may show no interest in it. When a prospective buyer comes into the Office to look for listed properties these agents will tend to avoid showing or recommending your property to them. The days and weeks will pass and nobody will come over to view your property. As the listing period approaches the end your listing agent may visit you and suggest that the price be lowered. If you do that your property may become more interesting to the selling agents because at a lower price it might be easier to sell.

DIRTY TRICKS

As a buyer there are certain tricks you can apply. For example you can make a list of the faults in the property then do up a list with the cost to fix each. In reality you might be quite happy to live with the faults. But if you do come up with a list be sure to have a couple of the items on the list priced below what it would cost to fix them and the rest higher using the rates professional tradespersons would charge. Present them with the list which should be typed in four columns including the fault, the materials, the labour and the total to fix it. At the bottom of the sheet have a total in $. This list could be used to effectively reduce the asking price.

Any offer would start at the new asking price that is the original asking price less the cost of repairs less a discount. The trick here is that the original asking prices should have been set by using the actual condition of the property. But by giving a list of the faults you are effectively reducing the price below what it had already been adjusted to. It would be fairly easy to go thru $20,000 to even $50,000 in repairs depending on the condition of the property.

Focus on the Problem Trick

Every real estate property has at least one problem. If you are a buyer your objective is to obtain the property at the lowest cost. So what you could do is identify the main problem and then focus on it. Keep on going back to it. Try to identify what it would cost to fix the problem. If it is the roof say that you prefer a certain type of roof replacement such as a steel roof but that it is more expensive than the standard roof. Say that you are going to get an estimate of the cost to repair the roof. Go back to the agent after talking to a few roofers and tell him what the highest bid was. That amount effectively comes off the asking price. Then focus on another problem. Pick a problem where expensive trades would be required to fix it. Those costs effectively reduce the asking price. Then make your offer noting the approximate cost of fixing the problems plus an additional discount. Your offer is now several thousands dollars under what the owner's projected lower offer is. But they will begin to focus on the repairs that are required. There is a lot of psychology working here. But the effect may be that you will acquire the house at a much lower price than simply offering a lower offer without identifying the problems that need to be fixed. In realty the problems may not need to be fixed and you could try fixing some of them yourself or acquire a lower priced trades person to do the work.

Lie about other offers

Tell the agent that you are looking at several properties and you will take the best deal. This places a lot of pressure on the agent to convince the seller that they should accept your offer because you have other properties that you are considering and it may not be wise to present a counter offer to you.

THE ASKING PRICE

Setting an asking price is a bit more complicated than you might originally think. Here is why.

If you set the asking price too high it will reduce the interest in your property with some buyers. This means that fewer buyers will actually look at your property and the chances of obtaining an offer and a sale are also reduced. This does not mean that nobody will look at your property and it does not mean that your property will not sell. If a buyer is looking for a property in your neighborhood and yours is one of the few houses available they may request to look at it anyway. They may even place an offer. It is entirely possible that setting a higher asking price will filter out buyers so that just the highly motivated ones contact you.

A Realtor will help you set the asking price. I have some problems in this area. A realtor will use the actual selling price of like properties to suggest an asking price. My problem with this approach is that I feel that each property is different. Yes there may be some similarities but there are also differences and how does one account for them in the asking price. Also some owners have invested several thousand dollars in extras for their properties. How does one account for that? Add to that thought that a lower priced property will likely be easier to sell and more likely to generate offers and this is how the realtor collects a commission,

UnREAL-ESTATE CANADA

We have three parties here. The owner or seller wants to obtain the highest price. The buyer wants to pay the lowest price. The realtor wants a sale so would be willing to support lower priced offers. On a 300,000 property at 5% commission the realtor can make $15,000 at the asking price or if the buyer offers 10,000 less the realtor still collects $14,500. So well the seller takes a reduction of $10,000 the realtor only takes a reduction of $500 and a commission of $14,500 is much better than nothing if the property does not sell.

THE OPEN HOUSE

Most houses do not sell through an open house. The process is time consuming for realtors so many prefer not to hold open houses. Some Realtors will claim that a sale occurs at every fifth open house so 80% of them do not generate a sale. Some people derive their Saturday entertainment by driving around looking at open houses. They may have no intention of actually buying a house and no resources to do so.

You could look at this another way. If you held five open houses then mathematically there is a good chance your home will sell. If you look at this from a Realtor's point of view then if they have a lot of listings open houses could take up a lot of their time. Perhaps the time would be better spent replying to individual expressions of interest from the MLS listing or the ad in the paper or their online website.

The Realtor only makes money when a home sells. So they will be using their time to generate the most sales. Now we have a problem.

From the seller's prospective they want a sale for THEIR home and they really don't care how many other homes the realtor sells. So if that means several open houses then go for it. Your realtor will likely use this as an opportunity to ask you to reduce your asking price with the logic that a lower asking price will attract more prospective buyers. But do you really want to do that?

LOOKIE LOO

Some people just want to look at your property for sale. They have absolutely no intention of buying it. They may have no money to buy it. They may be nosey neighbors. They may be crooks looking to case the joint or buy something at a low price. They don't care that they use up hours of your precious time.

But there are problems. They could be the parents of people who are looking for a new home. They may tell somebody about your property who will be more interested in buying it. Or they may be just goofs out to do something interesting.

If the red flags go up and you feel uneasy about these people simply avoid showing them the property. Be polite but firm. Realize that there is a small chance that you may be losing a prospective customer. When in doubt show them the property but don't let them walk around by themselves unless the property is empty.

QUICK VS SLOW SALES

Sometimes a sale will take only a few hours or days once the sales agreement is signed. And occasionally the seller will receive an offer for greater than the asking price so that they will agree to the sale ASAP. When this happens everyone is happy. The buyer is happy because they have the property they want. The seller is happy because they got the price that they wanted and the Agent is happy because they did not need to work very hard or long to get the sale. But when the seller starts to think about it a bit resentment builds that the Agent is being paid a large amount of money for less than a week's worth of work! Nevertheless the happiness at getting their price makes it acceptable.

Then the second thought arises. Perhaps they should have gotten more for the house and should have asked more and maybe the Agent suggested that their asking price was lower than it should have been so that they could sell the property faster! In some cases that is exactly what happened. In other cases it was just a matter of luck that the right buyer came around at the right time. But as you can see there are issues.

And what happens when the sale takes several months to complete. Some properties have been on the marker for over a year. And of all the properties for sale not all of them ever sell at least at their original asking prices. So after a few months there is pressure from the Agent to lower the asking price. This presents another problem!

Will the lower asking price actually generate a sale or will the sale have happened anyway because the person who finally buys the property would have bought it as the higher price? Here you need to consider just what the market is doing. If it is going down then your chances of selling the property increase as you decrease your asking price. In a steady market with low sales volumes it is possible that your chances of a sale will increase if you lower the price but it is also possible that the sale would have occurred anyway. In a rising market if you priced the home at a fair price and several months went by but the market was still rising I just don't see the logic in lowering the asking price. As the time goes by the price should seem lower to prospective buyers anyway because all the other prices are increasing. So the point here is that when you set or adjust the asking price for your property you need to be aware of the state of the market. Is it steady, increasing or decreasing in price and volume?

THE REAL COSTS OF WAITING FOR A SALE

Many people find it difficult to calculate the actual costs of holding a property that is for sale. Consider the case of a homeowner who moves from Ontario to BC to take on a new job. They place their Ontario property up for sale and month after month no sale occurs. What is all this costing?

Opportunity Cost – first of all you need to know how much equity you have in the property. This is not as easy as you may first think the main problem being that it hasn't sold yet so you don't know what the selling price will be. This amount will need to be an estimate. Let's say that the asking price of your home is $435,000 and you hope to get $400,000 out of it after paying the commission and negotiating with the buyer. Let's also say that you have a mortgage of $200,000 remaining on the property. So your estimated equity in the property is $200,000. If you had that money you might put it in the bank in a certificate of deposit and earn 5% on it or $833 a month. So by having your equity tied up in the property you are incurring a loss of $833 a month.

Mortgage Cost – Your mortgage cost is represented by the interest you are paying on your outstanding balance and let's say that you are paying 4% or $666 a month

- Insurance cost – Likely about $50/month
- Local Taxes   -Likely about $300/ month

- Utility costs   Likely about $100 a month
- Maintenance costs   about $100 a month
- Repairs and maintenance about $200/month

In this case your monthly costs would like be approximately $2250 a month or $27,000 per year. If you add in travel costs to and from the home and other miscellaneous or unexpected expenses you could be looking at about $30,000 a year to maintain your empty property. This is a shocking amount of money to just have your house sit there empty waiting for a sale. If you are living in the home then the numbers are different as they represent your normal living expenses.

What I am trying to do here is underline the importance of obtaining a sale in a reasonable amount of time. That time will vary significantly depending on if we have a buyers or a sellers market. For example in a sellers market with strong demand a home could sell between two weeks and a month. But in a slower buyers market it could take several months to sell a home.

When you know how much it costs per month to sell your home you are in a better position to change the asking price. In most cases it would seem to make more sense to drop the price by significant amounts than by small increments. In the case of a home asking $435,000 consider dropping the price to $399,000 rather than say $415,000. On one hand you are taking a significant loss on your equity but if it generates a fast sale then you are saving $2250 a month if you are keeping the house empty while you live in another province. If you drop the price in small increments of

$5000 then you may end up waiting several more months for a sale.

YOUR FIRST OFFER IS YOUR BEST OFFER

Yes it is possible that the first offer you receive will be the best offer. It is also possible that the first offer will be the worst offer. This is a fact one will only know after several months with a healthy dose of hindsight. It would be totally incorrect to apply this phrase when the first offer is presented.

And yet when your real estate agent arrives with that first offer there is the tendency to offer up this phrase in an attempt to close the sale. But it is not this simple. Your agent may have other good reasons for suggesting that you accept the offer. He or she may genuinely feel that it is a reasonable offer given the market conditions and likely future trends. Your agent may be correct. What do you do?

First consider the offer. Are there conditions attached like a home inspection and approval of financing or sale of an existing home and or a late occupancy date? While that is an offer it is a weak offer because there are so many conditions that the buyer can take to get out of it. How close is the offer to the asking price? The closer the offer to the asking price the stronger the offer. But you still need to factor in the conditions.

Consider your financial situation and is the marker rising or falling and what time of year is it? You are building up to a decision –should you accept the offer or not or should you counter offer? If you counter offer you are actually rejecting the buyers offer and requesting that he or she make a larger offer. Your risk is that the buyer will say no and the offer is dead.

I once sold a house in Victoria where we had several people looking at it until finally we got our first offer. Our agent suggested that we take it and we agreed and to this day I am happy with the decision all factors considered. Accepting an offer on real estate is high drama. It is a tough decision. You need to make that decision.

My point here is that if you make a decision on acceptance or declining the first offer it should be done by considering as many factors as you can including the ones mentioned here. Try to be as unemotional as possible despite the fact it is an emotional process.

CLEVER SELLER TRICKS

I am not a Real Estate Agent. But I do have experience in Banking, Financial Management, Auditing, Small and large business. I have owned several businesses. So I am going to suggest some ideas that you may not have seen in Real Estate and they might or might not work. I think that under certain conditions they are worth a try! Here goes.

If your house for sale has a two car garage place a boat, motor and trailer used but in good condition in one of the spaces. You should be able to acquire a suitable one for about $3000. Be sure that it is spotless and waxed. Include that and your lawnmower and hoses and outdoor equipment in the sale. This will have the effect of diverting the buyer's attention from the price to the fact that they also get a "free boat" which would likely be unaffordable after they spent all their funds purchasing your property. In fact offer them the option of having the furniture that you don't want to take with you as a part of the sale at the asking price.

BROKER COMMISSION

When a sale occurs two commissions are paid one to the selling broker and one to the buyer's broker. Then they share their commissions with their real estate offices. No sale? No commissions.

The incentive for real estate agents to sell your property is the commission that they are paid. One fairly standard rate in British Columbia is 7% on the first $100,000 and 3.5% on anything above that. In Ontario the standard rate is 5% Rates are competitive and although the agent would love to charge you more if he did you would go to another office. So lets consider the commission paid on a home that sells for $400.000.00

- 7% on first $100,000   = $7000
- 3.5% on the next $300,000 = $10,500
- total commission   =$17,500

It is entirely possible that the property could sell in a week in a rising market. It is also possible that several months would be required before the house is sold. But the commission is exactly the same! This is incredibly stupid. Why should the commission be the same if the house is sold in days vs being sold in several months?

To confuse things a bit we now have competitive commission rates being offered. One that I reviewed charges 3.75%. Let's review how that might work comparing it to the standard commission above

3.75% of $400.000 = $15,000 Your first thought might be that the discount brokerage is only saving you $2500 which is not really a lot of money on a $400,000 sale in fact it is only 0.006% not even a full percentage point.

There is another problem here. Let's say that your house is valued at $200,000 and another seller has a house valued at $400,000. Which house do you suppose that a real estate agent will try harder to sell? Using the standard rate shown above on the $400,000 rate the total real estate commission will be $17,500 and on the $200,000 house the commission will be $10,500. And yet think about that fact. The amount of work is precisely the same! So why would an Agent try just as hard to sell a $200,000. Now it is possible that the market for a less expensive house is larger but it also might be possible that people who can't really afford the house will take up the Agent's time showing it.

Most people do not understand how the commission is split up. There is the seller's agent and the buyer's agent and the seller's brokerage and the buyer's brokerage so the commission is normally split up equally as follows :

$400,000 property = $17,500 standard commission

- $4375 Buyer's Agent
- $4375 Seller's Agent
- $4375 Buyer's Agent Brokerage
- $4375 Seller's Agent Brokerage

So most people think that when they sell a property their agent gets the commission. Wrong. Their Agent only gets 25% of the commission! So in the case of a less expensive home say the $200,000 home the Agent would receive $2625.00 and they still need to pay sales tax on it so they only get $2625.00- 341.25 = $2283.75

As you can see commissions are relatively easy to understand when you look at the numbers and follow the money. The results are sometimes a bit surprising but it gets worse.

What if you were a Real Estate Agent and you acted both as the Seller's Agent and as the Buyer's Agent? In other words as the Seller's Agent you were able to find a buyer and were able to present the buyer's offer to your seller and your seller accepted it and the sale was successful. You would then receive both the Seller's Agent commission and the Buyer's Agent commission! This is called "Double Dipping". This is a fairly simple concept too but again ….it gets worse!

UnREAL-ESTATE CANADA

Some Agents have been known to apply techniques to avoid allowing another Agent to bring a prospective buyer to your property for sale. They may even do this so that a friend or relative can purchase your property at a lower cost than you might otherwise receive with more offers from other Agents Buyers. And then they may work with that buyer to resell your property to yet another buyer at a price several thousands dollars higher than you were paid. I would expect that something like this would more likely occur in a rising market and possibly in a falling market too if it looked like the bottom of the market was approaching.

There are two major reasons why you need to be aware that unethical behavior sometimes occurs in Real Estate in Canada. The first is that an Agent will ONLY make money when the deal is complete and even then the entire commission is usually split between up to four players –the Seller Agent the Buyer Agent and both Brokers that that both Agents work for. Because there are so many Agents in Canada well over 110,000 of them the average number of sales per agent is relatively low. For example the average Agent in Vancouver had approximately 11 deals a year. This is an active market. Some agents have fewer sales per year. So clearly the Agents are often short of cash and they are desperate for commission income. This is an incentive to act unethically to obtain that commission income.

The second major reason for unethical behavior is that commission income is a small fraction of the total sales volume in a real estate deal. In most cases 95% of the funds entirely avoid the Agents. Yet they see these huge volumes of money being exchanged for property. Some properties are in excess of one million dollars! So there is a second major incentive at work here for the Real Estate Agents to participate in the actual acquisition of property and it's resale so that they can not only make a commission but also make additional income on the increased value collected in a subsequent sale. This sort of event occurs in a rising market or when a property is offered for sale at much less than it's actual market value. And there are tricks that an Agent can use to obtain a low price listing. Should they be able to do that they could direct the sale to a friend or business partner who would then resell the property and split the gain.

Imagine the following situation. An older senior has decided to move to a nursing home after loosing their spouse to old age. The Agent talks them into listing their property for $325,000 knowing full well that all it needs is some paint and it could be easily resold for $425,000. The widow signs the sale agreement. The Agent calls their friend and advises them they have a property for sale for an excellent price. The friend offers $300,000 and the Agent talks the widow into accepting the offer. The friend has the house cleaned and painted and some very minor repairs made costing them $10,000. Then the property is placed back on the market for $425,000 and sold for $400,000. The profit is approximately $90,000 and the friend and the agent split it. So the Agent makes $15,000 commission on the first sale and $45,000 on the subsequent sale for a total revenue of $60,000. Ask yourself if this was legal? Now ask yourself if this was ethical?

Here is the problem. When large amounts of money are involved in a financial transaction many people want a slice of it. They want as much as they can get from it! There is an ethical way of doing business and an unethical way of doing business. And I will tell you right up front that not all Real Estate Agents would do something like this. But my point is that some would. And this is why in any Real Estate deal you must approach the subject objectively and be aware of exactly what is happening with your money. Forget about the smiles and stories and free coffee and lunches. Do the math.

And if you are a buyer and your Agent takes you around to several properties to see they are not providing you with a "free service" While they receive no income if there is no sale if there is they obtain a portion of the commission that the seller pays goes to them. So think about it. There is a Realtor driving you around to see properties and spending time with you but what they are really trying to do is talk you into purchasing a property because if you don't do that they not only get any payment they also need to pay all the expenses associated with taking you to the properties.

ALTERNATIVES TO TRADTIONAL REAL ESTATE

Traditional real estate would be a house or apartment or condo. But in 2017 Canadians are looking to alternative places to live because costs are going up and incomes are not. So what happens when you cannot afford a house? You normally move to a condo or an apartment. But then the condo and apartment prices go up and you are spending the major portion of your income on that with few dollars left over for other things in life. So now what do you do?

Some young people are moving back home to their parent's residence and living in the basement if they have one or sharing rooms in the house. The numbers are staggering but for some strange reason neither the media or the governments seem very interested in it. If you look at the actual numbers in 1981 vs 2011 in 1981 27% of kids between 20 and 29 lived with their parents but in 2011 over 42% did and the population of children between 20 and 29 was 4.3 million. Obviously the fact that young Canadians were unable to find jobs and unable to afford their own living quarters is very important. The trends are scary. I was not able to find recent figures for 2017 from stats Canada but this is one area you may wish to investigate. There is another problem here too because as time goes on the costs of maintaining homes is going up too and what we are seeing now are parents selling their family homes and moving into apartments. So while one alternative that we are seeing now are children moving back home there are other things happening too.

Because younger Canadians cannot afford their own homes they are beginning to share residences with friends as another option. If two or more couples combine their incomes and purchase a home with separate living quarters in it then they can share the home. They form a type of partnership or joint venture and instead of being house poor with a house and no money to live they now own a house together and still have enough money to meet their other expenses. There are problems. What if they have a disagreement or what if one person loses their job? It could get messy. But in some cases the idea could work and it forms a successful option for house prices which are too high to afford. Something to consider.

A trailer or motorhome is also an option to consider. We owned both of them for several years and lived in a Trailer in Calgary for a few months and a motorhome in Victoria for a few months before purchasing a home. Stats Canada in 2011 reported that 183,510 people lived in moveable dwellings (trailers, motorhomes, boats, and trains). I suspect that number is much lower than the reality in Canada today. If you check out our trailer parks they all seem quite crowded these days. Our marinas are also crowded and although their official number of spaces for liveaboards are low the actual number of people living on board are much higher. How do I know this? We lived on a large sailboat in BC for over three years and I saw that first hand. There are thousands of people living on boats in Canada that our census has never counted.

And there is another alternative which very seldom gets into the media and which even our governments are not aware of and that is the thousands of Canadians who are living in their vehicles. It could be a van or a small trailer or even in some cases a car but if you check out expensive areas like Vancouver or Toronto they are there. I remember that when I lived on a sailboat I meant a nice woman who was living in her van in Victoria during the summer with her 6 year old child. I also discovered areas in town there where people who lived in their vehicles often parked at night. Some people even camped out in local parks! So we are not talking about a few dozen or a few hundred we are talking about thousands of Canadians who are living in their vehicles and motor homes in areas such as parking lots, parks, industrial areas and even residential areas. And this is often seasonal. Insurance for a year for their vehicle could be approximately the same as rent for one month at an apartment.

There are also new styles of small housing that are developing in Canada. Conversions of shipping containers have been progressing for decades and their costs for the initial container are quite low. You can purchase a used 20 foot shipping container for approximately $2500 or less and a used 40 foot container for about $4000. The problem is finding a place to put it but people are doing that too. They are also experimenting with micro houses which are cabin sized living quarters some of which are moveable on wheels.

We could go on but at this point I just wish to make the point that yes there are alternatives to traditional real estate and we have thousands of people in Canada today taking advantage of them despite the fact that most of them are not approved by local city by laws.

Why? Because the municipality is unable to collect taxes from these people and they make use of city services that taxpaying citizens support. But the problem is that these folks don't have enough money to pay for apartment rents or standard housing costs. So the municipality realizes that if they make these alternative housing options illegal that they might have to pay more taxpayers money to provide living quarters for these people. Is it a mess? Absolutely. Is the government doing anything to solve the problem? Nope. Did I provide you with the facts? Yes. In 2016 we had 8000 millionaires from foreign countries migrate to Canada and purchase expensive homes and yet in 2016 we have thousands of Canadians living in alternative housing because they can't afford any traditional Canadian housing. Is that fair? Nope.

ANIMALS AND REAL ESTATE

Most people like bears unless they are in your back yard.

When you pay for your property in Canada you have this mistaken concept that you own it and in certain cases the animals may have an alternative point of view. There are a couple of things that you need to do. First of all you should be aware of the fact that there are several animals and marine life in Canada that will cheerfully bite and or eat you. Then you need to know what the best response is to prevent this.

And here is the problem. The majority of the Canadian population lives in a 100 mile band of land clinging to the border with the USA and most of the population exists in just a few communities in that band. Although dangerous animals occasionally visit most of them live in regions north of this band in relatively unpopulated areas. So you say what makes that a problem? What it does is set up a general opinion in peoples minds that all is well and that they are safe and that one should not harm animals in any way because they are just being animals. Or to put it another way millions of Canadians are incredibly stupid when it comes to animals and keeping safe.

Let me give you a few examples. When people visit national parks some of the dummies actually try and feed bears! Yes there are signs saying don't feed the bears and warning you that you will face up to a $25,000 fine if you do but they still do. And because a wolf looks a lot like a German Shepard they will feed wolves too or think that they are safe to be around. The list goes on. We also have mountain lions, polar bears, rattle snakes, wolverines, eagles, sharks, whales and they all can harm you if you are not careful. And just to scare you a bit Canada has over 25,000 Grizzly Bears over 475,000 black bears , over 60,000 wolves and each one of these "nice animals" could eat you. And if you think that your are safe in southern Ontario where most of the Canadian population is located watch out for the Massauga Rattlesnake that lives down there with you!

And while it would be nice to stop here I better mentions something else. Should you wish to go hiking in the woods or go climbing in mountain areas or go out on the water in small boats because of Canada's very restrictive gun laws you are not allowed in most cases to bring a firearm to protect yourself.

If you have a raccoon problem in your back yard you are not allowed to solve the problem by shooting the raccoon you must hire a professional trapper to come in and remove them and move them to a safer place. So what is the solution if you have property shared with dangerous wildlife? Be prepared. That might mean obtaining a fire arm license and having a safe place to store your firearm so that it is available if a dangerous animal appears in your area. That also means not allowing small children to play in wildlife areas without you being there. If you are living in the city this is usually never a problem but if you have property or are visiting low density population areas where wild life exist you must understand the risks and have some method of protecting yourself.

If you see a bear cub STAY AWAY because if you even get close to it the bear will attack you. If you see a deer with a fawn STAY AWAY or the deer will attack you. How do I know this? A few years ago I was in our back yard and saw a deer a few hundred feet away then I noticed she had a fawn near her. She looked at me and then started stomping her front hoof and I left immediately. It was a warning to stay away! Then there was the time we were climbing a mountain in the Rockies and on the way down we came across a fresh grizzly bear track in the mud going across our trail. It was huge! So be prepared! I once was out snorkeling and then noticed a 15 foot shark beside me but that is another story and that happened down in the Caribbean. I love the outdoors and wildlife but you do need to take care. Or else.

WHAT GOES AROUND COMES AROUND...

A financial transaction ends when the funds have been transferred and when the asset is delivered. Or does it?

When people enter a financial transaction they will both have expectations that may not be covered in the sales agreement. For example they may have an expectation that the property will be cleaned to a high standard. But what happens if only a light cleaning was done and the people moving in need to bring the property up to a higher level of cleanliness? Perhaps the rugs are not clean. Perhaps there is dust behind counters or in closets. Perhaps the washrooms are not spotless. Now emotions start to run. A feeling of resentment begins to build. Does it end here? No it does not.

The people moving in will talk. When they meet the neighbors they will mention over time that you left the home in a dirty condition and they had to clean it. They will yak about it to their workmates. They will harbor resentment towards the seller forever. And eventually the bad vibes will bet back to you. **Because whatever goes around comes around.** It is one of the natural laws of the universe.

When you sell a property it is not the worst idea in the world to send over some flowers or a bottle of wine with a card to the new owner to welcome them to their new home. Don't buy a cheap bottle of wine or some cheap flowers either. Why do this? Because it will come back to you and it is a nice thing to do. The new owner will appreciate it and tell their friends. Your reputation will be enhanced.

You can also ruin your reputation quite easily in a real estate deal. When you move out take everything even the toilet paper. Take all the grounds equipment like rakes and hoses and shovels. Take anything that isn't screwed down. Take all the hangers in the closets. By doing this you will establish your reputation. You did this because you didn't get the price you wanted so you thought you would get even! And that will eventually get back to bite you on the bum.

Things will quickly dissolve into a tit for tat contest. The new owners will toss any mail out that comes to the house with your name on it. You only gave them one set of keys although you had four sets.. They will be worried that you have retained a set of keys and could still have access to the house if they went away for a vacation. Now they will need to re-key the locks at considerable expense and they will blame you

Another way of looking at unreal real estate in Canada is that our lifespan is so incredibly short. Consider that Canada is 150 years old but that our First Nations have lived here for thousands of years. In takes 360 payments during a time span of 30 years to pay off a property at the standard mortgage payments and of all the residences in Canada Stats can reported that over 58.6% of households had a mortgage. The housing prices are shooting up and so is the amount and the cost of the mortgage and the residential living costs are rising more rapidly than incomes. So clearly there comes a point when the standard 30 year payment period will be too short to pay off your huge mortgage.

I would like the end this book on a good tone but while there is a lot of good on the way there are some problems to solve first. Clearly Canada is headed for a real estate disaster and a huge drop in prices. This will result in some form or depression like what happened in 1929 with the stock market crash and extended on to the dirty 1930's. You simply cannot have prices rising to the point where Canadians can not afford to live. Something must give. And that something will be real estate prices. Will I be wrong? This book was published in May 2017 and if you are reading this in 2020 and nothing bad has happened then I was wrong! But hopefully the information about the reality of real estate in Canada is helpful to you and helps you live a better life! Now for the pending good things that will happen soon!

One thing that I did learn over the years is that people adapt. And Canadians are very good at adapting. In fact Canadians live in one of the best countries on the planet because we understand how to live well. That is what is happening now and what will continue to happen in the future. At onetime in Canada it was possible to get a job that paid a reasonable wage and to get a mortgage on an affordable house and pay it off over a standard mortgage period. But in 2017 this is no longer possible for an increasingly large number of Canadians so what will happen? How will they adapt?

Canada does have some options that other countries don't have. We have trillions of dollars of natural resources and millions of square km of available land. So with a bit of work from all levels that work in real estate today we should be able to fix the problems that we face today! And there is the unexpected to consider too. We have a pending earthquake for our West Coast. We have climate change occurring melting our Arctic ice. We have a crazy leader in North Korea threatening nuclear war. We have religious violence. We have new levels of automation in both the manufacturing and service industries that are resulting in the reduction of jobs. We have billions of dollars of crime occurring on the internet and we have new technology that tracks everyone's activities and generates information that big business uses to market their products. So there is no doubt that times are changing. And those changes include real estate.

Good luck! And have fun!! **UnReal-Estate Canada** is one way that you can look at real estate from a different perspective. And when you have a better understanding of what is really going on you will be in a much better position to make the best decisions. There is a danger in depending on just one source for your information about real estate. Each group in this area has their own objectives. You can receive excellent information from each group and that will place you in a better position for deciding the best approach. And remember each person in each group associated with Real Estate is trying to do a good job and earn a decent income for themselves and their families. I suggest that you respect that fact. That does not mean that you must agree with everyone it means that you should listen to them, try your best to decide if the information is correct and helpful and move on.

There is nothing better than living in a nice home with your family and friends and enjoying life and having fun! Have fun and if you have suggestions for future editions please contact me at ron@battistonpublishing.com.

Cheers!   Ron Battiston

UnREAL-ESTATE CANADA

www.ingramcontent.com/pod-product-compliance
Lightning Source LLC
Chambersburg PA
CBHW021546210326
41599CB00010B/329